Absolute Optimist

Absolute Optimist

Remembering Eluned Phillips

by

Menna Elfyn

translated from the Welsh
by Elinor Wyn Reynolds

HONNO PRESS

First published in the Welsh language in 2016 by Gomer Press
First published in the English language in 2018 by Honno Press
'Ailsa Craig', Heol y Cawl, Dinas Powys, Vale of Glamorgan,
Wales, CF64 4AH

1 2 3 4 5 6 7 8 9 10

A catalogue record for this book is available from the British Library.

The cost of translation has been underwritten by Cymru a'r Byd (Wales
International), the Welsh North American Association, the North America Wales
Foundation, Dafydd Evans and other individual friends of Myra Thomas Lawrence.

Published with the financial support of the Welsh Books Council.

ISBN 978-1-909983-80-9 (paperback)
ISBN 978-1-909983-81-6 (ebook)

Cover design: Ruth Rowland
Text design: Elaine Sharples
Printed in Great Britain by Gomer Press

The translation is dedicated to Myra Thomas Lawrence, a good friend of Eluned's, who has been a longstanding leader of Welsh American life through her vision and generosity.

Contents

Acknowledgements

'For me, winning the Crown is like a huge wave breaking without warning on golden sands.'

Eluned Phillips

In this account, you will experience waves of happiness and rough currents that will bring you into sunlight and sometimes take you to the edge of the rocks. This has been my experience whilst putting this book together, and the many friends whose names are mentioned below have been witnesses to this maritime journey. There was something of the Atlantic in Eluned's personality; she sailed close to the wind but managed to navigate her way around the literary poetic world without once asking for help or sanctuary. Yes, she succeeded in making her life a jolly one, and her friends made sure that she did not land on a desert island.

The American poet Mary Oliver said, 'Prayers are needed for a person who writes a biography.' My prayer was answered by some of Eluned Phillips' friends, relatives and neighbours as they opened their hearts to me. I should like to thank them for their generosity when discussing one who had been a lasting influence on them. This book would not have seen the light of day without them; the deep affection conveyed and their effervescent testimony to her gave me such pleasure for close on two years. Thanks therefore to the following:

Ann Evans, Bryan Evans, Gareth Rowlands, Andrew Gilbert, Gwenno Dafydd, Ann Morgan Evans, Rhiannon and Jeff Lewis, Caroline Roper-Deyo, Dafydd Evans, Trixie Smith, Phil Howells, Jackie Edwards, June Gray, the Reverend Dr Wynford Thomas,

Tim and Hettie Jones, Haydn James, Roger Hopkin, Wyn a Carol Calvin, Michael J. Lewis, David Fielding, Rosemary Beard, June Lloyd Jones, Angharad Blythe, Mererid Hopwood, Idris Reynolds, Rona and Barbara.

I wish to thank Ann Evans especially for entrusting all of Eluned's literary works into my care. This biography has benefitted so much from browsing these works: notes, letters and exercise books. Thanks to my sister, Siân Elfyn Jones, for her assistance with the manuscript. A special thanks to Gareth Rowlands for giving me copies of some of the programmes he made about her and for reminding me always that she was a sparkling thing that shone her light across all who crossed her path.

Thanks also to Gomer for their usual care and to the energetic editor, Elinor Wyn Reynolds, for her diligence and her vivacity in steering this book to print. Indeed, her enthusiasm for this book was an impetus to get it finished in time. And thanks to her also for all wise counsel during the editing process.

The reader may sit in peace, whilst navigating the occasional storm of Eluned's life.

Prologue

Over the years, I have specialised in closing the doors on hurt.
[A letter from Eluned Phillips to a friend, 23.11.88]

There is something nostalgic about November: a yearning, a feeling of loss, as the tattered, speckled leaves fall to the ground. I'm driving towards Cenarth, looking for the essence of somebody special. But it's a dark afternoon and the leaves fall in front of my car and my tyre-treads leave the impression of their end days on the tarmac. The leaves will soon be absent from our consciousness for another year, until spring comes and the trees become clothed once more to make us vibrant again. The leaves that fall on the way out of Cenarth and on towards Yet farm are a memory of a similar fate that befell the pages and leaves in the books of poems by Eluned Phillips. Perhaps her poems were palimpsests, in that her handwriting seemed overtaken by pages in other unpublished volumes of poetry with their white leaves that would show the layers of history from end to beginning. Like looking through the rear-view mirror rather than the windscreen in my car.

As I guide my car along the road, I think of Eluned driving a Jag, at a time when nice little girls sat respectably in the car next to their husbands. I am looking in my rear-view mirror and she appears as if she's back to front; in my mind's eye I see her stepping towards her century in 2014, confident, talented, but not without her worries. She seems back to front, too, because she succeeded in fooling everybody about her age as she refused to say how old she was. That secret was revealed during her ninetieth birthday: born in 1914. And yet, a year passed before her birth was registered – a

1

sign maybe that she was before her time or that others were behind her times, always trying to catch up with her.

A garden of remembrance was opened by Beulah Community Council to note and celebrate her birth on 27 October 1914. She shared the same year and day with Dylan Thomas, another poet from Wales. Indeed, she admitted that she avoided sharing the date and month of her birth because of that very reason, as she would have been compared or contrasted with the remarkable talents of the man from Swansea. But, in contrast to him, there was no birthday dinner and nor was there a visit by the President of Ireland, Michael D. Higgins, as happened for Dylan. There was no evening's feasting in London, with invited poets noting the occasion nor were there readings of her work in America, even though she too made her mark there. What she had was a simple and appropriate celebration given by the Beulah Community Council, and a standing stone noting her place honourably in the small village of Cenarth. A fitting celebration for her own people. Professor W. J. Gruffydd talked of the three subjects that are an integral part of our fabric as Welsh people: religion, locality and death. And this tribute to Eluned shows that she held fast to her chapel in Bryn Seion, and even though she spent time away from Cenarth, this was the place she returned to constantly. This is where she was born and spent most of her life, as a proud member of the community. It was a tasteful, non-ostentatious celebration that was given by the people who knew her best, clear testimony to the fact that she was held very dear by her community. But I believe that Eluned the poet was one of the greatest enigmas of Welsh literature in the twentieth century. It is no surprise that I failed to find the memorial garden on my first journey to Cenarth. I expected to see an obvious sign noting exactly where it was. I have since learned it is through mysterious ways that one discovers anything about Eluned.

I turned my car back towards home without seeing the garden or the stone, though I had seen it on Google along with pictures of the people who were present at the celebration. Somehow, failing the first time and returning home without finding it was almost like looking for the spirit of the departed. Failing to find her becomes a motto in a way. Work written about her is rare and her published work is even rarer: nothing but one thin volume of poetry and an autobiography in English. Did Eluned Phillips just walk mysteriously through life or was it a device adopted by her for reasons that became clearer to me as I wrote this book? During her lifetime a veil was drawn over her, a much less obvious covering than the white robes of the Eisteddfod Gorsedd.

In Wales some are revered and praised during their lives, as poets, as Archdruids and as lynchpins of the Welsh literary establishment. Others are left on the sidelines during their lives and, indeed, even after they have shuffled off this mortal coil. It is accepted (if not acceptable) that history is written by the victor, by those who are in power and have authoritative influence. So I ask myself, why are some absent because of others? Is it because that they do not belong in the traditional societal tapestry?

In Eluned's case, she was a woman, and unmarried at that; she hadn't been to college and worse than that, in the narrow-minded nature of Wales in those times, she was by nature an itinerant person. To some, she was almost like the gypsies that she praised in poetry, the people whom 'Mam', her grandmother, would spend her time with as a midwife on Banc y Shifftwn (Gypsy Bank). In an article in the *Tivy-Side* it was said that she was 'well known and respected, both locally and internationally. Eluned was an inspiring character who gathered friends and admiration wherever she travelled'. Reading these words in English stung the conscience because of the lack of respect shown her by certain individuals, the very people who should have acknowledged her unique talent.

Having returned home from my short journey in the car, I realised anew that there was a need to tell this remarkable woman's story from beginning to end. The difficulty that faced me was the one referred to by André Gide in his 'notebook':

'the artist needs a special world to which he alone has the key'.

In Eluned's case, she learnt early on how to lock doors and to live within her own world. How far might I be able to open some of these doors? Two days after my failure to find her garden, I opened the car-door again and went looking, in the right place this time, and turned to the right by Cenarth bridge where the falls create a powerful water-force. I left the car and walked under the bridge and on towards the garden, by the road, a stone's throw from the river. It was obvious to me that I should have found her the first time, had I paused, deliberated and persevered. This I took as a moral as I prepared to write about her. I should have to drive my words attentively and tread carefully to open the door on her life.

I wrote a poem once about 'Afon Cenarth' ('The River Cenarth') that notes the duality that the river offers a poet:

Mae dwy ochr i fywyd	There are two sides to life
fel sydd i afon Cenarth	as to the river Cenarth;
y naill mor anystywallt	one is so unruly effervesce
yn byrlymu	into waterfalls
rhaeadrau a ffrwydro	frothing and exploding battles
o'r ffrydiau	white dreams from the springs.
frwydrau a breuddwydion gwyn.	

The second half of the poem alludes to the stillness that can be felt on the other side of the bridge and it is an exceedingly good place to fish, so they say, if you know where to drop your line. My poem finished with the two facets stitching themselves into the fabric of life. When I went for the second time to Cenarth and found the garden, the river-level was high. As I crossed the bridge back towards Newcastle Emlyn, I could swear that the flow of Eluned's life was also lifting her up from her incognito state – because apart from the two occasions when she received great praise at the

Eisteddfod, there was a profound silence and mystery about this extraordinary woman.

It is time to take the rod to the water, and catch a wondrous sewin.

Early Years

Sara Adeline Eluned Phillips was born in Glynia, her grandmother's cottage near the village of Cenarth, a mile or so within the boundaries of Carmarthenshire, west Wales. It was 27 October 1914, two months after the outbreak of the First World War. On her birth certificate her mother, Mary Anne Phillips, was recorded as being a maid and an X written by her grandmother, Margaret Phillips, confirms her place of residence. Where the father's name should have been, there is only a line and a space. He is not named. In her autobiography *The Reluctant Redhead* [1] published by Gomer Press in 2007, Eluned writes that he was killed in the First World War, but according to her earlier book, *Pwy oedd Pwy* (*Who was Who*), he was a builder-farmer [2]. No mention is made of his family or their presence during her childhood. From the 1911 Census we also know that, three years before Eluned was born, her mother was a single woman working as a farm maid for Thomas Rosser, who was sixty-nine years old and receiving a teacher's pension. It was his wife, Margaret Rosser, who was recorded in the Census as being the farmer, so it was she who employed Eluned Phillips's mother, Mary Anne, to work at 'Yet' (Gate) farm, Cenarth. In the 1911 Census, Eluned's mother was recorded as being a monolingual Welsh speaker and Eluned recalled how her grandmother, too, spoke only Welsh.

There is some uncertainty regarding the family history of the little clan who lived under the grandmother's roof. It is not known whether Margaret Rosser knew or was related to the grandmother. And did Eluned's mother end up as a maid at Yet farm through

---

[1] Eluned Phillips, *The Reluctant Redhead* (Gomer Press), 2007.

[2] Eluned Phillips, *Pwy Oedd Pwy* (Cyhoeddiadau Modern Cymreig), 1983, p. 51.

kinship or some other social connection? Eluned called her grandmother 'Mam', which was common practice in those days, but she called her own mother Mary or *Mari fach* (little Mary). It was just an endearment, Eluned said, adding that they were great friends but acknowledging, too, that the informality was frowned upon by some of her acquaintances: 'it was a sinfully unconventional thing in the twenties, and I was given a telling-off from nosy people for being so forward. But Mari and I understood each other completely. There was not a hint of disrespect – just a sense of intimacy .'

Eluned's sister, Margaret Elizabeth, had been born two years previously and was known as Madge. Another family member who came to live with them was Eluned's cousin from the Swansea area, Carbetta Mary, who was called Get – or Carbetta '...if I was feeling out of sorts.' Eluned described her as 'my big sister,' and recalled how she was a brilliant storyteller but a very strict disciplinarian too. One other cousin also lived in this cottage, namely Agnes Phillips who was seven years of age in 1911, two years older than Get.

In 1922, they crossed the river from Carmarthenshire into Cardiganshire and moved into a substantial house called Glanawmor. The nest full of children having outgrown her grandmother's cottage, and the pressure of needing to provide accommodation for so many, prompted the decision. Eluned was eight years old when she moved to Glanawmor along with her grandmother, her mother, sister Madge, and Get. Agnes, however, stayed in Glynia with her husband, David Garfield Morgan, and their son Gwilym. Later the three of them moved to live in the Hen Ysgoldy (the Old Schoolhouse), behind the church in Cenarth, renting the bottom floor.

Glanawmor was surrounded on all sides by old oaks, six acres of land with an orchard, and Awmor stream ran through its land as it meandered towards the Teifi river. What change of fortune enabled this extended family to move to such a substantial place, is not known but it has been suggested that there was someone in the background offering the support which allowed them to move to a more suitable place to raise a family of girls. That would also explain the payments made for piano lessons and a boarding school in London. There are some locals who still speak of the large lorry which arrived in Cenarth from London, leading to much discussion about its contents and destination. It became quite a talking-point as it contained a piano delivered to Eluned's home. This demonstrated the family's effort to give the best possible start to their children's lives even if it was difficult to make ends meet. Eluned admits:

> This entirely agricultural area was full of big farms and little smallholdings, some ten acres to start off with and we had to live on what Mam was able to produce from it.
>
> And I challenge any clever farmer to have a better understanding of the nature of land and weather patterns than she had...or better bargaining skills against the odd deacon who had forgotten his chapel principles in the commercial hive of the mart. Mam wasn't one to be wrongly put down...and from cow to cow and acre to acre, we established ourselves.
>
> [from Eluned's personal papers]

She recalls how difficult things were for them when she was a child. The land around Cenarth was almost all owned by the Cawdor estate:

> ...there was no such thing as buying a piece of freehold land, and even less opportunity if anyone was too trusting when it came to an agreement. Those buildings would end up adding to the Earl's estate, often unfairly. And that happened time after time in our family ...and it was no surprise at all that someone of Mam-gu's strength of character rebelled against this unjust oppression.
>
> [from Eluned's personal papers]

An interesting story is told of how her grandmother dealt with everybody in the same way, no matter what their social standing. Eluned tells how Lord Cawdor came to the cottage once in his very grand car to talk to her grandmother. The precise reason for his call isn't mentioned, simply that he happened to arrive at the same time as her grandmother caught sight of Daniel Cwmllwydrew walking by, rather uncertain on his feet having had one too many in the village inn. According to Eluned's story, Lord Cawdor had to wait for half an hour while her grandmother sorted Daniel out and got him safely on his way. One wonders what would have been the purpose of such a visit. Was this the only time Lord Cawdor called at the cottage? Even if that was the case, it is easy to understand how she made him wait, whatever his status, and gave her attention first of all to an old man on his unsteady journey homewards. It may not be much of a story, but it underlines how her grandmother treated the lowly man and the aristocrat in an equal manner.

It seems that material hardship, however, had no adverse effect on the family. The hearth was a warm and happy one, filled with joy, where storytelling was an everyday aspect of family life and the door was open wide to welcome people in. However, no mention is made of many other family members other than Anti Hannah (Auntie Hannah), Eluned's mother's oldest sister, who became a legend in her own right as a fisherwoman who fished the Teifi river in her coracle. Upon her husband's death, a little before the Second World War, she too came to live in the house. In the years to come, Eluned paid tribute to these women in the family for the way they succeeded in making ends meet to 'raise us as children'. This gave her a particular confidence and the household seems to have been full of joy.

In Eluned's autobiography, *The Reluctant Redhead,* an entire chapter is devoted to Margaret Phillips, her grandmother, where she is described as a Solomon-like mother. Eluned recalls 'Mam-gu was the boss in our house.' Clearly she admired her grandmother greatly: 'Mam-gu was the most beautiful woman I'd ever seen and she was a like a queen in our household. Her poised strength set her apart from everybody else. She was the Solomon of our area, settling marital disputes or neighbours' quarrels.'

There is little mention of the male lineage in the family, though it is said that Thomas, Margaret Phillips' father, emigrated to Boston, Massachusetts, leaving his wife and ten children behind in Wales. The intention was that they would follow him in time but Thomas was killed in an accident, and so his family stayed in the Teifi valley carving out a life for themselves there. Eluned makes a passing reference to her grandmother's eight brothers, all craftsmen: carpenters, millers and cooks. However, despite the vagueness surrounding her nearest male relatives, she took pride in being able to trace her family ancestry back to 1011. She states that Sir Henry Jones, who was a member of the New Model Army in the Civil War, was related to her and that he missed out on a knighthood due to some trouble or other in the seventeenth century. In 1867, two of her male ancestors went out to the Welsh settlement in Patagonia and so, said Eluned: 'there wasn't a single man in our home for me to remember... it was the women in our house who influenced me.'

It was clearly her grandmother who ruled home and hearth, a fearless and generous woman. She would travel on her own to the market in Carmarthen over the mountain from Newcastle Emlyn, returning sometimes late at night with only an iron-tipped stick to defend herself against any villainous attack. She was a woman of character, Eluned's staunch supporter and great ally, and one who grounded Eluned deeply in literature. Since Margaret Phillips had been born in Aberdwylan farm on the banks of the river Cych, an area of importance in the legends of Wales, she would regale Eluned with the stories of the Mabinogion and feed her imagination with the tales of the red-eared hounds. It was 'Mam' who saw something in the young girl, something worth nurturing – her love of words. '*Cer amdani 'merch i*' ('Go for it girl, give it your best shot') was her mam-gu's advice, Eluned recalls.

One of Eluned's clearest memories of her grandmother was being taken by her to see the gypsies when her grandmother's services as a midwife were needed there. The story goes that gypsies would camp just outside Cenarth, in a spot called Banc y Shifftwn by the local people. That was how it was referred to in *The Reluctant Redhead*, and translated as The Gypsy Embankment; however, that may have been a mistake and the name was in fact Banc y Sipsiwn – '*sipsiwn*' being the Welsh word for gypsies. However, I rather like the word '*shifftwn*'. Isn't that what gypsies did – shift from place to place, just managing? They would come to this spot nearer the birth of one of their children knowing that Margaret's midwifery skills were close at hand. In this way, Eluned came to know many of the gypsy families of Wales: the Lovells, the Boswells, the John Evanses and the Duttons. After a birth there would be much rejoicing, a bonfire would be lit and a feast prepared; her grandmother and Eluned, if she had been brought along, would be invited to take part in the celebrations. She notes how she once recoiled at having to eat a hedgehog.

She writes romantically of the travellers who came to their door at Glanawmor and how her grandmother would take pity on them, and offer them food and advice. After her grandmother's day this role became her mother's, and later Eluned herself continued the tradition of extending the welcome. It was said that the travellers or 'tramps', as they were known, knew where the best places were in all areas; they knew which farms had open doors and who showed kindness towards the poor.

Although the home was not a wealthy one – they lived from hand to mouth in general – generosity would still be shown to those in need. Eluned inherited that generous quality, and she always had sympathy and respect for those who were in dire need and those who lived on the fringes of established society. She understood their way of life, and when she grew up it seems that she herself inherited a wandering spirit. She wrote a poem in praise of them but the final line is stinging, condemning the ones who held them in contempt:

The kiss of the sea, the wind's hum,
On the tiny caravan – a palace,
And the little Irish girl of a tinker
Her heaven on the blue place.

Resting from the many tormentors
Those brusque to her innocence,
The little Irish girl of a tinker
Embracing her tiny place

Little Irish girl of a tinker
Her gaze to the horizon beyond,
She flees in her mind before nightfall
From the crowd who call her 'dirt'.

Little Irish girl of a tinker
And her question is also curt;
To the kiss of the sun and the wind's hum
Why God, do men throw words that hurt?[3]

In her autobiography she refers to some of the other tramps who called by, longing for the characters she knew as a child at Glanawmor. She presents a somewhat romanticised view in her recollections of them, feeling a sense of dismay that 'the Welfare State took my tramps away from me.' She remembers the regulars who used to call and characters with names such as Daniel Jones, Trampyn Tal (Tall Tramp), Twm Berllan (Orchard Tom), Prothero Bach (Little Prothero), Paddy Gwallt Hir (Long-Haired Paddy), Dic Poli, Twm Shot – all were 'old friends who would give us sparkling conversation in exchange for a meal.' She recalls too how 'Twm Berllan was an experienced gardener and saw to our roses every year; Dic Poli was an authority on Lloyd George … and Paddy, Paddy was very fond of his country's whisky and song. He'd sing me the same Irish song every time.'

[3] Ron Davies, *Llun a Chân* (Gomer 1983), p. 8.

It's quite possible that those visits nurtured in Eluned her grandmother's talent for listening to those who came to her door and her policy of 'an open door for neighbours and all troubled souls.' Glanawmor was a place of comfort and help to all those in need. However, it seems that Eluned cultivated within herself a kind of duality – of being open to others and yet keeping herself to herself during her lifetime. On the one hand the family door would be open wide for all, and on the other Eluned learned, through bitter experience perhaps, how to close the door firmly on her personal life. However, her friends and family might not entirely agree with the metaphor of a closed door; with kindred spirits she was completely warm and easy-going.

Her gratitude for her upbringing, and the values it instilled in her, knew no bounds. In a programme of memoirs for radio she stated:

This is where I think my independence of opinion was formed. That, and the fact that women had succeeded in making ends meet to bring us up as children. This gave me a particular confidence. For example, I was never one to believe that a man's earnings were one of the main recommendations in a marriage. Oh no...a totally equal freedom is what would appeal to me. There's something hateful about arranged marriages...like a kind of fairground sale. And this used to happen when I was young...especially amongst rural farmers. It still happens of course in France, India, China and so on. I'm not sure that some farming families in rural Ceredigion aren't completely blameless, even now. I don't give tuppence for all the fuss about equal status for women; I've never felt less than equal. When I felt the urge to go travelling on a camel in the African desert, and when I found myself by accident in a harem in Casablanca ... nobody could prevent me from doing these things. Oh no ... if Mam-gu was willing to sail to America with no more than two sentences of English, I'm not going to miss out on life's adventures because I happen to have been born a girl.

[from Eluned's personal papers]

The above words reveal just how fearless Eluned was in all that she did. She completed all kinds of adventures and thanks are mainly due to her grandmother, 'one who laid out the dead and who was the midwife at a birth.'

The following poem is a loving tribute to her grandmother and conveys everything about her influence; it was found amongst Eluned's papers. Written originally in Welsh, this translation was one which she wrote herself and she may have read it out in America where she was often invited to Los Angeles and the *Cymanfa Ganu* (a festival of congregational singing) with the South Wales Male Voice Choir. It's interesting that she has kept to the metre form of the *'englyn digynghanedd'*. The *englyn* is a four-lined poem in which each line contains a specific number of syllables, and where a strict metre is observed, using the rules of *'cynghanedd'* where consonant and vowel sounds correspond and rhyme in different ways. Eluned's poem adheres to the syllabic pattern of the lines, but she writes without using *cynghanedd*. It is a form which she used in her poem *'Clymau'* ('Ties') in the National Eisteddfod in Anglesey in 1983, and one she uses often in her work.

My Grandmother (Mam-gu)
Her gift of genes as dowry – gave me
a dynamic entry,
to a world of imagery
and to the beauty around me.

Her memory remains in picture – her eyes
pools of tranquil splendour.
And her tenderness a sure
helping hand out of a gutter.

Midwife to gypsy clan Boswell – Dutton,
John Evans and Lovell;

15

their caravans' magic to dwell
and Mam-gu there an angel.

Her gift of silent listening – and her
patient way of advising
helped all with troubles calling,
made every mountain seem a hill.

The world's misfits adored her – as she
travelled miles to give succour.
Her footprints will be there,
fixed in concrete forever.

This is a joyous translation, and Eluned's ability to use assonance 'splendour'/'gutter', 'sure' as well as 'calling' and 'hill' plays beautifully on the ear.

•

I have already referred to Anti Hannah, Eluned's mother's eldest sister. After her death, a stretch of the river Teifi was named Hannah Rees' Pool, immortalising her name. This was where she would sit every day until well into her nineties, fishing rod in hand, enjoying a spot of angling. It was a magical place and she never returned home without at least one fish. She was a rod-and-line fisherwoman and, according to local talk, a dangerous fisherwoman – to the extent that experienced fishermen would phone to enquire whether Hannah was already out fishing that day. If she was, they'd stay away because there wasn't a hope of a catch if she was already out on the river. No wonder she was given the freedom of the Cenarth waterfalls by Captain Charles Fitzwilliams, the owner. She became a well-known figure by the famous falls, settling her blind husband at the door of the cottage nearby while she fished in her special pool. Everyone was amazed to see Morgan the cat at her side, dutifully carrying each single fish caught up to her husband, Peter, and laying it at his feet without as much as taking one bite. She would also take her clock with her so that she knew when to return to make her husband's lunch. Despite the family's poverty, Hannah would always have a few spare fish to share with needy people.

Pictures of her can be seen in places like the Emlyn Arms Hotel in Newcastle Emlyn, and another by Eluned herself in the hallway of Glyn-y-mêl which she liked to boast had reached the many corners of the world. That is probably true, since people come to visit the falls from all over the globe. Anti Hannah appeared with Eluned in a film, *Troubled Waters*, in her final years and she died in 1968, three months before her hundredth birthday.

In a radio script entitled *Brethyn Cartref* (*Homespun Cloth*) created by Eluned with the title '*Pysgotwyr Glannau Teifi*' (*Teifi Fishermen*), it is Hannah's voice that is heard telling her story:

ELUNED: It's been a long while since you started fishing, hasn't it, Anti Hannah?

HANNAH: Oh yes, eighty years. I was told off often for running down to the Dwylan river when I lived in Aberdwylan as a child. I would go fishing on the sly and Mam would want me to wash the dishes or some other dull task.

ELUNED: But you kept alive to fish in spite of all calamities.

HANNAH: Well yes, though I would be close to starving on many occasions. I would forget about everything when I was at the water's edge.

ELUNED: Well, of course, you would even take an alarm clock with you.

HANNAH:	That old clock has been the butt of many a joke. I'd put it on the rock nearby and set the alarm to when it was time to catch the bus into Newcastle Emlyn to go shopping, but I might as well admit that if there was a plucking or two on the line, I would turn the alarm off and live all the day long on fish.
ELUNED:	And you were sure of catching enough.
HANNAH:	I got fairly decent catches – but I would spare some, you see, for those boys that hadn't been as lucky. The fishermen's wives didn't understand a thing about fishing, so there would be hell to pay if their husbands dared to go home without a fish.
ELUNED:	And did you fish using the same fishing rod every time?
HANNAH:	Of course, a hazel rod cut from the hedge. That's what I used every time – it's good to catch everything – trout, sewin, salmon. I nearly lost it once...
ELUNED:	I remember that escapade well, it was when you caught a fish so big that it took your rod and tackle with it, and one of the local boys jumped in to the river thinking it was Hannah Rees that had gone under holding on for dear life to her rod.
HANNAH:	He was quite right – it wasn't often that I let go of my rod or of a fish.

The script went on, with others contributing to the programme and Eluned in control in her usual relaxed manner. This is a snapshot of two women who were totally at ease in their own skins, as is evident in the poem Eluned wrote about Hannah in Cardiganshire dialect, a poem full of vitality, crafted neatly and with no waste:

Anti Hannah –
(Queen of the Teifi)
A bubble of infectious humour
Dancing from mischievous eyes,
An embroidered, lovable face,
Old country corn without the chaff.

The magic of the Mill
And the merriment of the kiln house
Ascends the ladder of memory
To white wash the dark clouds.

The wild tales rollicking
As she watched the roasting of the grain;
Today her garment of joy is fading,
Our yesterday is the today that has passed.

The Queen of the Cenarth Falls
Who challenged the avid anglers
From her coracle on the waving waters
Today is silent in the bonds of the graves.

But who holds sway in the cementery home?
The man-made grave is not hers truly,
When the salmon comes home to the Teifi.

[from Eluned's personal papers]

When Hannah lived at Glanawmor she could be quite a handful, according to Eluned. When the phone rang she was the first to answer and, before taking any message, would pester the caller with questions, discover the secrets of his life and form a great friendship in no time. Eluned would take her in the car to the local towns where parking could be difficult. Upon returning to the parked car, she could be sure that Anti Hannah would be in full flow of conversation with a police officer or traffic warden. She was also a great teller of tales and a bit of a poet herself. Eluned described how Anti Hannah's love of words could sometimes be problematic for her as she tried desperately to meet a deadline for handing in her script for a weekly soap opera on the BBC, and her aunt would insist at the last minute on regaling her with a story or launching into a recitation. However, Eluned concludes this story by conceding that such interruptions, despite being rather frustrating, always ended in great hilarity thanks to her aunt's genial personality.

There was one person who succeeded in riling Anti Hannah and that was the poet and family friend, Dewi Emrys. He would come to stay in Glanawmor occasionally and at such times either one or the other had to be kept apart in what was called a no-entry zone. Eluned remembers how both regarded themselves as consummate fishermen and when it became a matter of discussing sophisticated issues, such as tying fake bait, civil war was on the horizon. Both were also complete egotists, full of self-importance; and had the poet Cynan, also a keen fisherman, also been staying there, there would have been even more drama.

In a radio script broadcast the end of the sixties, Eluned portrays Anti Hannah:

> It's a pleasure to record the wonderful influence that came into my life at the start of the year – Anti Hannah came to live with us. Her husband, who had been blind for many years, had passed away and she was alone.

She was a dear and colourful character and settled down to become one of the household until she died two years ago aged ninety-nine. One thing Anti Hannah taught me – it's not the years that age a person. She was as lively in her mind and spirit as when she came to us a quarter of a century ago.

When anyone asked her age she would always reply 'Twenty-six next New Year's Day' and since she refused to let the years grind her down she continued to live a full and enjoyable life. She'd read, compose poetry, write stories, knit, fish – enjoying every moment of life... Many people across the world know of her – she's been filmed, painted and portrayed in papers and magazines...she was the Queen of the Coracles and the Teifi river. The house would be full of humour when she and others such as Dewi Emrys or Cynan held competitions to tell shaggy-dog stories about the fish that got away. She was never the one to give in first.

Cynan wrote a letter to Eluned sympathising with her loss when Anti Hannah died in 1969. It was a warm tribute to her (note the opening greeting):

Dear Crowned Bard Eluned,

I can easily accept and understand and sympathise with your striking turn of phrase 'that a grey sky has fallen across the green of spring in Glanawmor'. I well remember your Anti Hannah as a welcoming matriarch, her colloquial conversation like pearls.

•

Who would deny that Eluned could write very entertainingly herself? That gift of storytelling, inherited from the women in her family, should be no surprise. She had been raised in the sound and rhythm of legends and light-hearted stories, narrated by people who knew how to create their own entertainment at home. One neighbour of theirs said how he and his family would often pay them a visit, but the Glanawmor family never visited others. And why would they need to, since they were self-sufficient in their own

21

company and entertainment? The urge to entertain was in Eluned's blood and that urge was developed further as she arranged events, wrote sketches and songs to welcome back and cheer the spirits of returning servicemen during the Second World War. She was considered a born entertainer, and this desire to contribute to her community became an important aspect of her youth. There are reports of how she was encouraged to take part in discussions and cultural events in her chapel, Bryn Seion. She comments that they were fortunate in having no minister at the chapel for quite a long time, and because of that everybody had to pull their weight in the services, following the instructions of two deacons, Ben Jones and Richard Rees. There is no doubt that the chapel's influence was a formative one, as she became a Christian. She insisted, despite attending services in places of worship across the world, that nothing gave her the same thrill as when she attended Bryn Seion, where she was accepted in both senses of the word. In *The Reluctant Redhead* she writes: 'I have fond memories of the chapel of my childhood. I used to sit and stare in pride and awe at the sculptured *sedd fawr* (the big seat, where the chapel deacons sat) and the pulpit, hand-carved by a blind man. John Miles, Wern-goy, was a distant relative, so I felt I was entitled to acknowledge him with reverence and joy.'

Eluned's praise for the ministers who preached there and influenced her as a young girl is fulsome. She would call by the Rev. D. D. Walters, known as Gwallter Ddu, when he had retired, and lead the blind man to the chapel by the hand. Eluned knew of his reputation as a poet, and she liked to share her earlier poetic efforts with him. Because of his blindness, she felt confident in his company. Later she learnt of his great scholarliness and his ability as a minister to convince an audience, and from him she learnt about Karl Marx for the first time as well as many other famous people.

Even more suspect characters came to stay in Glamawmor too, sometimes for extended periods of time. There was a kind of garden house, a small thatched building known as the '*Gegin Fawr*' (the Great Kitchen), at the back of the house; it was an ideal place for guests, the inference being that the family kept lodgers for money, bed and breakfast and fishing – this was a time before hotels and guesthouses became popular. This kind of arrangement must have supported the family financially. There were plenty of fish for all-evening gatherings. Who knew if these fishing gentlemen that came to stay, many of them professional people, brought their own alcohol for late-night socialising. There is no doubt that there were no better lodgings or a warmer welcome at a stone's throw from the river.

One of these lodgers was a man who worked a local milk-round for the family. He hailed from Brittany and the only words of Welsh he knew were '*Bore da*' ('Good morning'). He was given the nickname of 'Bore Da' by the villagers whilst he was delivering the milk from a wooden cart with wheels underneath that made it look like a pram. Other anonymous visitors from Brittany deserve a futher mention in another chapter, but Glanawmor appeared to be a house with its doors wide open to everybody. It was said that Glanawmor had a licence to serve people after the local pubs had shut, but the residents refused to take money for any drink. Perhaps, according to some, they had no wish to turn it into a business. Perhaps they, like many locals of the time, made their own beer and were generous towards folk that called late at night. Did these women enjoy such jovial company, knowing full well that the men who frequented the pubs had more colourful tales to tell?

Another person who contributed to the happiness of Eluned's upbringing was Get, Eluned's cousin. I can remember them both passing my window on their way to the shop when I lived in Cenarth for a couple of years before settling in Penrhiw-llan. When I had a miscarriage in 1977 they were the first to call to see me, with a basketful of fruit and delectables to raise my spirits. This was a time when people would actively avoid talking to a mother who had lost a baby, because of the awkwardness of the situation. Eluned and Get felt no such difficulty. They did not come to 'sympathise', merely to raise a smile, and and they did this with aplomb. It was, after all, a time when I would not want to leave the house in case I saw a baby's pushchair or a child walking holding its mother's hand. As they left Glan yr Afon, I was given an invitation to come for tea, which I readily accepted. At their home, Get reminded me of the parable of Mary and Martha as Eluned sat talking to me while Get organised the tray and the afternoon-tea: beautiful sandwiches and tiny cakes. I remember Eluned laughing, saying that it was mostly '*chas y gegin*' (a 'chase round the kitchen') in their house – her unique description of rushing around the kitchen at the last minute to hide any mess. This turn of phrase chimes exactly with Eluned's personality and perhaps also with her way of composing poetry. I remember that I avoided saying that I too tried to write poems. It was probably just as well that I did not share this, as I would not have been able to hold a conversation with anybody about the process of writing. Years later, I came to know that Eluned suffered the same shyness that prevented her from talking about her work and explaining the way she wrote. Within the year, we had moved to Penrhiw-llan and I lost touch with Get and Eluned and lost the chance to invite them back for tea with us. And with that I also lost the chance, perhaps, to nurture a kind of friendship that might have been between us. But isn't setting oneself apart and treasuring privacy an integral part of being an artist, and indeed that of being a woman artist?

But I still remember the warmth that was apparent between her and Get and their close relationship. The letters Eluned sent to friends after Get's death show how deep their understanding and love was of each other. Eluned wrote a touching poem in memory of Get that showed the extent of her loss:

In memory of Get
In Glyn-y-Mêl, a carpet of snowdrops
When you went away,
And the dew of spring morning's pearl showers

24

Eyes full of tears , that day.
That purest of days, did they discern
Seeing you leave that there'd be no return?

You were brave in facing the future
And the long Armageddon,
Your hand on cheek as you said *adieu,*
Changing land all of a sudden,
So gentle and light, like the mischievous breeze,
The feather of a wren fluttering with ease.

The tears today how they linger
Stalactites they loom;
And the mist of *hiraeth* over the whole world
Without sun or moon,
A tempest came to spoil a carpet so pure,
The footprints of death is what you endured.

But spring's welcome will follow all grief
And the grave released,
For Faith renews the wounded heart
With a portion of peace,
And the Greatest Artist will return and dazzle
A magic carpet at Glyn y Mêl for all to marvel.

It is difficult to imagine Eluned's grief at losing Get, the two having
been 'sisters' and friends since childhood. And as she related tales
of the women in the family it was obvious that Get meant a lot to
Eluned, not only as an adopted older sister but also because of what
she offered Eluned as a storyteller. She saw Get as a milestone in
her life. During her early years Get lived for a while in Swansea and
was brought up hearing English before finding a home in Cenarth.
According to Eluned:

She opened a new world and Get had a way with a story, English stories – Robin Hood and similar tales – and I would hang on her every word. I'm sure that this was the best education I could have as regards storytelling in English. She taught me songs in English, too, so that I could sing in the many concerts held in the church hall or the schoolhouse, as the locals would have it.

[from Eluned's personal papers]

But of all the English Alice-like stories that Get would tell, the tale that totally captured her imagination was a Welsh one, the story of Nest, the Welsh princess. Eluned says: 'She engendered a glorious pride in me for the history of my country. Nest was in my dreams every night, and it was a child's paradise to go with Get to Nest's Castle, in Banc y Brain, by Gellidywyll, near Cocsed, a huge wooded glade, where there were the remains of an old mansion.' Only a person with a lightning imagination could have written a comment as thrilling about the effect of an old tale upon her. It is ironic that the historical princess Nest is the eponymous subject of Eluned's last great work, yet to be published or performed as a musical. But even though Get was a prolific storyteller in English, the 1911 Census states that she was monolingual Welsh. Was this a mistake, or was it bashfulness about using English in public?

It is possible that we think of D. J. Williams, a local west Walian author, when we think of the importance of the 'square mile' to an author, and the square mile between Cenarth and Abercych is equally as significant to Eluned and the kind of poet she was in her early years. At seven years of age she wrote a poem which was submitted without her knowledge and published in the local paper. A local forester from the Cawdor estate, Tom Morgan, Garreg Lwyd, saw the poem and told her mother in no uncertain terms that there was no way that Eluned could have written that poem. Eluned was summoned to the house and a pencil put in her hand, and made to sit at the table. Her mother asked the man to give her a subject on which to write, and he chose a subject close to his heart

26

– the woodcutter. Eluned proceeded to create a poem about the man as a murderer because he had cut down her favourite tree. Her poem ended that quarrel. In her teenage years, Eluned was also given lessons in *cynghanedd*, strict metre poetry with internal rhymes, by Mrs Clement Davies in Newcastle Emlyn and this also shows how keen she was, abetted by her family's encouragement, to succeed as a poet.

She wrote numerous verses for different events and in honour of local characters. Of her native area, she states: 'I'm sure that Cenarth in the twenties was quite poor and despondent like many other places. But to us, born here, there was plenty of fresh air, and nature, working overtime, had woven its beauty like a warm coat around every one of us to keep the poverty of the time out.' And through thinking of the 'warm coat', one thinks of her walking to school every day, some two and a half miles to Abercych, the next village along, in all weathers. 'And in spite of the distance, the meagre sandwiches and a bottle of cold tea sometimes, if I was lucky, I enjoyed every day in school… I careered through the classes at full tilt and passed to go to Cardigan grammar school before I was ten.'

Eluned's thirst for education became obvious even to the Moshtir or Master, the headmaster at Abercych who was a sweet and kind man. Recalling those years, she came to the conclusion that the headmaster did not believe in secondary education for girls. In fact, she maintains that she was not given more than one night of homework preparation for the scholarship at the county school, the 11 plus as it was known. It is suggested that he was so indifferent about further education that Madge, her sister, missed the chance to sit the exam, the result being that her mother had to pay for Madge's schooling. Eluned admits that since she had succeeded in getting a place, Madge would have done so standing on her head, because she was 'more able than me'. It was, Eluned maintains, through the perseverance and confidence of her mother and Get to 'keep things going at home', that the two girls were 'given the best education possible'. Indeed, Madge came top of the girls in her year at University College, Aberystwyth, and she shone in her science studies, following a career as a scientist in a laboratory. Due to diligence at home both, in due course, succeeded in their chosen fields. It is also interesting to note that after marrying and moving to Stafford, Madge would lead services and preach in English in local churches as an acknowledged lay-preacher for many years. Both sisters became resolute in their faith as well as dedicated to their respective professions.

But a new and exciting period was awaiting Eluned, as she prepared to leave her square mile and turn towards an unfamiliar world in London at the beginning of the thirties. It is not clear why Eluned did not go to college like Madge. According to one of the family, they believed that a time in London would be beneficial to her. Eluned went to a private school, the Bestreben High School for Girls, situated at 197 Willesden Lane, London. Bestreben was one of many private schools on this road at the beginning of the twentieth century.

It is not clear either how it was possible to obtain a place at a private school for Eluned at a time when the family lived in straitened circumstances. Was there a generous benefactor to help with the costs? And how was this school found in the first place? It was suggested that this happened through the Cardigan school headmaster's contacts. Eluned herself does not understand why she was sent there. She says in her autobiography:

When I left Cardigan Grammar School I was sent to London to a boarding school. I'm not quite sure why, but I think the family's reasoning was that maybe I would dislike the noisy wicked city and would want to come home and settle for going to university and becoming a teacher. My mother's friend Katy, trying to explain to an inquisitive neighbour, said that I had been 'sent there to be polished off'. Sorry, but the polish was obviously the wrong brand. I didn't shine, but, step by step, I entered a life totally different from the one of my home village.

28

It is no surprise that a nosy neighbour asked about her departure to the school. The fact that Eluned was away at a private school when the family had no visible means to send her there would have been the talk of the village. Once again, Eluned is reticent to explain the reason for sending her to Bestreben and as was her wont, she manages to silence any enquiry by using humour.

During Eluned's childhood, her home at Glanawmor was no 'nest of poets' as in Gwenallt's poem 'Rhydcymerau', but they were a household of talkative women; their lively loquaciousness would have won the hearts of neighbours and visitors alike. This was also a place where harmony and sharing duties was an integral part of life, and they would welcome anybody to come and share in their company, to become a part of their world and their existence.

London and Dewi Emrys

Even though Eluned had been accepted at Bestreben school for girls in London, she said very little about the education she received there. In one interview she said that she was awarded a scholarship but she did not specify whether this meant that her family did not have to pay for her to go to that particular school. It was suggested by a member of her family that the school was a kind of finishing school though Eluned herself noted that she failed to acquire any polish whilst she was there. It is likely that she learnt how to write letters and been given instruction as to how to navigate a typewriter; she was an exceedingly accomplished typist throughout her life. Eluned herself said that she took a course in journalism, but there is no evidence regarding where the course was held. One thing is certain, she did later learn to master the computer exceedingly well, doing so in her nineties. She bought a computer and was given tutorials by a local company in Blaenachddu, Capel Iwan, BCC IT, who now have their offices in Newcastle Emlyn. She baptised her first computer Siencyn, and after its demise, she named its successor ap Siencyn ('ap' meaning 'son of').

What can be extrapolated from Eluned's time in London was that she benefitted from the kind of education that was prevalent for girls in particular at the time, where they would learn how to keep minutes and book-keeping. It would prepare her for a good career in posts other than the usual jobs available to girls of her standing, such as going into service or working as shopgirls. The fact that she had secretarial skills explains why the court clerk insisted on employing her to help in the courts years later. It is not likely that he would have dared employ her based only on the fact that he was a friend of her mother's; the experience gained in the city would have furnished Eluned with the secretarial capabilities which ensured that she was more than able to execute the work at hand.

She did not say much about the private school and there are no archives of information held at the British Library or in other libraries in London other than notes of the address and the names of the teachers who taught there. Eluned said that she stayed in London after finishing her education and tried to live off her earnings through writing romantic stories for magazines and that amazingly she succeeded in getting her first story accepted at her third attempt. The information about these stories is scant but Eluned gives the impression that she enjoyed the hustle and bustle of the city to the full and that she took advantage of networking there – essential for a fledgling writer with high hopes.

'Not been to London,' is a saying used in rural Cardiganshire for someone deficient in some aspects of life. It is not suggested that Eluned failed at any point during her time at the school, and she also succeeded in seeing a little of life outside school walls, sneaking out with her friend Joan, the daughter of a senior diplomat in India. Between them, they had the time of their lives roaming the streets of London. In *The Reluctant Redhead* tales are told of the two of them going to the pictures and finding themselves on Fleet Street, where Eluned hoped to bump into the famous Welsh poet, Dewi Emrys. This indeed came to pass through Joan's brazenness when she introduced herself to Dewi so that she could introduce her friend Eluned to him.

To a girl from the country, London was a totally new world and heralded a seismic change in her life. Even though Britain in the thirties was in the midst of dire economic problems, Eluned does not give the impression that these constraints had any effect on her or her city living. It was a period when women were being given more prominence in society, especially after contributing to the war effort during the Great War by doing 'mens' work, and by 1928 every woman over 21 was given the vote. This was a time for women, especially unmarried women, to enjoy their newfound freedoms – convention and taboos would be put aside and women would enjoy entertainment into the evening. This was the time of popular women's magazines, a time when fashion and leisure activities came into their own. It is no surprise therefore that Eluned took advantage of the changes in society when her time at the school came to an end and she decided she would stay in London and try her luck with the numerous magazines available. As Eluned wrote under various pseudonyms, there is no way of verifying in which magazines her work was published; she even maintained that she wrote for Mills & Boon.

Eluned does not mention going to any Welsh chapel in London, nor does she mention any of the many Welsh societies that proliferated at the time. After all, there were thirty-one Welsh chapels in London in 1938 just before the start of the war[4]. One of those was in Willesden, within reach of Bestreben school. Surely the school would not have refused permission for one of their pupils to attend a service of their choice? She does not mention any cultural Welsh societies that she might have attended, even though she had been a key member of such societies at home. It is also strange that Eluned did not mention bookshops in London, especially Foyle's bookshop. In 1931, William Griffith became the head of the Welsh department at the establishment, named Foyle's Welsh Depot, which also published books in Welsh: books like *Williams Pantycelyn* by Saunders Lewis in 1927 and *Llydaw* by Ambrose Bebb in 1929. The impression given is that Eluned immersed herself totally in the English world whilst she was in London. Not that this was strange. It is possible that this society held more appeal, and that there was more romance in mixing with people from other backgrounds. I believe that the key to this mystery lies in the fact that Eluned saw this new world as one that appealed to her curiosity. This, as well as the fact that there is a sense, perhaps, that Eluned

---

[4] Huw Edwards, 'Llawenydd a Llanast', bbc.co.uk/cymrufyw 17 October 2014.

suffered a little from an inferiority complex. She says this of the Café Royal on Regent Street, where the poets and artists congregated:

> to someone from Cenarth, the Café Royal in my younger days was not a home from home. It appeared to me to be forever bursting with odd, creative geniuses, like Edith Sitwell. I was in awe of her, but also had a somewhat envious admiration of her courage in bellowing out her poetry to all and sundry through the hugest old-fashioned gramophone-trumpet I'd ever seen. She appeared to have a cast-iron self-defence against the world. No doubt it was Dewi Emrys's concern for my welfare that kept me, almost compulsively, hinged to this mottled crowd.

She fell for the exotic, the unfamiliar; in the middle of this rag-tag bunch, this motley crew, she saw the genius in every artist she got to know and was utterly convinced of that, without seeing the excellence in her own work. Yet it was in this kind of circumstance that she was introduced to Augustus John by Dewi Emrys. John described Dewi as a friend, 'but who was also taking fatherly care of this lonely girl from Wales.' She talks at great length in her autobiography about Augustus and says that they were birds of a feather even though, 'our only point of contact was our wayward impulsiveness of acting first and getting into complications afterwards.'

Eluned writes in a revealing way of her first meeting with Dewi Emrys, and it was the start of a complex friendship that lasted until his death in 1952:

> a friend in Bestreban [*sic*] ... Joan, was an optimist to delight my heart ... before long we learned to dress in high heels and fiery red lipstick ... and down the fire escape we would go until we reached Fleet Street. I was innocent enough to believe that by walking along Fleet Street, the muse would surely strike. But even for a naughty child out of school without permission, there came a prize. I got

to meet Dewi Emrys for the first time ... And through Joan's enterprise we eventually spoke together. I spoke to the Bard of the Highway – this was a milestone that totally stood out...

In another part of her notes, she says:

Life was vibrant and there I was, in my element, in the midst of the giants – Dewi Emrys, Augustus John, Caradoc Evans, Dylan Thomas, Roy Campbell, Edith Sitwell and other bohemians of the time. But without a doubt, the biggest of these in London was Dewi Emrys ... the connection continued back in Wales. He became a regular visitor to our house, and even though I did not compete in literary competitions, he urged me to do so many times, and his influence remains a blessing.

Eluned admits that she wrote very little poetry during her time in London, and perhaps Dewi Emrys' fame as a poet of national standing was more of a draw for her at this juncture rather than her desire to see him as a mentor. Then, having got to know him as a friend her admiration of him deepened, as well as her pity for him. Perhaps it was his death that galvanised her into writing a paean of praise to him and it is fair to say that winning in the Cardigan Gŵyl Fawr in 1965, with this *pryddest* (long poem in free verse) to Dewi, under the nom de plume of Rebel, was her first significant success as a poet. She only published a short extract of the winning poem in her biography of him, *Dewi Emrys*, published in 1971 by Gwasg Gomer.

In her copy of the poem *'Mieri lle bu Mawredd'* ('Thorns Where There Once Was Grandeur'), she had stuck a photograph of Dewi and underneath, the caption, 'With respect to Dewi Emrys'. The series of poems begin in Rhos y Caerau; there are four parts to the poem, following his formative years along the pathways of his life towards Pwllderi.

The adjudicator was the *Prifardd* (Chief Bard) R. Bryn Williams who stated that 'this poem creates subtle images, savouring a sense of atmosphere of place'. He went on to say, 'Here is an artist who can convey an image in very few words.' He closes by saying: 'This poet rises above the others in originality of thought, also as a craftmaster, but above all else, as a poet. Here is an affectionate poem.'

Eluned must have been thrilled with this success for she kept her copy of the poem, even though the copy had faded somewhat over the years, as well as a photograph of Dewi on the manuscript cover. It is a mystery why did she not publish this poem along with the rest of her work in her sole published volume of poetry, *Cerddi Glyn-y-mêl*, (*Glyn-y-mêl Poems*) in 1985. Had the poem appeared in her book, it could have proved her poetic abilities in creating a richly-layered *pryddest*, and an unequivocal testimony to her authenticity as a poet.

One explanation for her not publishing the poem was that she had heard by then of the mean rumours circulating – that Dewi Emrys was the true author of her poems – and did not wish to give the naysayers an inch to stretch their stories further.

If this was behind her decision not to publish, then it was a sad state of affairs. Another reason for not publishing the poem in the biography might have been because, as an unassuming person, she had no wish to promote her own cause as a poet. I have no doubt that the inclusion of the whole poem would have been enough to silence the whispers once and for all, but she did not see things that way. Before working on the Dewi Emrys biography, Eluned, as the secretary of the Ceredigion Wayfarers, organised the publication of a tribute volume of Dewi's poetry in a book called *Wedi Storom* (*After the Storm*) published by Gomer in May 1965, some months before she won the Crown at the Cardigan Gŵyl Fawr. The book was edited by the Rev. D. Jacob Davies and the crowned bard W. J. Gruffydd. This is what Eluned said in the foreword to the book:

When Dewi Emrys died, the Ceredigion Wayfarers decided to remember their president in a practical manner.

A committee was formed to raise funds and the committee is deeply indebted to all who contributed, to Sir David James, and to the Gorsedd of Bards' Committee for their help and support. It was Dewi Emrys' wish that he should have a memorial stone in Pwllderi, and the committee decided to remember him in three ways:

a) To erect a memorial stone in Pwllderi.
b) To give an annual prize in his name in the Englyn competition in the National Eisteddfod.
c) To publish a commemorative volume of his work.

The Archdruid Cynan and the Reverend William Morris were chosen to select Dewi Emrys' poems and the committee is greatly indebted to them. Tribute must be paid to the late Reverend Seymour Rees for his careful work collecting and keeping his friend's works and for putting them on loan so as to facilitate this selection.

Here is *Wedi Storom*, in rememberance of Dewi Emrys – poet, man of letters, preacher, lecturer and a man of great character. I hope this volume is given a reception worthy of its author.

Eluned Phillips (Sec.)

Cenarth

Inside my copy of *Wedi Storom*, bought in a secondhand bookshop, there is a page with the words; '8/- in credit. 26/8/65' – a rather ironic motif considering that Dewi Emrys died without a penny to his name. And yet, through the kindness of the redoutable Ceredigion Wayfarers, led by Eluned, his name was honoured in a volume that was a celebration of his work. This is not the only kindly act performed by Eluned for her literary hero.

Some years later, Eluned started on a biography of him, writing to a good many authors, poets and critics. Her foreword to that biography, *Dewi Emrys* (Gomer, 1971) shows much affection, perhaps undeserved, on her part towards the subject of the book as she mentions how he started to pour out the story of his life to a select gathering in Glanawmor at the unearthly hour of five o'clock in the morning. Her description is a heartfelt account of how they had been listening to Cynan relating his experiences earlier in the night. She says: 'After the feast, Dewi was starving, as usual and he adjourned, along with a well-known barrister, an artist friend from Paris and me, so that we could raid the pantry. And then Dewi stood centre stage.'

The conversation between the two is revealing as Emrys talks about Pwllderi. He repeated a wish he had made a year or two earlier, when he said that he would very much like to have a large stone erected in his memory in Pwllderi, Pembrokeshire. Then, out of the blue, he turned to Eluned and 'commanded without ceremony':

'I want you to write a book about me. Do you promise?'

I promised innocently, without counting the cost of trying to capture a shooting star. I asked one question only: 'Do you want me to tell the whole truth?'

Both sunrise and the people present waited to hear his answer:

'What do you mean, eh? I'm a large enough bird, aren't I, that anybody can take a pot shot at me?'

I did not ask another question; within the year, there were strangers living in the Bwthyn. (Dewi Emrys' home.)

Only a person who had the ability to tell a subtle tale could have written the line: 'Both sunrise and the people present waited to hear his answer.' And the sentence mentioning the strangers living in the cottage within the year is Eluned's terse but eloquent cameo of their relationship: 'I promised innocently.' At times, Eluned's gentle nature gives rise to surprise. The word 'innocent' is one that appears many times in this biography. And it appears to describe her in the context of Dewi more than in any other, as we see that she had promised to complete a task of epic proportions when the number of his long poems written for competition was considered and as far as his colourful character was concerned. But she kept to her word and that also is an intrinsic part of her character: her steadfastness and dedication to her friend.

When it was time to write about him, she says, 'I only included the facts that I could prove in this book.' But the following sentence is a disturbing one for the reader. Eluned admits:

> I agreed to leave out an important part of his life-story at the insistent request of one who had a close connection to the poet in his personal life, as there was a possibility, it seems, of creating an adverse psychological reaction were I to reveal the truth. The purpose of the book is not to stir any kind of reaction, nor to profit from giving publicity to the unfortunate twists and turns of life.

Perhaps a more ambitious biographer would have enjoyed revealing potentially salacious details about the contentious poet. And in retrospect, perhaps the door should have been opened slightly on every aspect of his character and personality, even if it did bring his name into disrepute. But to Eluned, the 'insistent request' as well as the 'adverse psychological reaction' were strong enough words to persuade her that the welfare of the 'living' was paramount. What was the important part of the whole of the personality that was not to be revealed? It is a pity that she was not brave enough or able to express what is clearly a grave historical omission.

The revelation of secrets in biographical works often depends on the cooperation and permission of those who know the subject, in particular if the biographer himself has no personal knowledge of what is kept under lock and key. It is also easy to imagine that a man like Dewi – an egocentric, selfish man who believed his poetic powers to be unrivalled – would not have wanted to appear in a less than favourable light to someone who worshipped him. Was it his colourful carefree larger-than-life personality as well as his poetic talents that appealed to her? He seems to have had a charismatic personality that appealed to the women of Glanawmor.

It was an open-hearted home welcoming all kinds of individuals, from geniuses to wayfarers.

What becomes clear is that the family – this house full of women, as Eluned describes them – welcomed not just local travellers but well-known gentlemen as guests to stay in their midst. Indeed, among the ones to stay there had been the Archdruid of the National Eisteddfod, Cynan, Dewi, the artist from Paris, and a renowned barrister whose name is never mentioned. It was in the presence of this kind of society that these women thrived; they craved learned company and the opportunity to deepen their own knowledge of culture through giving them a generous welcome to the house, time after time.

Eluned's Dewi Emrys biography appeared twenty years after her initial promise, and the loss of her only literary friend weighed heavily on her. She kept her word, as she put all her energies into chronicling and sifting through his achievements and his lack of success in the eisteddfod competitions. It is likely that an arm's length perspective through the passage of time gave her a clearer objective view of her subject and the way 'this colourful and well-loved character disappeared from Wales'. As she traces his life and disappointments perhaps her feelings towards him intensified in that he too, like her, had 'been born outside of his time'. This is what his contemporary, the poet and author Caradog Prichard, had to say about him: 'It is a great shame that he had not been born half a century earlier, so that he could have shone in the high-flown eloquence of the last century, or that he should have been born seven centuries ago and have been in the company of Dafydd [ap Gwilym] and the true artistic masters of *cynghanedd* (strict verse).'

Do these comments also echo Eluned's own feelings about herself? There were other qualities that made Eluned and Dewi's temperaments allies when she says, 'One of the great tragedies in Dewi's life was that he did not get the chance to go to university, and a bitterness collected inside him towards the more fortunate ones and he insisted on challenging them constantly.'

When she looked for the opinion of literary critics and academics on Dewi's work, Eluned says this:

> I sought responses from our foremost critics and scholars. There was great interest in Dewi Emrys as a person, and they were invariably willing to offer a mature opinion after being given time to study his work; there were few who were familiar enough with his works to give a direct opinion. In spite of all the controversy in the press and the national prizes, and the books he published, there was never any mention of looking at his work in detail.

This same comment could be applied to Eluned herself as she tried to right the wrongs made to Dewi. By the time the book appeared in 1972, five years had passed since she had won the Crown in Bala in 1967 and all the unkind mumurings about her own authenticity had spread through the 'establishment' and across the country. I too feel guilty, because my first thought when I began on the task of looking through Eluned's work in order to interpret it was that I should hold an inquest on Eluned Phillips as a person. But Eluned's style was not to wallow in self-pity, as Dewi did, and for this she reprimands him:

> The fact that he had written poetry, almost without exception, about his own lack of luck, his exile, and against the society that he felt was persecuting him, made his work monotonous and deceitful; it made it pedestrian rather than great. He was so obsessed by this – that he failed to touch the social excitement that could have ignited his imagination. After all, he had lived though two world wars and yet he wallowed in his own self-pity and self-preservation. Even in his masterpiece, 'Pwllderi', he insisted on hurling stones against his nation. I remember him saying to me that he was the sailor in the poem – and that Wales has ignored him and cast him aside:

And the poor sailor shouting from the rock
Shouting and shouting, shouting and nobody answering,
And only the birds on the rock hearing him.

He said that the 'demons' in the poem were 'the scholars'. But strangely enough, Eluned defends them by saying: 'He had been in the shadow of this spectre for all of his life. I believe now that the academics were close to the mark, and that it was the eisteddfod competitor and the dramatic preacher in him that were his main enemies as he tried to measure his literary standing.'

Eluned showed her critical perception with her precise comments. These unbiased comments by the author of the biography show clearly that she could, in spite of their close friendship, see his literary failings more than anyone.

However, Eluned, the benevolent benefactress, did sympathise with his fragile nature – she filled the pantry shelves in the Bwthyn and bought meals for him. She said that 'the innocent child was an essential part of Dewi.'

She took pity on him because he had been caught between two lights: the respectable world of the Wales of the time, and the more challenging and bohemian world that was spreading across Europe. A conversation between them reveals his capricious behaviour:

Perhaps because he was a Welsh preacher, he was never given the chance from the beginning to be an out-and-out beatnik in his time. He was unable to accept his tumultuous marriage or his romantic dalliances with an open honesty like a bohemian. There was all the distance in the world between him and his friends, Augustus John and Dylan Thomas. He liked to think of himself as Dafydd [ap Gwilym] the troubadour, but when I questioned him about women, his answer was that it was they who chased him throughout his life and that he was incapable of avoiding them. And if he was unable to reach the artistic heights of bohemians

41

from other countries, undoubtedly the memory of him as one of the most vibrant characters in twentieth century Wales remains.

Eluned Phillips accomplished a remarkable feat in compiling such a detailed biography of Dewi Emrys. She collected material from various sources, and interviewed many critics and poets. Some of the responses appear in the book. Yet I found some interesting letters received by Eluned following her requests for responses to Dewi's work. Perhaps it was her slap-dash approach that meant she asked many people to write 'a paragraph or two on Dewi's poetry'. But this would have been anathema to some discerning critics who took their responsibilities seriously. Indeed, Derec Llwyd Morgan responded in a courteous manner by noting that very point and saying, 'poetic criticism is the subject of an essay or an independent article, in my opinion'. A fair comment; and he added, 'Thank you for inviting me to make observations on Dewi Emrys, but I doubt greatly that such observations should appear in a biography written by somebody who knew him as you did.'

Eluned also received many warm and encouraging letters, like this one:

Baner ac Amserau Cymru,
11, Bryn-teg
Denbigh

Dear Miss Eluned Phillips,

I am gratified to hear that you are nearing the end of the task of completing the biography of Dewi Emrys: it was time that one was written of him. I should like to help you by expressing my opinion on an old friend's poetry. I shall do so with pleasure, but there is one difficulty – I am up to my ears at the moment (along with Euros Bowen and Eirian Davies) trying to work our way through 37 long poems for the Crown at the Ammanford National Eisteddfod! And around a dozen novels for the Literature Medal at the Pontrhydfendigaid eisteddfod! And there are poems yet to come for Rhydfendigaid! You see that I have – in a weak moment – promised too much. If you can wait until the work is done, then I will help you. I'm afraid it means waiting until the end of May. All right?

I wish you every success with the important work of creating a worthy memorial to a poet whom I hold in great regard.

Faithfully,

Gwilym R. Jones

Eluned received many letters that spurred her on with the work, like this letter from Alun Llywelyn-Williams that ends by saying:

I am truly sorry that I have to refuse you, because, as you know, I enjoyed your winning poems at the Bala Eisteddfod greatly and I should like to repay a little of my debt to you if that were possible.

Most sincerely,

Alun Llywelyn-Williams

A warm letter also came from Bedwyr Lewis Jones in April 1970 that notes, like others, the fact that workloads are heavy and asking for more time to write his contribution. He closes the letter by saying, 'I enclose a letter regarding *Cerddi '70*, inviting you to send a poem for the book'.

All in all, the letters are courteous about the book. Eluned kept the letters carefully but it is obvious that many could not accept the invitation to contribute because of the pressure of work. There are other warm letters from people such as Pennar Davies and Gwyndaf. And even though some responded, academics and crowned poets and well-known critics, there is no evidence to show that Eluned received anything from Dilys Cadwaladr – a crowned poet herself, having won in the National Eisteddfod in Rhyl in 1953 – who was the mother of Dewi Emrys' daughter Dwynwen.

Little is known about the relationship or the dynamic between

Eluned and Dilys, nor at that time of the relationship between Dwynwen, Dewi's daughter, and her mother. But there are a few letters kept by Eluned that attest to a cordial friendship between Eluned and Dwynwen that continued after Dewi's life-time. These letters are in English:

[Address not revealed]

My dear Eluned,

It was very nice to see you and also to see the MSS – it looks very good and you've done some remarkable research. Pity you are prevented from saying a lot that's important, but I'm afraid it is always the way when relatives are alive. I suppose complete biogs can only be written when the subject has been dead about 200 years!

Of course, I'll be glad to see a copy MS and approve it in writing, *to save you any later trouble* [handwritten].

Do let me know when you are coming next, a few days before if poss., so that perhaps you can come for a meal and meet a few literary types etc. I have quite a lot of interesting friends who would be thrilled to meet you. Also I should like to see the whole text of the poem at the end of the book, which was most effective.

Warm wishes,

Dwynwen

In a letter to a friend, many years later, Eluned admits her surprise that some people believed her to be Dewi Emrys' lover:

Glyn-y-mêl Cenarth,
Castellnewydd Emlyn
Dyfed SA38 9JP
16.2.88

Dear Friend,

... It is a great shock to find out recently that half the world thinks that Dewi Emrys and I were lovers. Nothing is further from the truth and it had not struck me at all that anybody should make such a statement.

... I'm truly sorry that I'm drowning you with all these exclamations. Please forgive a sinner. I must go now to move the dust from one piece of furniture to another. Sam (the new baby in the family) is on his way to Glyn-y-mêl. I must introduce him respectfully to the place. I hope that ... is still enjoying life. At the end of the day, even though I moan, I must admit that life is worth living.

With very warmest wishes
Luned

By the way ... 'They' are at it again ... this time they are adamant that I am the author of *Teulu'r Mans*.[5] Lord preserve us! Sorry for the rush.

It is difficult to believe that this piece of gossip didn't come to her attention before 1988 as the stories were quite widespread. Indeed, the first thing I learned about Eluned was this supposed relationship between her and Dewi Emrys. The fact that both Dilys Cadwaladr and Eluned had won the Crown at the National Eisteddfod was bound to create a 'two and two makes nine' situation, as Eluned had it. It also shows how innocent she was, that she would not have considered that tittle-tattle would certainly have taken root in the perverse minds of some people.

Perhaps it is because Dewi had spent periods in Glanawmor as a family friend and as an avid fisherman that these rumours started. She had also been a member of the Ceredigion Wayfarers, established by Dewi, and in full view of 'field gossip' – Eluned's way

---

[5] *Teulu'r Mans* (*The Manse Family*), was a contentious comedy series aired on S4C at the end of the eighties 1987-90, and not the radio series of the same name scripted by Eluned in the fifties.

of describing spreading stories. But was she foolish to keep such a close and unwavering attachment to such a contentious figure? Indeed, ultimately it damaged her good name.

It is difficult to understand what hold Dewi Emrys had on such a gentle personality as Eluned Phillips. Today it could be seen as similar to the way groupies follow famous singers everywhere and look upon them as beyond mortal. There is something peverse in thinking about her in this context as an immature young girl, losing her head over a man twice her age. Whilst accepting that this was foolish infatuation, it would be expected that having grown older and experienced a little of the world for herself in Paris and then in Cardiff, that she would have found her own writerly path, without carrying the burden of such an overpowering personality as Dewi.

But Eluned remained close to him and revered him throughout her life. Her unstinting effort in remembering him, even after he died, is disappointing as it gave the cynics free rein to doubt her integrity and independence of thought as a poet. It is easy to understand why some believed that her relationship with him had been more than just that of friends. Indeed, she was at fault for not taking off her serf's cloak once she had established herself as a talented scriptwriter. Even in her later years, she would often refer to him in her conversations about poetry. To her he seemed to be the greatest Welsh poet of all time. Suffice to say that the insistent praise – possibly unwarranted – she bestowed on him tarnished her own name as an award-winning poet. It is ironic that as a result of her unending admiration of Emrys, her own name should be sullied among people throughout the country who saw in her the malign influence of her 'wizard'.[6]

---

[6] There are materials and detailed and revealing notes in her papers, as well as some of Dewi Emrys' work, not used by her in the biography.

Paris in the Thirties

After the end of the Great War, artists flocked to Paris, and the twenties were christened *les années folles*, the crazy years. In the thirties, too, the Romantic movement was at its height, and the image of the artist as a genius was prevalent in some circles. On the left bank of the river Seine, on the Boulevard du Montparnasse and at the Rue de Rennes crossroads, there were cafés and watering holes aplenty, and many Breton restaurants. Here was the heart of the artistic and intellectual life of Paris. According to Jean Cocteau – an artist much admired by Eluned, and whom she accidentally trod on one time while he slept on the floor in Edith Piaf's flat in Montparnasse – Paris was a place where poverty and luxury coexisted. Some would be at their wits' end, living on next to nothing for the main driving force there was that of composing and creating artworks. Others succeeded in living communally and paying a low rent for the privilege. Often there was no water or heat, with rats living like kings, but the tenants didn't give a fig because their attention was focused elsewhere. Some of the stars of the time were: Picasso, Apollinaire, Jean Rhys, Max Jacob, Joyce, Hemingway, Ford Madox Ford, Ezra Pound, Max Ernst, Rousseau, Giacometti, André Breton, Jean Miró, Degas and Gertrude Stein. As well as the famous ones, there were hundreds of would-be artists or hangers-on who were eager to capture some of the sparkle given off by the stars.

It is not known exactly when or for how long Eluned Phillips lived in Paris, and we do not know where she lived in the city or how she supported herself financially while she was there, other than in family accounts. There is no mention of her having to wash dishes like George Orwell, nor is there evidence of feasting in grand restaurants. Whatever sustained her, the experience was an eye-opener into the kind of life that an artist, somebody who wished to write, could achieve. It is highly likely that she became besotted, like a kind of *flâneuse* on the streets of the Paris *quartiers*. Perhaps she, like the novelist Patrick Modiano, echoed the way that the mystery of Paris influenced her. In the *Guardian,* October 2015, Modiano discussed with Euan Cameron his early childhood in Paris, which he wrote about in his book *Pedigree*: 'It was there on Rue Fontaine, Place Blanche, Rue Frochot, that I first brushed against the mysteries of Paris and, without quite realising it, began dreaming of a life for myself.'

It was this creative powerhouse that that captivated Eluned one day and she found herself totally mesmerised by the beautiful, romantic city. If London was considered a city that was at the other end of the earth from Cenarth, then for Eluned discovering Paris was even more of a wonder. And Paris in the thirties was a vibrant and exciting place to visit.

From the outset, when she was released from the confines of Cenarth village life, there seems to have been a duality in Eluned's personality. Her feet were firmly planted in rural Wales and yet they touched fleetingly and lightly on the European continent's terra firma and beyond. She travelled to different places at a time when not many people crossed the water even for short holidays. She went on her own, even though she was a woman and unmarried, something frowned upon by people who believed that a woman's place was in the home, looking after her husband or tending ageing parents. But Eluned was no long-suffering 'spinster'. And she was certainly not raised in a conventional family, but by a strong group of women who believed fundamentally in having control of their own destiny.

From the time when she arrived in Paris, she fell for the city because of its international and exotic appeal, and that gave her carte blanche to behave as differently as she wished. The climate was perfect for creative adventures, populated by artists from all manner of persuasions, from the world of music, literature, theatre or art, who bounced ideas off each other.

Again, the impressions of Eluned's time in Paris are fleeting, even if it heavily influenced the rest of her life. Perhaps Paris was the definitive moment in her life precisely because it was so different from 'sleepy' Cenarth, Eluned's description of her village. Her eyes were opened to seeing another way of life without any restrictions or constraints. The bohemian city was a stark contrast to the Welsh-village respectability that she had been subjected to in rural west Wales, even though members of her own family were not puritanical, and her extended family by all accounts quite unconventional in their views of the world. But crossing from London to France was much easier than spending a whole day on a tortuous, meandering journey trying to get back home to west Wales. She does not mention exactly where she stayed, but Joan, her friend from Bestreben school, had a brother who was a musician in Paris and in no time they were both drawn to the magic of the Bohemian Left Bank. Occasionally Eluned managed to smuggle songs by the young composer Jean-Noel Pierre, which Joan's brother recorded in France, over to Britain, but details are scant as to the kinds of songs they were and how illegal her part was in these escapades. It is difficult to imagine the young Eluned as an experienced criminal. Was it naivety that led her to agree to do such a thing? Did she perhaps not want to disappoint her friend? This was a time when she claims to have consorted with rebels and those who liked to take risks. And through socialising with people who held different values from her own, she got to make friends, and especially with one kindred spirit, a Breton, who captured her heart. But telling of their meeting requires the introduction of another person who became an important lifelong influence.

As a result of her friendship with the musician Jean-Noel Pierre, Eluned met Edith Piaf and visited her at her home. She said that Jean-Noel asked her one night if she would like to meet someone special and after answering enthusiastically that she would very much like that, she found herself at Edith Piaf's flat. This is how she described the experience in pages of notes written in Welsh: 'down into the depths of the earth like a mole's cell, a forgotten cellar on the Rue Pigalle, the dampness creating pictures of death on the walls ... Piaf was just a set of eyes and a nose, her body like a cocoon rolled into four large black coats to keep the cold and the devil out.' She goes on:

I was asked out of the blue one time how I would describe Edith Piaf and the answer that came to me was 'Unexpected.' And indeed, having thought, I cannot better that description. That was the appeal: the mixture of virtues, failings and genius. Most probably it was the same combination that gave that unexpected power to her voice. And she was never as unexpected as that first night that I met her ... in the light of one candle I saw a chair in the middle of the floor, and sitting in it a thing similar to an Egyptian mummy, almost buried under a load of black coats – four, when I counted later. In the middle of the blackness, I saw a nose with a cold-white forehead where a beam of light shone.

I decided that my friend was pulling my leg and I took little notice when I was introduced as someone from Wales. Jean-Noel Pierre took a bottle of wine from his pocket and placed it in front of her, urging her to sing. But I felt nothing but pity that we should be harassing someone who was so unhappy and low, that I suggested that it would be better if we went. To my great surprise, this half-alive body shook free of the chair, peeled off her coats and started to sing. And this totally unexpected voice, and totally electrifying – with a voice the colour of oysters – an exciting combination of raging waves breaking on the rocks and the tender waves of summer kissing the silken sands.

And as Piaf herself had been totally unexpected, I understood afterwards that we had caught her in one of her melancholic periods. She asked me to come and see her in ten days. I felt an imperative that I should indeed meet her, and this is how the chance came for me to know the unexpected.

[from Eluned's personal papers]

There, on that first night, she heard her singing about the little girl scratching a living on the streets:

She was born like a sparrow;
She lived like a sparrow
She dies like a sparrow.

Later, Eluned wrote these words about her, calling her 'Llwyd Bach y Baw' ('Little Grubby Sparrow'):

O little grey birdie, singing nightly
in Paris, play City of throngs;
the crowd uncaring, rushing and mocking
their ears deaf to your songs.

Like an Angel from high, Louis Lepleé came by,
he recognised the prayer in the voice;
he saved the young girl from the evil whirl
of Rue Tryon, street of rapists and vice.

O, little grey birdie,
dressed so shabbily,
singing so pluckily
in the rain in the City,
and pleading nightly
manna for the hungry.
O, little grey birdie.

Non, rien de rien.
Non, je ne regrette rien

You flew high to freedom, from your evil Sodom
and other destructive parts.
You set yourself sights, reaching immortal heights
your voice captivating all hearts.

With emotions afire, you remain to inspire,
enticing with powers yet unheard.
The whole world loves you, loves you, loves you.
Little sparrow, our little grey bird.

Non rien de rien.
Non, je regrette rien
Our Little Sparrow, our little grey bird.

She published this song in 1997, with Pen Dinas Publications, Los Angeles, USA, and the following words appear on the front page of the score:

Presented to Lord Gordon Parry and the South Wales Male Voice Choir: 'Llwyd Bach y Baw' (A tribute to Edith Piaf) Soprano Solo, Harp, Male Voice Choir.

Words: Eluned Phillips. Music: Michael J. Lewis.

The song by Eluned is described as, 'an enchanting melody by Michael J. Lewis to the words of Eluned Phillips'.

Even though the information about her time in Paris is scant, with little evidence of actual experience, Eluned emphasises that she identified with the myriad of artists that congregated in Edith Piaf's flat. She spent nights there at the edge of the Bois de Boulogne, where some would sleep on a sofa or chair, but there was not much in the way of furniture there. 'The only furniture was the piano, a radio and a television, a record player, chairs to sit on and various low tables to hold the essential glasses. And there were travel bags underfoot everywhere. She lived to sing, that was her life.'

Eluned's reports were not always consistent; in her autobiography she states often that Piaf did not use more than one room. In other notes, not published, she says that Piaf had nine rooms and that she would only use three of these. Of course, she could have used one large room for the friends that called to stay the night, and her own bedroom to escape the hangers-on, as well as another room for special guests. There is no evidence that Eluned stayed on her own at Piaf's home,the only mention of her being there, late at night or until the small hours, in the midst of a motley crew. It is certain that being a part of the throng opened the door for Eluned to meet other famous people, the most distinguished of all being Picasso.

From her autobiography: 'I have always known that it was sheer luck that I met Edith Piaf on that momentous night ... It was a kind of surreal life visiting Piaf in the Bois de Boulogne...' In that large room there would have been a number of instruments and a large piano: 'To this day, I don't know how I fitted in. But I did.'

'The totally unexpected and totally electric voice' is the poetic description of this magnificent woman who was to influence Eluned for the rest of her life. In comments made in the 24-30 April 2015 edition of the *New Statesman* the author Tracey Thorn says of the way that we react to hearing a singer: 'When we respond to a singer, often we don't really see or hear the actual person. We see and hear an imagined version of them, a projection of our own needs and desires.'

Given that she had piano lessons and wrote the words for songs, it can be surmised that Eluned had an interest in music. She would not have called herself a musician, perhaps, but she had musical aspirations. Jackie Edwards, the owner of a hairdresser's in Cardigan attested to the way she would sing with zeal, either in chapel or under the hairdryer.

On camera, in the programme she made on Edith Piaf for S4C produced by Gareth Rowlands in 1994, Eluned is seen reciting part of a poem that she wrote for Edith. This poem was not a part of the poem which became the runner up at the 1967 National Eisteddfod in Bala but another poem, called *'Trioleg yr Oet'* [Et Tu

Triolet], published later in *Hel Dail Gwyrdd*[7] (*Collecting Green Leaves*) and in her book *Cerddi Glyn-y-mêl*[8] (*Poems from Glyn-y-mêl*). Eluned admits that she failed to attend Edith Piaf's funeral in 1963 as she was in America. She was given a chance to light a candle in the church that refused to hold a memorial service to Piaf. The church officials had to capitulate, partly because her many supporters were so vocal. In the television programme Eluned says that she would recite this little poem every time she visited Paris and Piaf's grave at Père Lachaise cemetery:

A flame eating Time in the flesh
in a fierce storm;
your candle's faith darkened
No sun, nor moon, or stars

A rose in the bleak wind withering
though water our offering,
Death came came, unwavering
bundling you into the earth.

Yet you still remain, your sweet voice
gladdening the long night;
Above the storm, a nightingale's song
she is the joy of my night.

Even though it is difficult to know how much time she spent in Paris, the place was a formative influence on her career as an artist. In her autobiography, Eluned gave three place names as chapter headings, 'London, Paris and Cenarth', as if they were related, ending each time back home in her own square mile. There is no doubt that returning to the cosiness of Cenarth was a comfort to her in spite of her city roaming; London and Paris were possibly mere stepping-stones to

---

[7] *Hel Dail Gwyrdd*, Menna Elfyn (ed.) (Gomer, 1985).
[8] *Cerddi Glyn-y-mêl*, Eluned Phillips (Gomer, 1985).

her... These are two facets to Eluned's personality: the way she loved the rowdiness of cities but also ultimately craved the simplicity of rural life.

What, I wonder, attracted her to Piaf? Was it a sense of ambivalence as to the absence of their fathers? Perhaps they identified with one another in longing to succeed, raising their voices so as to be embraced by others for their talent. Even though Eluned admitted that she did not possess much of a singing voice, the two women 'sang' in the broadest sense of the word, as Eluned later 'sang' her poems to audiences worldwide. The two were also religious and adhered to a simple faith, though Piaf believed in miracles and was more literal in her interpretation of the Bible than Eluned. This is how Eluned explains Edith's spiritual path:

> For me, perhaps the most unexpected vein in her personality was the depth of her religion. And this was not something temporary or a fleeting thing. She believed with the innocence of a child, absolutely, in God's miracles. When she was four years old, she nearly lost her sight, but somehow she was given restorative treatment which she never forgot.

There is another perhaps less obvious reason for Eluned's admiration of Edith Piaf. She was known as someone who worked hard with the French Resistance, in that she smuggled enemies of the Nazis out of the country during the Second World War. Eluned notes that she knew of at least one who was grateful for her help, though no name is attached to the story, In her own memoirs, she admits that she followed in Piaf's footsteps and saved nationalist Bretons from capital punishment.

She mentions another reason in her autobiography why she was to fall so hopelessly for the city of Paris:

> Paris has been known along the years as a city of lovers. Anyone who has walked along the Champs Élysées in the spring sunshine

when the chestnut trees are full of bloom, or at night when the flowers are about to close their sleepy eyes, must have felt the blood in their veins dancing with the hope that around the corner might be one's own special joie de vivre. So be it. The unexpected can play see-saw with one's life.

She admits that she was not particularly enamoured of the parties and the nights on the tiles: 'I have never been an enthusiastic party animal, preferring a quiet talk with friends or soft music but the Left Bank was always aglow with invitations and, in Paris, you do as the Parisians do.'

Eluned lived one day at a time, embracing the exhilaration of life and the society and friends that enveloped her. If there is a constant that runs through her life, it is her admiration of people. To an extent, they are portrayed sometimes in a somewhat hagiographic way; they appear to be above mere mortals. This can be tiresome for the reader, as she elevates indiscriminately whilst at the same time portraying herself as of little importance. She praises enthusiastically people like Augustus John, Picasso, Jean Cocteau, Dewi Emrys, the Archdruid Cynan, and a host of preachers and personalities from her own community. At one level this is commendable but on the other hand it is regrettable that she did not see herself in a similar light to those whose praises she sings. And again, this is what she says in a letter about these people:

Glyn-y-mêl,
Cenarth
Castellnewydd Emlyn
Dyfed SA38 9JP
16.2.88

Dear friend,

... And on top of this, the most damning phrase is the one about Augustus John. Here again, almost everybody in Wales – especially in the media – insist that I am the only Welsh woman to have ever met Augustus. Every time there is mention of the man, the media are instantly on the phone begging for an interview. I refuse every time and suggest definitely that there are others who certainly know him better than I. But nobody listens . . .

It's the same with Piaf. Everybody thinks that I was the only one to ever meet her.

Eluned

Yes, Eluned got to know Piaf to a certain extent and wrote passionate poetry about her, which would have won her the Crown at the National Eisteddfod in 1967 had she not won with another poem. But the evidence that Eluned had been a close friend of Piaf's cannot be verified and even though Piaf, according to Eluned, made a promise to come to Wales, she did not visit. So, one can assume that Eluned's life-long admiration of Edith's talent was tinged with a strong element of empathy for her. The two women had, after all, challenged the patriarchal society and they both experienced some personal freedoms whilst living in the bohemian environment of Paris. It is possible that there were similarities in their personalities: the retiring element, a mask to hide behind, an apparent public confidence that both had to maintain. The two perhaps also craved the warmth of companionship whilst being reticent about being the centre of attention due to their renown.

After Eluned came second in the National Eisteddfod in Bala, 1967, for her long poem on the life of Edith Piaf, she asked for the poem to be returned and as a consequence there is no copy available in the National Library of Wales. Searching in her papers, I came across a complete copy of the poem. It creates a poetic portrait of Edith Piaf, her lowly beginnings, her journeys 'from pavement to pavement / from hellish cellar to hellish cellar':

Folds (an extact)
(in admiration of the genius La Mome Piaf-
Edith Piaf – France's great singer)

I buttoned up my name on the winter coat of the world
With the black drops of the sheep.
La Mome Piaf,
Roof bird,
The little blue tit of the dirt.

A mother of necessity!
The troubadour getting coins from café to café;
Her ego in tune alone with the taut strings
to gather the genius in me...

leaving her prey red on the step of shop's door,
the window black and the night craving a hustler.
Bloodhounds licking a face and the scandal of tongues.
A hand in glove sneaking the other way,
And the breast heavy with the sign of the Cross.

The world careful.
...Poverty !
Since there was no shepherd at hand to carry me to his fold.
He fled in the dead of night,
Covering his ears from the harsh wind of the Great War.
I was insignificant.
The pride of the mother of Edith snatched from the Cavell of the
heroine
a stamp on my nakedness
and mother , a cuckoo turning her back looking for another nest.

The villages of two grandmothers
and the years of me playing hide and seek

between the beards of the thistle and the dandelion's clock.
... the quarrel
an eternal cloud between me and forget-me-knot.
And I never savoured the cowslips
but on the wallpaper of the clubs of the devils' company.

My spring tied to my father's caravan from place to place
and from circus to circus.
The dirt a smile on my face,
Every looking-glass blind in my seven years of bad luck.

... I grew in life's race
from blow to blow of the erratic mothers like irresponsible moons.

The fervour in the poet's descriptions is shattering as she describes the harshness of Piaf's life. But there is some light in the poem when she comes to her Christian faith:

One night funereal – the moon a bogeyman wandering
the thorn remembered the dew of blood.
And a wand in the hand of Saint Thérèse bowed.
Leading me to the fold of Liseux.
And to the Altar of Light.
'Our Father, thou art...'

Ond the tenth day of worshipping on my knee
God extended his miraculous light
And carnal candles danced.

... 'In the shadow the fold
there is room aplenty...'

The lonely feet crunching ice on the loveless lane.
The street's night a tight hand to the song in the heart's prison.

Getting closer to a smile
A word or two
At the breath's tightness in passing by
To the chance of a body in the fold of no man's land.
Sweet Mary!
The handful of stones in the hand of those lucky ones!
Is God from the Bench of the Living Things
Summoning a skeleton from the cold to put out the fire of passion?

There are emotional passages to the poem, and the part that best conveys this is the expression of Piaf's agony in losing her only child through illness. In her longing she would ask, 'Is there meaning to life?' This resulted in her turning to others for succour:

Between the thorn and the nettles of the nine months until birth
the love of a mother grew.
And from the bad luck of night, Marcelle came to model my flesh.
With the craft of lip's pride, I mended the fence.
I desired her in the fold of the heart.
And there was no wandering for the two years of borrowing her.

But what does the wolf of death know of grief's separation –
On small little hands letting go of the throat?
The bubbling hoarseness retreating… to the darkness. Forever.
In the storm of the empty stomach the ear remains deaf
And Life is a comma above the hearth of mystery.
To follow the way of my head, to the fold of forgetfulness
In the cellar of La Nouvelle Eve, earlier known as Gomorrah…

In the drugged life
the songs of the heart were mute.
The crying so desolate like babes in their wet nappies.

It is easy to understand how this poem caught the imagination of the adjudicators of the competition for the Crown at the National Eisteddfod, with a freshness and newness of theme that would have been totally foreign to Welsh language poetry in the sixties. In the same way, Eluned succeeded in giving testimony to a momentous life and the torment of a woman in a capricious world.

The Bretons

It is no surprise that Eluned was reluctant to mention her connection with the Breton nationalists during the Second World War, as the history of the different factions within the movement was complicated. She is just as vague whilst telling the story of her love for Per, the charismatic Breton. Even though the relationship runs like an unbroken line through her story and memories, the mystery of the love affair remains as if she had 'shut the door on torment/suffering'. She presents the experience as a romantic tale, the kind of story that she loved writing to earn a living while she lived in London. What part did illusion and what part did reality have in these stories? Some documents, which she kept show that she was besotted by the Bretons' ideal of self-government for their country, even if hoodwinked by their sincerity for the cause. This later led to bitter disechantment on her part.

It could be said that Eluned's love for Per was chiefly responsible for her dealings with this nationalist movement. But which Breton nationalists remains a vexed question; one group or cell believed that siding with Hitler and Germany would allow them self-government, thus realising the desire not possible under the French government.

She talks about Per in *The Reluctant Redhead*:

He was a Breton called Per living outside Rennes. He spoke Welsh, having learnt it from a man originally from Llandeilo, who had been working in his village and who had given Welsh lessons to a few interested students. He graduated as a scientist and had been working in Berlin as a scientific correspondent. This was 1938, and we spent all the time we could together, whenever we both could be in Paris at the same time. He was sometimes uneasy, as there were rumblings of war in Germany beneath the surface. We discussed Wales and Brittany. We had so much in common ... Per was an ardent Breton Nationalist.

In under a page and a half she closes the chapter with these words:

As time went on, the bond between Per and me strengthened and I knew that it was not the impetuousness of a redhead that decided that here was my soulmate. Per was equally certain. When a declaration of war was too imminent for me to stay longer in France, Per and I made a vow on parting that even if we found it too difficult to communicate, we would meet again as soon as armistice was declared. With the optimism of the young we did not foresee complications ahead.

Many complications came to upset this promising relationship and its rosy future. As there was talk of war on the horizon, separation for a while made perfect sense at the time... And yet, the two succeeded in seeing each other for one last time and they walked hand in hand along the Champs Élysées: 'Not really believing, but with the stubbornness of youth, absolutely refusing to accept that our separation would be a long one.'

And even knowing what the difficulties were did not stop them from planning the future. Eluned said:

Per knew he would be roped in as a war correspondent. I, knowing I would be called to serve, would volunteer to be a Red Cross ambulance driver in France. I rattled off the reasons why I would be accepted. They seemed sound. With impudent confidence, we settled on meeting the moment the war was over. Then we would continue our personal slanging-match over which of our respective countries would have the first Parliament, Wales or Brittany?

But that debate did not continue. There were other considerations, as the effects of Parkinson's disease had started to take hold of Eluned's mother. Before long, she would also find herself assisting the magistrate's clerk in Carmarthenshire. But it would not be the end of Eluned's efforts for her Celtic brothers and Per's compatriots – far from it.

•

It is possible that it was a perfectly innocent mistake that when I ordered the notes of a Breton nationalist at the National Library I got, in their stead, the log-book of a Ceredigion shopkeeper. After all, it's easy enough to mistake one number for another. And perhaps this is a metaphor for the way that some Bretons were regarded and falsely accused of collaborating with the German enemy while others had been guilty of it. The story of the Breton nationalists during this uncertain and turbulent time is full of mistakes, of guessing and questions of interpretation. In an insightful article 'The Breton Collaborators and the Welsh Llenorion' in *Planet* 216, (Winter 2014) Rob Stradling writes about Louis Feutren of the Breton nationalist movement, who had collaborated with the SS in Brittany. In his article he refers to a vehement disagreement that arose in 2011 between the Welsh Government and the National Library regarding some soldiers that had been a part of the armed unit of Breton nationalists, Bezen Perrot. After the war, they had managed to escape to the Irish Republic. Some of them lived in Ireland and a dispute arose because Feutren had left £30,000 to the National Library of Wales rather than to the country that had given him refuge, with the proviso that the Library of Wales would receive his private archive. Rob Stradling succeeds in outlining the background history and the internal infighting that existed in Brittany during the thirties in the twentieth century. The Breton National Party had been perturbed by the sacrifice made by some quarter of a million Bretons during the Great War. A growing number of Bretons felt alienated from the

French state and feared for Brittany's future, its language and culture. After Hitler came to power in 1933 some Bretons, such as Olier Mordrel, a prominent journalist, felt that, when considering Hitler's foreign policy, Germany could be a friend to Brittany: 'France's difficulty equals Brittany's opportunity.' This is when Gwenn ha Du (White and Black), a secret terrorist cell, was born. Before Germany invaded France during the Second World War, some members of the Breton Nationalist Party believed that this was their chance to achieve independence. Others campaigned for federalism. Three nationalists apparently went to Berlin to discuss the matter and to make an agreement to support the Germans. But this never came to fruition. After Germany occupied France in 1940, the German leaders had no need for the Bretons' cooperation because an agreement had been reached with France to split the country in two – one half would be under German military rule, in Paris and the north, with the French state being governed in name only by the French in Vichy, in the south. Satisfying the German leaders was the only way to survive in that situation, and that is what the Vichy government did for four years until the end of the war. Even though the leaders of the Breton Nationalists tried to gain recognition under Hitler's new regime, so that Brittany would be considered a state separate from France, their attempts failed.

After the war there were raids on the hundreds who had been suspected of being Nazi sympathisers, and they were summarily punished, shot – some merely for being Bretons and nationalists, while others were imprisoned. Much of Brittany's population also sought retribution and de Gaulle himself did not show much mercy towards the Bretons' desire for self-rule.

This was roughly the background facing Eluned during the forties. Per was a fervent nationalist and, according to Eluned, was incarcerated, although little is known about whether or not he collaborated with the Germans. Eluned believed the story that he had been identified as a collaborator for the sole reason that he had a friend called Otto who was a German military officer. Whatever the truth, some of Eluned's closest friends maintained that he was tortured whilst in prison, which had greatly affected his health. So, post-war, Per was not the same healthy, idealistic man with whom Eluned had been in a relationship when the two were in Paris together years previously. Cruel war separated them and Eluned might as well have been on the other side of the world, safe as she was in the quiet hamlet of Cenarth, whilst he was in the middle of the conflict. There are no details of his wartime whereabouts or activities, but after the war news of him reached Eluned through the nationalists who had escaped Brittany for the UK and Ireland and, little by little, she tried her best to campaign for others who were in danger of being executed.

In 1945, in essence, Eluned was not too different from the leading members of the Welsh nationalist party. It is believed that they too were naive because they knew some of the Breton nationalists and were unable to accept that most of them would be part of a secret terrorist cell. Either that, or they felt sympathy for Bretons who were being persecuted. Many of those Bretons were highly regarded as literary people or scholars of Breton culture, which also appealed to their Welsh counterparts. A concerted effort was therefore made to try and save the lives of some of those artists, authors and teachers from what was viewed as a perversion of justice and to draw attention to the oppression of those who spoke Breton in Brittany. Eluned wasn't the only female writer who tried to save the lives of people who had been given a prison sentence. Kate Roberts and her publisher husband, Morris Williams, the owners of the weekly publication *Baner ac Amserau Cymru*, were appalled at the court case of Roparz Hemon as early as 1947 and had succeeded in getting the late Judge Dewi Watcyn Powell, then newly graduated from Oxford, to be an observer at court. The situation was seen as a human rights case as well as an expression of distress at the potential future of the Breton language. I could expand on the turbulence of these times and the twisted turns that lead to different perspectives on the period's history, but it is difficult without knowing exactly where the truth of the situation lay. History itself created the ambivalence of emotion and of thought gripping contemporary Welsh nationalists. The fact that the National Library accepted money bequeathed by an extremist Breton nationalist, against the wishes of the Culture Minister, Huw Lewis, confirms how polarised opinions were at the time.[9]

This example shows how divisive the history of the Breton engagement with the Germans is; even a hint of collaboration is still enough to raise the temperature and give rise to mixed feelings. As if war wasn't enough to separate them, there was another agony facing Eluned as she had to get to grips with her part in, or the possibility that she was consorting with, a faction considered to be nationalists who used violent means.

In telling only part of this romantic tale, I am aware that I am glossing over what is a far more complicated story in reality. It is a sad story of two young people who discovered each other during the heady days in between-the-wars Paris, and of their time together on the devil-may-care streets of the city. The threat of war undermined all of this within a year and put a stop to their promises to live together. Their dreams were shattered. The turbulent tide of history separated them. Isn't that what Eluned would have wanted us to believe?

The story is told in a semi-autobiographical film made in 1989, *Rhith y Lloer* (*Ruffled Water*) in which Eluned presented her life story to the scriptwriter Ewart Alexander, who conflated fact and fiction. The article written by the scriptwriter for the *Western Mail* on 1 March 1989 tells the story succinctly:

> *Ruffled Water* (*Rhith y Lloer*) is about a girl who lands herself in one hell of a mess. Is that it? Well, if you're prepared to stand in the drizzle ... there's more.

---

[9] The National Library promised that the money would be used to fight fascism.

The story begins in the late thirties and ends in 1945. It tells how politics of a marginal kind became mixed up with love of the universal type. It starts in Wales, crosses to Brittany with a glance or two at Ireland and ends in Wales.

So what about this girl, then? At first she treated her sense of nationalism with the sometime flippancy of youth, until she sensed condescension in London, and became converted in Paris. It may seem bizarre that some Bretons could see the German invasion of France as a means of liberating Brittany. Her Wales is, therefore, put into perspective and she begins to see the similarities and feel the difference ... she confuses her growing love of country with her love for the Breton she met in Paris. After all, it's not all that difficult to assume or toy with an alien set of values if your loved one happens to hold them strongly. The Romantic Notion and Romance are persuasive bedfellows at the honeymoon stage.

Things seem simple. All problems solvable.

But alas, the attrition of time, and the conspiracy of events force their compromises and, in some cases, herald a bitter dawning. Yet our girl, still perversely in love, still a convert to the simplistic Nationalist faith, won't give up her man, won't allow reality to intrude.

She can't understand, for instance, why, after the war, the French took such a vicious turn against some Breton collaborators. Summary trials and executions were the order of the day. The Bretons learned that independence presumes a correct choice of allies ...

So who's to dismiss our girl, real Welsh, real proud, as some half-baked country girl who went out into the world following her heart for all it was worth? There's something fine and (pardon the word) noble in staring straight at disastrous odds and deciding to go on ... at whatever cost.

But ... Our girl isn't an island. The delicate web of friendships and relationships are all the more cruelly sundered when the place in which it happens is quiet and in west Wales. It's all very well to shout your slogans, display your heartache, but sometimes you stand on other people's shoulders, other people's feelings, in so doing.

Our girl therefore, is driven into a corner, at odds with the people she needs most, and who care for her most. Gestures of support and caring are seen as unfeeling attacks. The offered hands of lover are perceived as talons.

With exhausted post-war Europe groaning under the effects of its cruel excesses, when millions were displaced by the cold fog of war, our girl with a self-indulgence born of the irresponsible, chooses an internal exile in the only place she can now be – home.

They say that home is where the heart is. Hers is elsewhere. She marks her days with this and that of earning a crust. She's been on an immense journey for a girl of her place, of her time. Yet, she's back where she started counting the days to the new beginning which she knows will never come.

All this agony and agonising is for nothing unless the story is well told and interests you.

Eluned's mixed reactions to the attention given to *Rhith y Lloer* can be seen in letters sent to the producer and director of the film, Gareth Rowlands:

> Glyn-y-mêl
> Cenarth
> Castellnewydd Emlyn
> 19.4.89

Dear Gareth,

... But back to the other story, I'm afraid. I'm still alive, but only just; nobody has attacked me physically yet, but it came pretty close to it. There are one or two questions that I'd like answers to before we close the door once again – forever this time, I hope. Do you have a few seconds to spare in the future? If you don't happen to be down in these parts, I am free to be able to choose my time to come to Cardiff.

Apart from the nosy people who have been burrowing in from the outside, there was very deserved praise for the production.
I hope everybody is full of joy
Warm wishes
Eluned

In another letter she says again how proud she is of the production:

Glyn-y-mêl,
Cenarth
[no date]

Dear Gareth,

I'm sorry that I'm so late again in thanking you for the tape. It has been a tough time here. But all was as I expected, totally effective. I'm truly proud that *Rhith y Lloer* has grown to be such a hugely important drama; you and Ewart are indeed a dynamic partnership.

But seeing Annie looking at me from the cover of *Sbec* [a Welsh language TV guide] was painfully shattering. The red hair and a coat exactly like one of mine in a picture that I have of me in the house somewhere! The Bretons beat even the Welsh for gossip and I know that there will be a reaction from one – I hope she doesn't go overboard and create trouble for others. Before this, I was worrying about Get's reaction to it – but that worry is over now and I have become well used to fighting for myself.

Please forgive this short messy note. People are still calling and my mind is shot. The tears at the moment are like stalactites hanging in my breast. It is hard, so hard getting to grips with the fact that Get isn't here to draw my attention. Time, will most probably, fill the void.

I wish *Rhith y Lloer* every success again – unfortunately, for me, it is too good and is sure to garner more than the usual attention.

Warm wishes to you as a family,
Eluned

Please let me know if there are any enquries about our friends in Ireland – I should prefer to know – I hope that I am worrying without needing to and that there will be a great silence!

Eluned's letters express pride in what was made of her story in drama form in *Rhith y Lloer*, but also a fear about the wider reaction to the drama. She refers specifically to some whom she knew and who were a part of the extreme nationalist movement in Brittany. The reference to Ireland is to the Bretons who emigrated there after landing in Wales. Was the allegation that Eluned had been more than a generous host and that she had been a part of the activities of the time, an intermediary, if not a secret organiser, to facilitate the escape to Ireland true, then? Was she, by 1989, feeling a little ashamed at having assisted the Bretons and uncomfortable about that? In her autobiography, she said that being reckless was a part of her being. Was her non-partisan innocence also an element of her personality? Maybe the passing of time had made her reassess the significance of her being so obliging?

There is one more letter praising the director, who sent a copy of the script to her:

> Glyn-y-mêl Cenarth
> Castellnewydd Emlyn
> Dyfed SA38 9JP
> 23. 11. 88

Dear Gareth,

Yes, I received the tape, and a little while after that, your letter. The tape shook me up and gave me a fright – leaping before thinking as usual ...

My reaction to the production? Superb. The tape still gives me a shock; it is so much more alive than the written script. I believe that you have created a masterpiece, and have mixed the different elements with masterly artistry. It is a powerful document and I'm so proud that there is such an appreciation of your work in France and Brittany. Is there a date for it to be aired in Wales? It is the people outside of Brittany who have been a concern for me all along the while, but however things go, this is *my* problem now. This programme is one of the best you have ever made – the best that anyone has made.

She says further that she would not have entrusted the work to anybody else apart from Gareth Rowlands, a sign perhaps of his sensitivity regarding those who would have wanted to dig to uncover her numerous secrets. Brittany was never far from her mind; even a decade before the film appeared there were letters sent from Eluned pleading on behalf of imprisoned nationalists. Among Eluned's papers was a letter from someone by the name of HH, urging her to campaign for the release of Jacques Bruchet. He concludes his letter with the words 'A thousand regards', the wording of the letter shows that it was written in reply to a letter from Eluned:

> Darlington
> Totnes
> Devon
> 18.9.75

Dear Eluned,

Many thanks for your letter. However I want only to tell you that Jacques is now on hunger strike (he started on Saturday [the] week before last – i.e. 10 days ago).

This was to protest against the decision of the examining magistrate refusing him bail. The appeal is to be heard next Wednesday (20.9). If his application is turned down again he will stop taking any liquid and then he is not likely to last long, since he has only one kidney (in addition to his heart condition).

Amnesty International will be discussing his case; I hope the French authorities have had a change of heart by then. There is no case against Jacques. His charge is 'conspiracy'. He is not indicted for the Versailles affair. The person who had charged him with this has since recanted.

All communications in his favour to be sent to the examining magistrate:

Monsieur Gonard
Juge D'Instruction

Cour de Surete de L'Etat
71 Rue St Dominique
Paris 7

I have already contacted y *Faner* & the Blaid.
You may have more ideas,
Cofion fil
HH

The letters from HH show that Eluned was very familiar with the correspondent, Hervé Le Helloco, known as Bob. Yann Fouéré refers to him when he writes about the struggle and the difficulties regarding exile and how he organised escape from Brittany for those under threat of prosecution there.[10] The rumours spread that Yann had escaped to Wales and that others would follow. He had to persuade many that their lives were not in danger and that they would have no trouble with the authorities. He also said that the sympathy that Welsh press demonstrated was a comfort because it showed the militants in Brittany, as well as public opinion, that they were not short of friends or support, in spite of the pressure from the French state.

The first Breton who came over was Gildas Jaffrennou, but the second to arrive was Hervé Le Helloco. Yann Fouéré says of Hervé:

---

[10] Chapter 2: *The Struggle and Difficulties of Exile: The Welsh Report*. Fondation Yann Fouéré. www.fondationyannfouere.org

After a botched trial, held in secret, he had been sentenced to death in absentia at the end of June 1946, shortly before I left the continent. It was certainly preferable that he should leave there and place a border between his persecutors and himself. He was an ideal recruit, as he spoke and wrote English far better than I did. Within three weeks he had completed the English translation of the brochure which I had written for Plaid Cymru. He had completed the work with the help of a Breton student called Robert Stephan, who had contacted us. Whilst I gave my classes at the University, he dictated the English version of the French text to him.

Eluned responded instantly to HH's letter and sent a message to M. Gonard:

> May I, on behalf of the Welsh fraternity, in a desperate effort to save the life of a Political Prisoner, Jacques Bruchet, 1928141-78, appeal most humbly for the granting of bail at this application tomorrow.
> E. Phillips
> Glyn-y-mêl, Cenarth, Newcastle Emlyn, Wales

It appears therefore that Eluned took charge of writing on behalf of the 'Welsh fraternity'. She was sent confirmation of receipt of her letters soon afterwards:

> Foreign and Commonwealth Office,
> S.W.1
> 27 September 1978

> The Secretary of State acknowledges the receipt of your letter of 21 September about the concern of Miss Eluned Phillips of Glyn-y-mêl, Cenarth, Newcastle Emlyn, over the detention of the Breton Jacques Bruchet.
> The matter is receiving attention and a reply will be sent as soon as possible.

Two years later, this press release was made by J. Bruchet, 1 rue des Cordiers, 35400 Saint Malo:

On the 11.02.80 I sent to the Council of Europe a written complaint against the organisation of the Cour de Sûréte de l'Etat in Paris.

In that paper I exposed the proceedings of the above court in the last trial of the FLB, in contravention of article 5, paragraph 3, and article 6, paragraph 1 of the European Convention on Human Rights.

My appeal to the Council of Europe is likely to be inadmissible, since the French State has refused to ratify article 25 of the said Convention, which gives citizens of the member countries of the European Community the right to appeal to European courts.

However my complaint is not a mere symbolic gesture of protest. In face of the rapid whittling away of civil liberties in France, it is the first step in the campaign towards a better protection of individual freedom, especially through harmonisation of the rights of the citizen in European countries.

Therefore the aim of my protest is twofold:

1) Warn public opinion against the dangers of judicial authority which is an exceptional court depending on the Executive.
2) Call on the Members of the European Parliament to start at once the process aimed at giving French subjects the right of individual appeal in European courts, which is enjoyed by the citizens of all the other Members of the Community.

Even though it was J. Bruchet who released the statement to the press, the fact that it is in Eluned's possession and that she kept a carbon copy of it suggests that she assisted with the translation. In her autobiography, Eluned alludes to the event, noting the following:

I had one more small tussle with the French authorities. We had a Breton friend, Jacques, who acted for his fellow Bretons in prison for their love of Brittany, and was himself in prison because he had taken up their legal grievances. He had developed heart trouble and his friends worried for his life if he was kept locked up without medical treatment. There were prominent and respected people in Wales, like the Archdruid Cynan, the poets Euros Bowen, and his brother Geraint, the Rev. Dyfnallt Owen and others, trying their utmost to get him released. He was due to appear in court and that, everyone feared, would further prolong his time without treatment. As usual when I was frustrated, my red hair genes would commandeer my common sense. With sheer recklessness, I cabled the judge sitting on the case with a heart-breaking sob story. It happened to be more or less true, because Jacques's wife, Elizabeth was bordering on a breakdown. When I confessed to this later, the ones who knew more about the French system than I did, thought I had done more harm than good, as the Welsh and the French have different temperaments. I agreed. But suddenly, Jacques was freed. I take no credit for that, but am only thankful that for once, the French faced up to their mistake in locking him up in the first place.

Eluned was busy helping the Breton cause generally, doing more than just writing a letter to a judge. She gave shelter to the nationalists who had escaped from France, as she admits in her autobiography. They brought the message to her that Per was all right but that many of his friends were in danger, and that the French authorities were attacking nationalists and sentencing them to death. They wondered whether some of these could be hidden in Cenarth before transferring to Ireland.

The result was that two Bretons, sometimes up to five, would be taken in at any one time. They were given a haven in the Great Kitchen down at the bottom of the garden in Glanawmor. As can well be imagined, the family were not too happy with the arrangement, but once again they showed compassion as they were friends of Per's and fully aware of how much Eluned missed him. Rules were set. If they were to be moved to Ireland, the command was that they were not to give the family their real names, in case those names slipped from their lips at a critical point in the future.

The story is an amazing one, and it's difficult to imagine Bretons hiding in a small village like Cenarth in the forties without the knowledge of the authorities and without anybody coming to look for them. After a while, Eluned came to hear that Per had been imprisoned and that he would more than likely be executed. Was there any way of saving him from his cell and bringing him under cover to Wales, and then taking him over to Ireland?

It seems that this indeed did happen and that he subsequently went from Ireland to America. There is no direct written evidence of this but we do know that Eluned visited him in California decades later. There are also new accounts from a witness, who is still alive, of the boats arriving in Wales and the places where they departed from Wales to Ireland.

Regarding the Bretons, I was told by locals in Cenarth about their presence and especially about Albert 'Bore da'. Yann Fouéré also tells the story:

> Bob Le Helloco had been able to settle more or less permanently with the Phillipses in Cenarth, near Newcastle Emlyn, where he delivered, in all weathers and in a handcart, cans of milk from the farm where he had found refuge. I went to visit him with L'Haridon, shortly after the latter's arrival. It was a rustic spot in a pastoral setting. The harmonious outline of green, partly wooded hills overlooked the river, alongside where the house and the buildings around it were nestled.[11]

This is testimony to Eluned's contribution to the nationalist cause in Brittany, to those who were persecuted after the war, and proof that her contribution was important. One of the stories in Yann Fouéré's

---

[11] Chapter 2: *The Struggle and Difficulties of Exile: The Welsh Report*. Fondation Yann Fouéré. www.fondationyannfouere.org

account is of interest as it was incorporated into the television drama *Rhith y Lloer*. This is how the story was told by Fouéré:

As for Paul Perrin he had already been arrested and imprisoned shortly after the Liberation. He had escaped from the law courts in Rennes during one of the court inquiry sessions for his trial. The incredible circumstances of his escape were widely talked about. He came to visit me in Wales in the autumn of 1947, in Tre-gib, and told me the story. He had been relieved of his handcuffs to go to the toilet and had been able to climb out of the toilet window which looked out onto a narrow and infrequently used street behind the law courts, which is still called the rue Salomon-de-Brosse.

Climbing out of the window, he had been able to reach a drainpipe and slide down it to the street that was five or six feet below. Admittedly, he had already reconnoitered the area during a previous inquiry session. Having regained his freedom and allowed the excitement his escape had stirred up to calm down, he took the train to Paris, disguised as a woman with some make-up on, and in the company of his fiancée, Mlle Le Breton. The latter, being a social worker, found work in Paris at the B.N.C.I. Bank, through Monique Bruchet, Jacques' wife, who was herself a social worker.

In order to enhance the drama the story is changed slightly in the film; the girl saves her lover, but elements of the true story appear in *Rhith y Lloer* – an imaginative if not somewhat a shadowy version of the reality.

Even though Eluned met up with her lover again some decades after they fell for each other, the chance to realise the desires of their early love affair had been lost. And even though Eluned travelled to Santa Monica, California, to see Per, his health was fragile due to the adverse effects of the experiences endured in prison. But she never forgot the thrill of that electric relationship. Eluned much later got engaged to a doctor in London, even wearing a ring on her finger for a while, but he was not the life companion she craved.

It appears that every relationship Eluned had after her relationship with Per was shortlived, and the family, who met the doctor only once, believed that she enjoyed her independence so much that going to London to become a doctor's wife would have stifled her. But in the same way, she kept love letters from another Breton man, someone who begged her to go and see him in Brittany, Indeed, his letters were awash with his love for her and he signs his letters with 'Yours, in love'. He says in another letter in 1978, 'Now the Eisteddfod is over will you find time to come over?' He sent another letter asking her to spend Christmas with him, but Eluned did not want to miss Christmas with the family. 'My dear love, sweet Eluned,' he says again in a letter, 'I slept thinking of you.' He tries to win her heart by reminding her of the lovely times spent together, finishing the letter with the imploring words, 'Was not this happiness?' There is another extremely loving letter talking about the time they spent on the beach and in the sea, and afterwards drinking whisky and making love. But she did not keep copies of the letters she sent to him, or if she did, pehaps they went up in smoke on the huge bonfire that she organised in her garden with her niece, Ann Evans at the end of her life. Why did she keep these letters if she did not agree to his requests to visit and to continue the relationship? Was it to remind herself that she was still attractive in someone's eyes? A touch of pride perhaps? Who would begrudge a beautiful flirtatious woman these feelings?

Pierre Loisel was the Great Bard of Brittany, similar to the Archdruid in Wales. Eluned talks about their close friendship in her autobiography:

Our National Eisteddfod of Wales Gorsedd has for years had a link with the Breton Gorsedd. The Breton Bardd Mawr would attend our ceremony, bringing the Breton half of the sword of peace to be united with the Welsh one. I had known the Bardd Mawr, Pierre

Loisel, for years: he would come and stay at my home and we'd travel together to wherever the National Eisteddfod was held that year.

She mentions one incident when he was staying at her home and how they went, with Cyril, a relation, to do some poaching one night as Pierre was keen to have the experience. She tells the story in a humorous way of how he fell into the river that night in the only white shirt he owned. Eluned had to wash the shirt and she admits that doing so was new to her, 'I'd never washed a man's shirt but I knew I had to add starch'. The result was this: 'The shirt luckily came out white enough but it could stand on its own. It was by this time after 4 am. I crept sheepishly upstairs and went to my mother for advice. I had to re-wash the shirt and add the requisite amount of starch. We got to the Eisteddfod and no one was any the wiser.'

Alongside Per and Loisel, there were other admirers. I know of one famous entertainer in Wales, the same age as her, who had said publicly to a member of her family that he would have liked to marry her, and that if they had married, then he would be related to the Phillipses. But this did not come to pass either. Nobody came close to the 'Per' of her youth. Eluned continued to hold on to the ideal of this unrequited love. But if she lost him as a companion, then she had the time of her life with other faithful friends over the years.

Eluned's history with Brittany is a diverse one. She agreed to help the Bretons throughout her life, and did so even though she did not succeed in assisting or saving the one who inspired her love for the Bretons. One senses that she had been furtive regarding her contribution to sheltering some nationalists, maybe because she had turned her back on the kind of 'nationalism' that created divisions and conflict. She had been disillusioned by white-hot nationalism throughout her life, and even though she was patriotic and Wales was a shield in her heart, the flame lit by Per and Paris had been diminished. More than that, her relationship with one of the factions that had retreated to Ireland caused embitterment. In her letters she mentions her fear of their anger, many times over. Here is another secret and mystery which she did not reveal in her lifetime. Even though she secured for many a safe and easy passage to the Emerald Isle, the communication between Eluned and the Bretons came to a halt. This part of the story deserves another book, if only the key to the locked door could be found. She liked to believe in 'Closing the doors on torments' as she states in a private letter to a friend. In the midst of works she left unpublished is a poem shedding some light on her love but more 'mystery' is embodied in her life and works. The poem does not have a title but it refers to Per, her lover, and in the first verse she depicts his part being played on the television screen. The film, perhaps, inspired her to write this loving poem, which is a mixture of conflicting emotions.

How could I separate the one on the screen
To the one I loved in a faraway land.
A beautiful image from the one I saw
Far from my reach in a darkened cell.
The family doted on your company, albeit
I saw someone else in your place, and hated it.

You managed to stir me from all I believed
Without me fully knowing you in the flesh,
Leaving me miming the question 'Why'
Was I held a captive in the net of fate?
The cruel longing overwhelmed me for long
In seeing your picture, the thrill of your song.

But one night, unaware, my heart took a leap
In opening a door that had been closed in my heart,
I saw not a shadow but the real man
Forcing me to face the truth from the start;
How thin the border between love and hate,
Harder still to measure the medicine of fate.

Now you're sometimes a kiss on a tired pillow
To entice me to the perfect isle,
At nightfall, I'm an aristocrat of wine
Lightfooted I arrive at the feast's dance,
And yet you're sometimes just a fallen star
Leaving me perplexed, lonely, safety's hedge – afar.

You won my heart with your enchanting voice,
Your face, your eyes, how they were full of smiles,
You took me on a magic carpet to the marvellous isle
The hamlet, eternally green, where no one grows old.
And if by chance I get to know you some day,
I'll understand then the secret of life's golden way.

It is enough to say that their relationship was a bittersweet one because of circumstances beyond their control. Is this at the heart of Eluned's hardy personality and her ability to weather all the disappointment and criticism that came her way? The flame of her love for Per remained undimmed. In 1992, in a church in Paris, she lit a candle in memory of Per, and according to a friend who witnesssed the event, she wept bitterly for 'the sun that never was'.

The Scriptwriter

The one whose work I held in great admiration, and whom I desperately wanted to get close to, was Jean Cocteau. I still clung to my twelve-year-old's ambition of becoming a great dramatist.

Eluned Phillips in *The Reluctant Redhead*

In the years following the Second World War, Eluned Phillips' name came to prominence firstly as a contributing scriptwriter to individual programmes for the BBC, and then working as part of a small team on popular radio series. It could be said that she got her first apprenticeship at a young age through creating drama and humorous sketches to entertain people. She understood humour and seriousness, how to write slick dialogue and how to create drama from the most comedic and tragic of situations. She learnt these skills not in a college drama department but within her community, with an alert ear and the astuteness of the author.

One day, during the war, unexpectedly another offer came her way, one that she could not refuse. Roy Evans, the Newcastle Emlyn court clerk, and friend of the family, called at Glanawmor. He'd heard that Eluned had returned home from London and as his law partner had been called up into the army, he was keen that Eluned should assist him in court. Eluned was not at home at the time, but when she got back she was sent at once to his house in Brynmarlog. Eluned was full of doubts when he asked her to take the job (as clerk of court), insisting that she did not have any office training nor any training in law either. Despite her protestations, he ordered her to be in the office by half past nine the following morning. She agreed somewhat reluctantly to assist him for three weeks, as that would give him enough time to get somebody else in her place.

83

When she asked when she should start on the work, his unexpected reply was, 'Now.' And so she did. Here was an end to Eluned's aspiration to help with the war effort by driving ambulances, but it is likely that the work – and her wage – helped her family and it was also a way for her mother to get her home with the family. This is how Eluned tells it:

> I was on my holidays, having just finished at London University, and I had settled the big conundrum in my life; I was going to be an author. But on that Sunday in September 1939 the news came of war. I strode home, and I was young enough to believe that victory would be all the closer if I went to the Army as a Transport Driver on the Continent. I was quite an authority on car racing, and had lost my way so often on the European Continent that I felt that I was an authority on that too.[12]

Eluned had never been inside a law court before and Roy Evans had three courts under his juristiction: Newcastle Emlyn, Llandysul and Pencader. As well as these he was also responsible for two county courts, one in Newcastle Emlyn and the other in Cardigan.

When Eluned arrived at the court that first morning, she was surprised at the number of people present, and she asked herself if there really were so many criminals in such a quiet town as Newcastle Emlyn? Roy Evans was also quite deaf and would fiddle quite often with his hearing-aid. It would fall to the floor regularly and as Eluned would try and retrieve it for him, often he would lean down to pick it up as well; the result would be a calamitous

---

[12] A radio conversation 'Women's Work during the War', for *Merched yn Bennaf* (Mainly Women), on Radio Cymru, a written piece in her papers. The date of the programme is not known and it has not been archived, but the series was broadcast from the end of the seventies onwards and it's likely that the programme would have been aired towards the end of the seventies or the beginning of the eighties.

banging of heads. The audience would delight in the performance. Occasionally, Eluned would find herself taking the part of the solicitor for the defendant if he or she happened to be without counsel.

It is easy to gather from what she says about these years of helping in the courts – six in all – that she got to understand human nature and to study it thoroughly at close quarters. The impression given is that she and Roy Evans understood each other perfectly, and that they each admired the other. After all, if not she would have given up the work and he would have found somebody else to do the work in her stead. But this is what Eluned says about him, and her comments show again how Eluned would praise talented men: 'A man with the sharpest mind, the most incisive insight that I ever met: a brilliant writer, a nephew to Allen Raine the novelist, in the lineage of Dafi Dafis, Castell Hywel.' So here are two kindred spirits working harmoniously together. It is little wonder that the working continued successfully for many years.

Eluned demonstrates her knowledge of the human condition in an essay about her experiences in the court, in a writing notebook:

So here I go ... to Llandysul Court. It was the first time I'd set foot in a Court of Law. I sat at the Clerk's table and saw a sea of faces in front of me. And I thought – all the black sheep of Llandysul must be on manoeuvres today. I understood afterwards that there was an audience there to listen every time alongside the criminals. The sadistic element? Or perhaps the courts of the land fulfilled the role of the theatres? And boy, were there dramas – comedies, farces, tragedy after tragedy.

An unmarried mother, eighteen years of age, up on a charge of infanticide ... A soldier causing malicious injury to his wife's lover ... A thirteen-year-old girl that no *remand home* could keep from wandering from one military camp to the next.

There was a great responsibility. What if I fined too heavily, or sent a man to jail for longer that his allotted time? The experience of sending a man to prison at all was awful enough. I remember the first time – a loquacious Irishman up before the bench in Pencader for breaking in to a building and stealing money and merchandise. *Breaking and entering* was the official term. The justices gave him six months of jail and I cried for the whole night. And even though I saw many go to prison after that, I had the same uncomfortable feeling – I could not countenance that prison was a place to rehabilitate criminals.

But there were funny incidents too. Like the farmer who had killed his pig without a licence and the poor creature's last screams had been heard by the Food Inspector. But somebody had seen his car in the nick of time and even though he searched the farm, there was neither hide nor hair of the recently departed. Perhaps the farmer had become too confident and had indulged in too longwinded a farewell with the inspector. Anyway, his little boy ran across the yard shouting, 'Daddy, Mam's fed up of sitting on the pig. Is it safe for her to get up?' Fair play to the justices – the transgressor was given a small fine for such a great comedy.

We had two regulars – two neighbours – and they could not see eye to eye on anything; the artillery would vary every time – a fist, a rake, a pitchfork. I often think, if Hitler had succeeded in coming over, that he would have met his match in these two. And even though the Court had bound them over to keep the peace every so often, the truce would be shortlived, and the two warriors would be back with handfuls of each other's hair as *Exhibit A* and *B*.

What struck me every time was that it was the people with small crimes that worried the most – the ones without a red light on their bike or without a dog licence. These people would do almost anything to keep their names out of the papers. The people with the big crimes had, it seemed, developed a thick hide. I learnt a lot about human nature in this unexpected role.

I really wonder; would I have been able to make a living after the war as a writer had I not been thrust unexpectedly into the middle of this life? I cannot help feeling impatient today when I

Eluned's birth certificate with only her mother's name noted

Eluned sits on the bridge in Cenarth

Eluned and Margaret (Madge) in school uniform

Eluned's home – 'a nest of women'

Young and carefree – Eluned and Margaret (Madge), books in hand

Eluned – happy and at ease

Eluned and Get – rolling their sleeves up and getting down to work with a neighbour

CANEUON I BLANT

AR GYFER YSGOLION DYDDIOL

Y Gerddoriaeth gan
PENCERDDES EMLYN
Castellnewydd Emlyn

Y Geiriau gan
LUNED TEIFI
Cenarth

J. D. Lewis a'i Feibion, Argraffwyr, Gwasg Gomer, Llandysul

CYNNWYS

RHAN I

3

20 LILI WEN FACH.

Cyweirnod **D**

Lil - i Wen Fach, O 'rwyt yn hardd!

Ti yw bren-hin - es lân yr ardd; Y

cyn-taf o bawb i god - i pen I

dder-byn y fen - dith ddaw o'r nen.

Tlws yw dy ruddiau, gwyn eu lliw,
Cefaist brydferthwch gwych gan Dduw;
A chennad a ddaw o'r Gwanwyn braf
I lonni y tlawd a gwella'r clâf.

24

21 Y FRIALLEN.

Cyweirnod **G**

Flod - yn del, â'i darn - au aur,

Chwyth-wyd dros dy ddisg - glair rudd?

Gwn yr hoff - ai llu dy gael,

Ar - os rhwng y dáil yng nghudd.

Friallen fwyn, ti ddywed im'
Ddod o'r Gwanwyn yn ei dro;
A oes rhaid i'r Gaeaf oer
Fynd â thi i ffwrdd o'm bro?

25

Eluned published her first songs for children in
Caneuon i Blant at the age of 12, in 1936

Anti Hannah – the fearless fisherwoman

Anti Hannah's lovely smile

Eluned, Anti Hannah and Get, after she had won her
first National Eisteddfod crown in 1967

Heavy snow in 1947; Eluned with Get and the Bretons, Albert 'Bore Da' and Robert

Dilys Davies (Mersi Fach) and Manny Price (Joe Long) cast members of the radio series *Teulu'r Mans*

Eluned's first success as a poet at the Cardigan Eisteddfod, 1965.
Eluned kept a copy of the critique and of the poem and also
a photograph of Dewi Emrys in bardic robes.

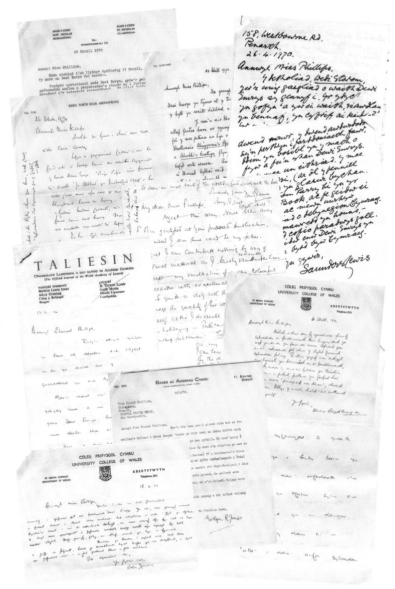

Some of the many letters Eluned received from well-known Welsh authors in response to her bid for contributions to her memoir of Dewi Emrys.

hear all the harrumphing and spluttering about four-letter words, because I remember on my first day in Court, being called to translate in a case of bastardy. The two barristers made sure that I lost forever any overly respectable puritanism, which I think is a part of everybody's constitution.

•

Apart from assisting in the court, Eluned was persuaded to translate occasionally for those who were unable to express themselves in English. Roy Evans addressed the court on one occasion and introduced Eluned as a qualified translator as she was a member of the Gorsedd of Bards in the National Eisteddfod and asked her to take an oath as a translator. At that time, she did not know many of the legal terms used but she succeeded in doing her work capably, and this gave her confidence to help with other cases in other courts. She maintained that she was a favourite of Judge Temple Morris, who would ask for her services whenever there was call for a translator in a particular case.

In *The Reluctant Redhead,* she said of that time:

I sincerely believe that those six years in police courts during the war did more for my career in writing than any college or university could ever achieve. You saw life in all its aspects. You saw the little oddities in people's thoughts. In a way, it was a rude awakening for me. Because of Roy Evans's severe deafness, and his absent-minded meddling with his hearing aid, I had to be prepared for all contingencies. Every night I had to take *Stone's Justice Manual* with me to study in bed. For a time, also, I was in charge of the two county courts and had to read the Annual County Courts Practice to keep abreast of the legal jargon. To add to my new burden, because it was wartime there were endless new government regulations out daily. It was quite a legalistic labyrinth.

This is just a taste of the colourful life that Eluned saw passing through as she assisted the court clerk.

She earned her place there as, by her own account, it took her many months to persuade Roy Evans that 'it was all over'. The yearning to return to London had taken hold and she wanted to start writing again.

But there was another change in her circumstance. One night a dinner had been organised by the Ceredigion Wayfarers in the Black Lion, Newquay. John Griffiths, a BBC producer, was the speaker and Eluned was seated next to him. She admits that she took against him to begin with, because he turned to her and said that he had no need of any scripts and that he had enough already. She speaks eloquently of the evening in her autobiography:

I was honoured to be seated next to the guest speaker. We had not met before and I began to suspect that my table companion ... was of a rather nervous disposition. He was assaulting his fingernails ferociously, biting down to the quick. He also kept on repeating that he didn't need any more scripts, that in fact he had enough to last him for at least six months. OK. So what? I wasn't offering him any. By this time he was making me nervous too, and I could feel my red hair beginning to tingle. I knew I had to do something; so, and as ever acting first and thinking later, I told him in no uncertain terms: 'Mr Griffiths, if you were the only producer in the whole world, I wouldn't offer you a script.' I gave him what I hope was a courteous nod and took myself away to the furthest corner of the room for the night. I went home with my thoughts in an incredible twist. The following day there was an enthusiastic appreciation of our guest speaker by all the Wayfarers. He had probably disliked me because I had gone to London to write in English. Did he think, maybe, I was a traitor to my Welshness? I felt a bit uneasy. But then, nobody had ever commissioned me to write anything in Welsh. And I had my dream.

She realised later on that somebody had pulled his leg about her, and had told him she wrote scripts too and made her living in London. She mentions that same night in the Black Lion in a green notebook in her personal papers, in Welsh this time:

> I know that John will forgive me for confessing that first night that I thought him to be the most provocative man I had ever met, even though my old friend Eser Evans tried to referee between us in his own inimitable way. I went home more determined than ever that I should cast my lot with the English.
>
> [from Eluned's personal papers]

It came as quite a shock to her when she received a letter the following Tuesday from none other that Mr Griffiths, asking for a script in Welsh. She tells the story:

> I went on to write, and from script to script, and from battle to battle, I started to be interested in writing in Welsh for a fee. There were many feature programmes and series like *Teulu Tŷ Coch* (*The Red House Family*) and *Teulu'r Mans* (*The Family in the Manse*) and it is to Mr John Griffiths that I must give thanks for keeping my nose to the grindstone. I was being given a chance to mix with Welsh producers, writers and actors and it made working in English more tedious every day. Trying to be fair to two languages constantly is a painful thing.
>
> [from Eluned's personal papers]

One can also sense the pride of being allowed to write in her mother tongue:

> I was being asked in my own country to write a script in my own language. And by a man I had thought impossible! I reminded myself sternly that redheads do not bear grudges. I cancelled London and there and then sat at home and wrote a script. It was accepted. Thereafter for years and years I wrote in Welsh, mainly

for BBC Wales with the occasional story or article for London magazines. I wrote well over a dozen documentaries, mainly about rural life. In those days, it wasn't that easy sticking a microphone under a nose and then asking questions. No, a documentary in those days meant, more or less, writing a play.

This is an insight into an important chapter in Eluned's life, explaining how she returned to her home territory and started to be a part of Welsh-language life. It was a world full of parochiality and by immersing herself in it she came to understand all the forms of human nature. It's certain that her work in the law court as a translator and as a fledging lawyer of sorts was an invaluable resource towards becoming a recognised and able scriptwriter. She went on not only to write scripts for popular series but also for single feature programmes. Perhaps it could be said that she was the first female professional writer in Welsh, totally dependent on the fee she got from broadcasting. Fortunately, the scripts she wrote are now held in the National Library of Wales, thanks to the kindness of Ann Evans, Eluned's niece and executor. In them, there is vibrancy, an effervescent humour and rural joyousness at its best.

> Thereafter for years and years I wrote in Welsh, mainly for BBC Wales, with the occasional story or article for London magazines ... I tackled all sorts of rural activities – *The District Nurse*; *An Auctioneer*; *Telephone the Plumber*; *Call the Vet*; *Gypsy Life*; *Harvest Home* etc. There was such a demand for radio programmes before the onslaught of television.[13]

There is a touch of pride and modesty as she talks about her work in creating the radio scripts. They were innovative in their day and reflected the audience across Wales which was entertained by them.

---

[13] There is a fuller list of programmes at the end of this book on page 273-274.

Because Eluned did not see them as high art, but similar to the kind of stories she wrote for the English magazines, she talks about them in a dismissive manner.

But they are of the utmost importance when evaluating her work as an author and they certainly prepared the way for her to reach greener pastures. They can be viewed as precursors to her ability to create characters and to conjure detailed and striking images; they are serious and full of humour, they fuse the shallow with the complex.

Eluned served her apprenticeship by contributing to *Teulu Tŷ Coch* first of all, and then was invited to join a panel of selected scriptwriters.[14] It may be said that this was the first Welsh-language soap-opera and that when it came to an end, John Griffiths created and devised another daily soap from Swansea called *Teulu'r Mans*.

Eluned was one of the main scriptwriters from the outset and she continued to contribute to the series six or seven years after its inception. She said that the series was so popular that the times of services in chapels in some areas were changed, lest the congregation miss any of the drama.

Strangely, she said that their names as scriptwriters were never mentioned at the time and that it was only later that their names came to be heard and known by their listeners. In that first meeting held under John Griffiths' leadership, the trio discussing the series from beginning were D. Jacob Dafis, Ifor Rees and Eluned. There are many rich turns of phrases from Eluned's locality in the scripts and she names some of the actors who made the series such a success, such as the actor Manny Price as Joe Long. Later other scriptwriters joined the group, among them: Eic Davies, Elfyn Talfan, Islwyn Williams, T. Llew Jones and others. Some of these names were considered lynchpins in the cultural life of Wales and between them they were responsible for some of the most popular

---

[14] *Teulu Tŷ Coch*, the story of a schoolmaster's family, a radio soap opera on BBC radio in the 1950s.

plays and novels of the time. It is regrettable that Eluned's contribution has not been recognised, that her innate talent in creating scripts isn't lauded along with theirs.

But it wasn't just in the world of radio that Eluned excelled, for she was given the chance to contribute to numerous television series such as *Y Sgwlyn* (*The Schoolmaster*) and *Y Gwyliwr* (*The Watchman*) and a few other individual plays. One play she refers to was the adaptation of one of D. J. Williams' stories where the actor Gwenyth Petty had to feed a calf from a bucket, somewhere in the countryside, and the calf's head got stuck in the bucket. It was always the hilarity of the situation that appealed to Eluned rather than the difficulty of mastering the skill of adaptation.

This fascinating collection of her scripts perhaps deserves further exploration. S4C's commissioning department would have benefitted from her natural talent for scriptwriting, but by the time S4C was established at the beginning of the eighties Eluned had retreated from the literary world and also from the wider Welsh cultural audience. Few outside her faithful circle of friends and admirers knew of her inherent ability to create muscular dialogue. And whilst remembering her admission that she would only send poems if invited to do so, it is unlikely that she would have offered the channel any new work herself. After she had won the competition for the *pryddest* at the National Eisteddfod on Anglesey in 1983, one would have thought that the commissioners and producers would have taken advantage of her creative acuity.

One of the few BBC producers who recognised her natural ability was Gareth Rowlands, who produced several programmes with her and these are still available to view. One such programme is that of Edith Piaf and and a television film based on Eluned's winning long poem from the Anglesey National Eisteddfod. But one of the most revealing television plays based on her life experiences was *Rhith y Lloer*, scripted by Ewart Alexander as detailed in an earlier chapter. However, by the end of the eighties,

Eluned had yet again faced derision and insinuations about the authorship of her second crown-winning poem.

A producer I worked with told me of her intention to make a documentary about Eluned in the nineties, but to no avail. She left empty-handed without being able to make any progress whatsoever in securing Eluned's cooperation. I understand that the door to Eluned's heart was closed and her suspicion of the media's motives affected her to such an extent that she rebuffed any such requests. The producer told me that it was a strange meeting, that she too was sceptical as to whether Eluned really was the true author of her writings. Refusing to cooperate was, I now understand, Eluned's way of defending herself and her means of self-preservation as a writer. She was, after all, once again closing the door on potential critics.

Despite the fact that Eluned possessed a warm, friendly and open-hearted personality she became more introverted. This introversion was in sharp contrast to the humour and satire evident in her early scripts from the sixties.

The two examples that follow are typical of the style of the *noson lawen*, (jolly nights) the homespun entertainment of the time with popular melodies and which we don't see from her later in her life:

> Sweet music hums in the harsh wind
> of the happy times that we lived,
> a merry crowd who made their way
> to the blue patch of the crossroads.
> Some joyful girls and cheerful boys
> how carefree they were, long ago
> when we'd spend those ecstatic hours
> and with the boldness of our youth
> we whitewashed all dark clouds
> on the blue patch of the crossroads.
>
> If the blue patch had a tongue, truth
> to tell, tall stories and magic tales

93

would spin on the blue patch of crossroads.
An echo of meeting our lovers
where full of mirth and laughter
we danced like silken feathers.
Oh, to bring back those hours to us
the old spirit of romantic Wales
on the blue patch of the crossroads.

Cats' Eyes
When the night is dark
and drivers get confused
as the white line disappears
until we fear the worse –
an elixir unrivalled is ours
the cat's eyes of course.

If fog descends its grey blanket
and all traffic is closed to its host,
and the hedges meld as one with the road
till the drivers are shaking and lost.
The road is alive with those little eyes,
Winking at drivers who arrive – alive.

The marks of the poet's craft appear in these lovely songs with internal rhymes echoing clearly particularly in the second song. Eluned also knows how to pile on rhymes in order to create a comedic effect, in keeping with the aim of the feature programmes, which was to entertain Welsh-language audiences and listeners. The fact that she worked frequently for the BBC also shows her ability to meet the requirements and the constraints of the various commissions. There is evidence of meticulous research in her work, for example when she tells the story of a mill, and traces it back as far as medieval Welsh laws . She notes the fact that the water-mill is a part of a man's estate to be bequeathed in a will and that it is not possible to move the mill or divide it. In fact, it was only an orchard or weir that was considered to be as important as a mill, and both were the only things that could be divided between families. Following a divorce, the mill's top stone was given to the husband and the wife was given the bottom stone and Eluned shared this detailed information in her composition in a subtle and precise way.

The notebooks that Eluned had left behind testify to her enjoyment of research as many of them contain the outline for scripts or synopses for structuring dramas. She loved learning and sought knowledge on every subject under the sun. It is not surprising therefore that she should win her first crown at the National Eisteddfod for a poem that depicted the great religions of the world in stunning imagery.

But how did she find such information? Let us remember that she spent most of her life in Cenarth, without a university library close by, so it is puzzling that she managed to educate herself with such ease? I shared with her niece, the librarian Ann Evans, my quandary. The question foremost in my mind was how did she come across the Quran in a place as hidden away as Cenarth? Ann confirmed that she did indeed have a copy of the holy book:

Yes, she did have a Quran. I think she was given it when she was in Morocco. And she found it fascinating. She got to know a family who followed the Islamic faith and she talked to them a great deal about it while she was with them. I think she began to appreciate the way their faith permeated their everyday lives. And she liked that. She said that she returned to the Quran at certain times in her life. She didn't elaborate on that.

That solved one question, and the mystery about her attraction to the book. Again, I doubted that a Moroccan family would own an English copy of the Quran unless, having received an Arabic copy, she later found a copy of the English translation. But what about other sources? How in the world did Eluned succeed in doing the research needed to complete her work and find the relevant books to do so? If she had done the research, how was it not evidenced in notebooks and other papers left by her? This is her niece's answer:

As for the rest of the research, she did spend a lot of time in libraries. Often when she was up in Aberystwyth – getting thrown out at closing time because she was absorbed in something or other. I do remember once my father and I had to dash up to Aber to return a pile of books that were overdue.

Cardigan library wasn't used as much, I don't think, as they would have had to obtain material from larger libraries anyway. Cardiff and Swansea I think were used as well, Cardiff more so as she was often there for other reasons. And there was the university. She was shameless in asking for help and information – she would ring up professors and academics and experts in the field at the drop of a hat.

I frequently got called upon to research authors and titles that she could request locally. I often wondered if her local libraries wondered where she got her information from! As she used to say – might as well use the librarian in the family! And copious notes on all sorts of things. Before she died, she and I spent some time – quite a lot – sorting papers out and so much of that was research notes she had made on all sorts of things. She had filing cabinets in the garage full of notebooks etc. We had a large bonfire. By then she could not even remember what work she did the research for.

She always had an A4 notepad with her and scribbled away constantly. Poor Get used to get into terrible trouble as she would move bits of paper in an effort to tidy up. And of course it was always some vital bit that she had moved!

Yes, books were a huge problem when we started to clear her house out. They were everywhere. Piled knee-high often. As a great many were obviously in Welsh, I contacted a bookshop in Cardigan; the owners knew Eluned and they had often researched specific titles for her in the past, and they came to the house and went through hundreds of titles. And they sorted them into saleable ones and non-saleable ones. So that helped a great deal.

Here is the explanation for the fact that much of her research work went up in flames. It is easy to understand why Eluned might want to destroy much of the notes she'd made over the decades. Was it to protect herself or was it so that she got her house in order knowing that the untidy drafts would be of no importance to anybody else? Of course, the less material she left behind, the less able people would be to sift through and pull to pieces her unfinished works. Her underlying fear was that once again some deceitful individuals would analyse her work, not for its virtues but in order to find more deficiencies.

Her unperformed play *Robot* shows her caustic talent when discussing a subject that was, like her prize-winning long poem *'Corlannau'* ('Sheepfold'), ahead of its time, or certainly not in keeping with the kind of subject-matter used in the sixties. I believe it was created sometime in the sixties or at the beginning of the seventies, as she wrote it on an old typewriter, and some pages of the play are in dark blue, a sure sign that she used carbon paper in order to make another copy. But only one copy remains, full of handwritten amendments. These corrections are in both Welsh and English, another indication that she thought simultaneously in Welsh and English. The play itself is written in richly colloquial Welsh but occasionally she turns to English to write the stage directions as if she was well used to working at the BBC, where often the production side would not be able to speak Welsh. Or perhaps her mind rushed back and forth between the two languages. Writing stories for English magazines would have been an influence and would have taught her to think in English at times, and yet her dialogue is full of the Welsh of the rural, monoglot society, puritanical, rough and ready.

It must be remembered that in the period when *Robot* was

created even the simplest computer was not yet commonplace. It could be said that she was innovative when she created a drama based on a group of scientists' invention, and it's surprising that one character is a female scientist also. Taking into account Eluned's dramatic output, Wales lost a playwright who could have developed to be of an equal stature to Wil Sam or Gwenlyn Parry, both highly acclaimed Welsh-language playwrights. Neither Wales nor the theatre perhaps were ready to embrace a female playwright, any more than than they were willing to warm to somebody like Eluned, a prizewinning poet. Once again the scripts she created show amazing imagination and remarkable humour – a rare thing in the rather pious Wales of the sixties and seventies.

The play itself chastises religion, something else that would have raised the hackles of the respectable Welsh-language audience and alienated them, even though Eluned herself was a practising Christian. But she was juxtaposing this satirical picture of religious life with worldwide scientific and ecological concepts in the play. This in itself was a revolutionary and fresh approach to Welsh language drama. The story moves between two groups and two mindsets opposed to each other. Eluned created something extremely innovative, therefore, when she satirised both worlds before the end of the play. Surely some of the words uttered about religion would have been deemed shocking to the chapelgoing Welsh-language audience of the sixties and beginning of the seventies. Perhaps today the play would not have provoked any such outrage.

At the beginning of the first scene of *Robot* we see two women, chatting in a very superficial way about this and that, but more often about him and her; then we meet a contrasting character, a man with his mind on religious matters and the end of the world, the polar opposite to their chatter. Into the mix comes a character called Ap Coel (Son of Belief), who is a journalist looking for the next new story. This is an excellent collection of characters used as a counterpoint to what is happening in the scientists' laboratory.

Even the name given to the journalist, Ap Coel, is an inspired name, as is the name of the robot, who is christened Anfarwol (Immortal). And who else would have thought of naming the interpreter, Wil Sffincs (Will Sphinx)? Between the satirical and the serious there is much drama. The play opens like this:

LIWSA and GYRTRWD walk past the laboratory chatting nineteen to the dozen.

JAMES ELISEUS HUWS, an ordinary man of religion, carries sandwich boards: 'Be prepared. The end of the world is nigh.' (This man does not know how to smile.)

AP COEL, a reporter on Y Clwt (The Rag), *the local paper. Poking about for news. Always standing around the doorway.*

THE SCIENTISTS stand in the middle of the stage.

ALL are selfishly engaged in their own business.

WIL SFFINCS comes along the main road in a wheelchair and on towards the front of the stage. He waits by the entrance. He is a link between the people on the outside and the Scientisis on the inside.

He acknowledges the different groups. Spotlighting on everybody in their turn.

WIL SFFINCS:	(*Referring to the Chatterboxes*) Yap ... Yap ... Yap ...
LIWSA:	Heti Belle Vue ... fur coat ... no knickers.
GYRTRWD:	Twm Rach ... going home in coffin assistants ... a light one like tallow. Yuck!
LIWSA:	And her, the *jifigŵ* in lime green and brown shoes.

GYRTRWD:	And crying in front of the menfolk, enough to fill a bath tub.
LIWSA:	That Dai Congeril's in the lock-up again.
GYRTRWD:	You don't say –
LIWSA:	His fancy piece has bruises the size of Maesteg cobbles ...
GYRTRWD:	Gosh ... and the Pen-top cock after Rod Eilan Pwll Du's chick.
LIWSA:	Meri Frances is in trouble ... Lord Jim's on the dole.
Y DDWY:	Yap ... Yap ... Yap ... Yap, yap, yap ... yap ... yapyapyap ...
WIL SFFINCS:	Yap! Yap! Yap! Nothing is sacred. Nothing ... Nothing ... Nothing ...

(*Turns to AP COEL*)

AP COEL
(*Y Clwt* reporter): Coel on news (*SPORT*). Each item is nicey-nice.

Everybody in the play has their own aspirations, apart from the scientists, but before we turn to them the dramatic microscope focusses on the minor characters who wish to better themselves. This becomes obvious with Liwsa and Gyrtrwd as well as Ap Coel, who has his sights set far away from Wales, where he believes great things are happening. Even though next door to him, as it were, there is an important experiment about to be instigated.

| AP COEL: | Fleet Street here I come ... here I come! The Press in Wales ... Auntie May's gruel. I'm going to London. I'm going to be a Welshman. |
| WIL SFFINCS: | (*Introducing FFWNDA-MENT*) James Eliseus. Man of religion . Bumble ... Bumble ... |

Bumble ... Bumble ... And he turns his arse towards the world.

FFWNDA-MENT: BE READY. THE DAY OF JUDGEMENT IS GETTING NEARER.

WIL SFFINCS: Tally-ho! Fallen-apple jam for the Old Pensioners. Chop suey for the fathers of bastards. GOD IS LOVE. Fly the striped pyjamas on the line of Life. It's the end of the world at two seconds to quarter to three on the thirteenth ...

The interpreter Wil Sffincs satirises the portrait of the great man of religion and makes fun of him and his double bill-board that says 'God is love'. His role is like the voice in *Under Milk Wood*; he discusses, extrapolates and makes fun of the whole scenario. Then he turns his attention to the main theme of the play, which is the desire of the scientists to create history and in so doing change the world.

(*Turns to the SCIENTISTS who are walking back and forth centre stage, taking no notice of anybody*)

SCIENTISTS: $X-Y + b.B =$ the bridge of the shoulder and muscles.

SCIENTISTS: Create! Create! Create!
WIL SFFINCS: THAT'S THEM. The Pill Posh-nobs, AI people, the Bombs and men without belly-buttons. (*He turns to the audience*) Quick! Lie down under under Granny's patchwork quilt. They probe with their clinical fingers, their soulless poking into the staring eyes of the future.

	(*He gives a slight shake of fear, then he introduces himself with great ceremony*) WILLIAM GENESIS JONES.
LIWSA:	Wil Sffincs to everybody else.
GYRTRWD:	Wil Sffincs to everybody else.
LIWSA:	Who is he? (*They shake their heads*)
WIL SFFINCS:	One of Mari's children (*Laughing*). Wil Take Every Side. With you. With them.
GYRTRWD:	Where did he come from? (*They shake their heads*)

Wil Sffincs is never short of words as he prattles against the changes and the events of the secular age:

| WIL SFFINCS: | Yesterday in Eve's garden, a gust of wind annoys a leaf. Today – Porthcawl and Porthaethwy. A blonde doll in a mini-skirt sporting her nappy. Tomorrow – who knows, will there be a body ... Will there be clothes. Will she have skin on her? |

BOTH:	Wil Sffincs ... Tiddly-winks ... Wil Sffincs ... Tidllywinks ...
WIL SFFINCS:	(*Chuckling*) As old as sin ...
	(*He jumps out of his chair*) As young as temptation. (*Does a little jig, then walks with a limp*) The world is a long journey of a thousand years ... (*He takes off a shoe. He looks at it for a short while*) Blimey! The mice of time have given the soles a battering! (*He hops and hits his forehead like a man pointing to a weakness of mind.*)

Hop and jump.

Who's in the Big House?
Who's out?
It's me today ...
It'll be you tomorrow ...

What is life?

Sam Pendulum's second-hand car with its
innards stretched to swallow the miles; a snail's
kiss on a cabbage's hump; a fire on Twelfth
Night; the smile of a rose; the pout of a three-
year-old; bingo; an empty grave; bumbailey.
And Dai Beca's whippet changing colour
between two races.
Hey! Let out the brake. The dawn is green.
And the world goes on.

We return to the superficial world of the girls who say nothing, it
appears, nothing but chattering about the material things that
everybody has, the minister's wife gets it in the neck constantly. What
they discuss also gives a flavour of the period in which the play was
written, or at least the relatively poverty-stricken society that was the
backdrop to the story. It is a portrait of those who desire the luxuries
of life, as the following dialogue shows, cutting across Wil Sffincs'
flow:

GYRTRWD:	What did you say, Liwsa ... Mrs Jincins the Mans?
LIWSA:	*Fitted carpet*, Gyrtrwd ...
GYRTRWD:	*Fitted carpet*. On the toilet floor.
LIWSA:	On the toilet floor?

(*Beat*)

GYRTRWD:	Yuck. *Fitted carpet.*
LIWSA:	The minister's wife.
GYRTRWD:	His feet must be cold.
LIWSA:	Hardly anybody goes to the evening service.
GYRTRWD:	Five and Dai Saved.
LIWSA:	And Bessie Bronchitis peddling the harmonium.
GYRTRWD:	Like a cyclone through a field of bracken.
LIWSA:	The scollops on her petticoat.
GYRTRWD:	Like the teats of an old Friesian.
LIWSA:	And Jack Phoebe staring ...
GYRTRWD:	And spills the collection plate ... (*Giggles*)

(*Beat*)

GYRTRWD:	But – *fitted.* [*Eluned has crossed 'carpet' out*]
LIWSA:	THEIR chapel wants to beat OUR chapel. Caersalem. Moreia. And a Split Chapel.
BOTH:	Religion!

(*They walk back past the laboratory*)

GYRTRWD:	But Liwsa ... *Fitted.* On the toilet floor.
LIWSA:	That's life. It goes on, lass!

(*They wait. They look at the Scientists*)

LIWSA:	What are they doing then? Do you know, Gyrtrwd?
GYRTRWD:	What are they doing then? Do you know, Liwsa?
BOTH:	Nobody ... Nobody knows.

The play moves from snappy turns of phrase, to sweet nothings said between the two neighbours, to the amusing monologue of Wil Sffincs as he pontificates about the world and his wife, with an obvious talent for a colourful way of expressing himself:

WIL SFFINCS: WILLIAM GENESIS JONES! (*Looks at his feet*) Adam's feet, my foot!
Hey! Did you hear my corns hooting as they raced through fields of grass ... Crunch-crunch on the throat of the worm (Hi, hi, hi! Enough for a year, Will Poacher).
Ransacking the grub's switch so that the world doesn't watch two naked people making love.
Lying totally drunk in Will Temperance's corn in the wildness of his night, and bathing naked in the sun's tears in Clywedog.
Stamping from gut to gut and trampling on the microbes of sin –
And the Old Boy's two black horns stiff. Thank you, Good Boy! And here's a little something! Dock leaves to tame the nettles;
Lord Emrys's pheasant egg for breakfast.
And Lady Llwyn-drain's lace handkerchief to wipe Sebastian the white tom-cat's nose. Hall-e-luh! We shall meet ... Far away in China on the Rhos-on-Sea Prom ... and behind the thistles on the building plot at Wilson Parade.

BOTH: Tiddlywinks ... Wil Sffincs ... Tiddly ... Tiddly ... etc ...

This is the the play's opening scene, which is deceptive as we do not hear much about a robot or about the scientists. Instead we receive a rapturous flow that excites the audience and makes them wonder and guess at what exactly the relationship between the different characters could be, if indeed there is any relationship. Bearing in mind that three characters have yet to appear on stage, it's obvious that the author has not been hampered by the theatrical requirements of our age, when a playwright is urged not to write for more than four actors. Of course, this play could be staged as a community play, and the way the drama unfolds suggests that it is some kind of slapstick comedy. But even though the dialogue is light, altogether the message is a serious one and there is great mental anguish involved in the process of creating a robot. The dichotomy is an exciting one. Here are the two facets most evident in Eluned's work: her ability to create comedy and an unbeatable situation comedy, and on the other hand, her ability to delve into intellectual depth with complex ideas. She pushes the boundaries of both. That is, she sees the comedy in human nature as well as the gravity of the creative, scientific drive that potentially could be terrifyingly dangerous. Perhaps Eluned herself did not know exactly how to weigh up the two things, thus creating confusion. The words of Liwsa and Gyrtrwd at the end of this passage, 'nobody understands' are a constant refrain:

WIL SFFINCS: Oops! One moment in life to wander aimlessly by the grave of civilisation, listening to the earth begrudging its shine to the headless angel's two arms and the magnificent stone in memory of the black and white saint of Pwllywhied.
Close your eyes, old son, against the clay! I never got my fill of girls.
But if you came back you would die of greediness.
Girls ... girls ... girls ... The cauldron is bubbling in the Scientists' laboratory ... (*He jumps about.*) Them. They're creating ... creating ... creating. Who ... Who ... Who will come from the cauldron?

LIWSA:	Did you understand, Gyrtrwd?
GYRTRWD:	Did you understand, Liwsa?
BOTH:	Nobody ... nobody understands ...

At last, after a fanfare of words, full of hilarity, the journalist Ap Coel reveals the crux of the play: there are three scientists attempting to create a robot that could transform the world of work. One feels the frustration with journalism and the million trivial things that seem to be important coming through this character:

AP COEL

(Y Clwt *office. Typing furiously. Does everything furiously. Takes out paper. Reads*): Laboratory mystery ... Three scientists are researching ... Doctor Paul, Doctor Pwyll and his daughter, Dr Sarffa. Creating a machine to do man's work. There has been a great expectation for the robot ... But what is happening

... Not much ... Not much at all! Nothing. NOTHING. (*Rips the paper into shreds*) Damn. Damn. Damn!

The Press in Wales (*Waves* Y Clwt *about*) – Y CLWT. Babies' potty paper ... Little Jones. And big James ... sticking the hands of duty into the folds of pockets and folding the conscience like a Sunday kerchief into the breast pocket of our Respected Minister. Thank you for being allowed to live ... Palomino Stallion and Gossamer Plain. (*Reading a few items*) 'Mrs Angharad Huws. Number Three ... Maes Twmdili. St David's Hospital (we bow to the saint). Observation! A spyglass then. The world has seen her varicose veins ... her appendix... her ulcers ... her gold-stones ...

Councillor R. R. R. Roberts. B.E.M. (*Parish Council*).

A chair for the Cwmpryfed [Fly-town] Eisteddfod.

Is there peace! The poet's wife is in the asylum. The house is full of dry rot.

Village in arms over sewerage.

The Bed-pan Band! Wonderful! Halleluiah!

As we cannot be certain when this play was written, we can only speculate that it has echoes of the kind of jokey material written in local newsletters. This makes the scenario a familiar one to us in Wales today. We see again the editor's satirical reaction as Ffwnda-ment, James Eliseus Huws, calls by:

(*JAMES ELISEUS HUWS comes up the road to the office*)

AP COEL:	Bloody hell! Another artefact from Wales, my country.
	Welcome. Welcome ... Mr James Eliseus. (*He shakes a chair*). Dry rot. Worry not ... It will hold your religion's weight.
FFWNDA-MENT:	Er ... I've hurried here. (*He sits down*)
	Halfway through toast and a soft-boiled egg.
	Er ... A letter for the religious corner. (*He gives him a large bundle of paper*)
AP COEL:	Hurrah! We'll sell millions of *The Clwt* tomorrow morning.
FFWNDA-MENT:	Er ... an interesting topic. Fundamentalism. Persuading people to come back...
AP COEL:	Back ... Where from ... Majorca ... Las Palmas

	... Cwmtydu ... or from bloody Llanfihangel-y-Cynrhon [St Michael-of-the-Grub]?
FFWNDA-MENT:	Back to the Bible. To believe it literally. The end of the world is at hand.
AP COEL:	Stodgy potatoes in the Foxhole storehouse.
FFWNDA-MENT:	Er ... beg your pardon ...
AP COEL:	Yes, beg ... And get nothing. Nothing, nothing. Absolutely nothing. No story. No news ... no flash on the horizon ... Fundamentalism ... *Y Clwt* and its religious corner ... (*Points to the SCIENTISTS*) What do you have to say to THEM. That's the news the readers want. The religious response to THEM over there ...
FFWNDA-MENT:	THEM over there ... (*Fumbling and peeping*) Er ... Them there ... er ...
AP COEL:	Yes. THEM. The Scientists. The people who hold our future in their hands.
FFWNDA-MENT:	Uh ... Them ... Dear ... dear ... Them ...Er ... I have nothing to say to Them ... Er ... nothing ...
AP COEL:	But if you religious people can't give guidance ...
FFWNDA-MENT:	We have nothing to do with Them. Er ...THEM ... Experimenting on monkeys ... and ... and ... mice ... and ... and ... frogs ... Yuck... what do they understand about the Bible ... About fundamentalism?
AP COEL:	Bloody hell! If that's the response of the Church ...
FFWNDA-MENT:	Very good. Very good, my son, your ideas are healthy.
	Hell! Hell and Heaven! Heaven and Hell! The foundations of our beliefs. Adam and Eve ... And the Garden of Eden ... And the Great God creating man on the Sixth Day ...

109

AP COEL:	On the sixth day – what the hell was the Union doing, that's what I'd like to know. Working six days. Smashing the rules to smithereens. Well – what was the Union doing? That's what you need to discuss. Look at things in the light of today. Not slobbering like a rotten pumpkin with its seeds all slops in the sentimentality of the past. Did you ever think what if Adam and Eve had been created anew? If the Scientists hit on a formula … Oh lord! Religion in Wales! *Y Clwt* and the religious corner. There's more kick to the Saturday night slops served in the Black than would ever come from the vineyards of Fundamentalia … Go back, Sir. To your toast and your soft boiled egg … The Church's slops are too weak to even cause diarrhoea. But as for Them over there – it's a potful of stomach-ache at least. (*Strides out – looking towards Scientists*) But what the hell are They doing. That's what I'd like to know. And that is what I'm going to find out. Take *Y Clwt*. (*Throws it*) Sit like a castrated cock on the compost heap of religion. (*Throws the bundle of letters to him*) Fundamentalism! In the age of going to the moon! (*He leaves laughing*)
FFWNDA-MENT:	(*Collects the letters and hugs them*) But the message for Wales. The Message … Fundamentalism …

After the Brechtian dialogue, the playwright now establishes the main theme, which is the attempt to create a robot. We also arrive, if we skip over some scenes, at the point when they assemble the robot. This situation itself would have been a huge and fascinating challenge for any theatre company to stage and the spectacle of seeing and using wires in science and medicine are commonplace today, be they wires to solve problems of sleep or to test patients for brain disease. The initial aim is to create something that has the ability as a robot to function for the good of people. Note how clever the names of the scientists are: Pwyll – a sorcerer, according to his historical name in the Mabinogi, and Paul – the apostle with a far-reaching spiritual influence in the world of Christianity. They order the robot to respond to their commands:

PWYLL:	(*Standing above the robot lying on the table – his feet can be seen by the audience. They move his arms, legs etc. Hold on to the fingers ... they stare at him in wonder.*)
	As flexible as fingers embroidering. (*to the robot*) Sit up then. (*The robot gets up*).
	Lie down. (*The robot lies down*).
	To think that he can do the work of a thousand men for a year in one minute. (*Turns to Paul*) Paul. Isn't it amazing, Paul?
PAUL:	(*Looking at his research*) Eh?
PWYLL:	A machine that has so much ability...
PAUL:	Goodness! Pwyll – the whole thing is so bloody exciting.
PWYLL:	Oh, light will come some day. Science amazes scientists often. But it will take time. Look at DNA and the problem of heredity. Fighting for years ... and at a strike, Crick and Watson succeed...
PAUL:	And I will succeed too, Pwyll. I will create an artificial brain.
PWYLL:	You will one day, I don't doubt ... Paul –
PAUL:	One day ... the thing is within reach now ... The cells are reacting. I can carry the elements

	from one cell into another ... from the brain and through the nerve systems...
PWYLL:	(*Somewhat uneasily*) There is life –
PAUL:	And it can produce its own energy ... Pwyll, this thought-process can run for ... well, for ever –
PWYLL:	But that would mean...
PAUL:	That we could give a robot a live brain.
PWYLL:	But that would be impossible ... the size and the cost –
PAUL:	I can get all the thought-patterns into this. (*Gestures to a small battery*)
PWYLL:	But...
PAUL:	Micro-circuits, Pwyll ... exactly as they made that tiny radar set. That and... I can do away with all the cells and complications. Pwyll ... at last we have a machine that can take over from man.
PWYLL:	But it would mean that man would have to continue feeding the machine...
PAUL:	It would mean no such thing. This would have its own mind. It would be able to receive facts and use them correctly like us. Goodness! Imagine! It can store a huge amount of information, more than man – and continue to work ... for ... for ... well, for eternity –
PWYLL:	That idea scares the hell out of me.

The play goes on with Pwyll – true to his name, Patience – inviting us to exercise patience while Paul is so excited about the discovery that he feels a huge urge to take the experiment further. He does not want to stop the research and insists on battling onwards in order to succeed in his task. He feels it necessary to share the the discovery with his fiancée, Sarffa – who is, by the way, Pwyll's daughter. Paul implores him not to tell her, probably because he knows that she would encourage him to develop the experiment further. Paul is also more ambitious than his soon-to-be father-in-law, afraid that similar developments in America or Russia would win the day. This is the dramatic arc in the play, as they disagree fervently about what the next steps should be:

PWYLL: The *risk* is too much. We haven't prepared ourselves, Paul. Let's use this robot to do the work that we know is within his capability.

PAUL: And let Russia and America win again? Goodness, Pwyll! The scientists of the world would give their lives to be in our shoes today. And if this robot is as good as you say it is, Pwyll ... imagine what it could do if it got a brain.

PWYLL: But we can control him as he is now, Paul. We will be the ones to program it. But give it the ability to think for itself –

PAUL: This would save man endless work. And nothing can go wrong. I'm sure of this, Pwyll. I can't afford for anything to go awry. Don't worry ... I'll take the responsibility...

PWYLL: There is something ... something ... unnatural – presumptious even ... in venturing –

PAUL: You're not talking like Dr Pwyll the Scientist, now. We scientists don't have the right to hide any of our discoveries.

PWYLL: But do we have the ethical right to go so far? To create a man – that's what you're attempting to do in reality.

That indeed was Paul's intention as he sees the possibilities come alive in front of his eyes. The quarrel continues. Pwyll cannot persuade Paul, who is determined that he is 'going to create a man' and he commands the robot to stand up. He tells Pwyll that all he needs to do now is to 'change the speed of the patterns through the nerve cells' and work on the equation 'until it becomes equal'.

PWYLL: Paul, please, don't do this –
PAUL: Not to do ... But that's unreasonable, Pwyll –
PWYLL: To create an artificial man. I am really afraid –
PAUL: (*impatiently*) Oh for goodness' sake ... why don't you take a pill for your fears then. This is a complex problem. And I need solitude in order to think again ... solitude ... do you understand ... solitude.
PWYLL: Oh, well ... if you feel that way – (*he goes to cogitate over the robot*)

Sarffa walks in to a tense situation and complains about Paul's total commitment to his work rather than to her. Even though she's also a scientist, following in her father's footsteps, she says that she's had enough of all the experiments without achieving anything, and maintains that she means no more to Paul now than his 'test-tube'. Then, gradually she comes to realise what he has achieved with the robot, and revels in his masterpiece. The name Sarffa is also revealing, since *sarff* translates into English as serpent and her personality is rather snake-like. She encourages Paul to push ahead with the experiment. As she had berated him once for being 'as unambitious as an Arab without a tunic', she now realises that she should side with him in order to see the experiment reach fruition. She encourages Paul to continue to create free will in the robot's head. As a character, she questions Eve's position and the Creation. She says: 'Symbols! Perhaps you believe that a woman caused man to sin. And that flippin' apple. Cox's Pippin, Granny Smith, Golden Wonder ... or Granny's Lady Fingers – Which was it, Daddy?'

Juxtaposed with the scientific and philosphical dialogue about creating life, the mortal characters of flesh and blood disrupt the scientific developments. Liwsa and Gyrtrwd return to the stage and the play creates different layers of contrasting characters so that the audience can identify with the varying worlds in the play and feel the excitement of the more challenging and intellectual elements. Once again this is the aim of Eluned's work throughout – far-reaching and otherworldly ideas side by side with the naked, flesh-and-blood reality of people who have their feet firmly on the ground. Her ear is alert to ordinary folk's speech as is evident in this passage:

GYRTRWD:	What did you say, Liwsa … Daniel next door?
LIWSA:	Building a lean-to, girl. An old coffin of a kitchen.
GYRTRWD:	She has children like sandwich meat.
LIWSA:	Out on to the yard to turn...
GYRTRWD:	Baby after baby.
LIWSA:	Like mushrooms in the Pissy Field...
GYRTRWD:	(Pills to India.) If the Pope was a woman... (*Beat. Walks back towards the laboratory*)
LIWSA:	Her in Number Five has bought a coat ... *Swagger*.
GYRTRWD:	Huh … not before time.
LIWSA:	That old cocktail cabinet –
GYRTRWD:	(*Sings while opening the lid*) *Drink to me only*.
LIWSA:	Yuck … A bellyful of gin. And forgetting the pill.

(*Pause*)

LIWSA:	She'll have to keep it.
GYRTRWD:	Her father's on the Council.
LIWSA:	And in the Big Seat at Moreia. Where will we all find space?

GYRTRWD:	Where will we all find space?
LIWSA/	
GYRTRWD:	(*Turns to the scientists*) What are They doing then? Yeah. What are They doing then?

A spotlight is shone on Wil Sffincs who once again pontificates about this and that in his usual style, confirming that there are different things happening everywhere: 'The sun shines on little Gwen in the Mumbles / it burns Ashu's skin in the Kashmir hills / and throws its aura on a primrose in the Furthest Field. We hear some of the characters coming forward; Ffwnda-ment, and Ap Coel, say this:

| AP COEL: | Light! By gum, it's Light! Your religion is like a mole's parlour ... Some light on the things that are going on here – this is where we need the Light. Knowing what the scientists are doing. THEM ... not you, the men of religion – who are trying to light the world. |

He says later on when giving Ffwnda-ment a piece of his mind:

A woman from man's rib! Jesus! If there is any truth to that story ... why not. The Scientists? Why let this business of creating man be a monopoly. It's a competitive world – and everybody's at it till death. And maybe it's time to have new men on this earth. We're a shabby lot at best ... oh hell ... if I could just get one look in there.

The play continues with the appearance of the robot christened Anfarwol (Immortal). At the beginning it is not intended that the robot should do anything more than react to Paul, the scientist's, commands, and then later on to Pwyll and Sarffa's commands. But when he is given free will, problems arise creating an extremely unexpected situation. There seems to be no way of controlling him and this causes consternation for the scientists. The play is clever in one sense because the characters are expressing extreme opinions. Sarffa is particularly strident in her views and expresses herself succinctly:

SARFFA: Nonsense. The earth had been in existence way before man appeared.
We know that the earth is one planet in the stellar system. And we know too that the day will come when our type of men won't exist anymore –

FFWNDA-MENT: They shall be swept away because of sin just like in Sodom and Gomorrah –

SARFFA: Sorry, Mr Religion. Nothing as intriguing. The weather will put a stop to us. The changes in temperature will make mortal man not able to live

Here we are confronted with one of the most profound issues of the twenty-first century. This extract illuminates Eluned's undoubted talent in creating a challenging play, that both entertains a wide audience but also probes into ecology, religion, mortality and immortality. The point at issue here is man's dilemma whether to control or refuse to control scientific developments. It was no small feat that she succeeded in writing a three-act play, and it's obvious from looking at the directions that she could see clearly the whole play being performed on stage. This could have been a successful play and deserving of performance by National Theatre Wales or any other professional theatre company. If only this play could be realised on stage instead of being kept in a grey box in the National Library's archives... It would also make an excellent radio play as the language and imagery is so rich and demotic.

It may be that the criticism of her poetry made her return to her former craft as a scriptwriter. Did she not get a receptive audience in her home village during the war when she and her sister took all the roles? Madge complained frequently that Eluned would wander away from the script and turn every play into an improvisation, thus creating confusion for her older sister. This tendency in Eluned to diverge from what was intended is revealed in *Robot*; this multi-layered play bears witness to her erratic nature.

In essence, *Robot* has extremely forward-looking messages. Calling the robot Anfarwol (Immortal) is an intriguing device and is inspiring in itself. After all, she was as innovative as Isaac Asimov in *The Three Laws of Robotics* or the Czech playwright, Karel Čapek, with his play *R. U. R.* or *Rossumovi Univerzální Roboti* in 1920 that popularised the use of the word 'robot', which comes from the Czech word for hard work or slavery. Eluned combines the seriousness of the subject-matter with the comedy of the characters as they demonstrate their ignorance of the technological implications. For them, it is society and its religion, or lack of religion, that is at the heart of their concern.

•

This is only one facet of Eluned's writing and it is evidence of an inquiring mind and the ability to deal with scientific and religious subjects to create interesting, dramatic and terrifying scenarios at the same time. There is another kind of script-writing that she did which was more educational and entertaining and it fitted perfectly with the commissions she received from the BBC. These are based on social matters that touch on the political.

Studying these scripts more closely proves that Eluned was a scriptwriter who possessed an ear for the vernacular dialogue of the society in which she lived. She could emphasise the comedy in situations and through various characters and, as is shown in *Robot*, she could go to the other extreme and explore the world of theological and religious ideas. This also brings to light how she thought and wrote her poetry. On the one hand, she gave the impression of being a country poet whose duty was to entertain, whilst on the other hand with her long poems she displays depth and insight. It may be that the two winning long poems are exceptional examples of an extraordinary inspirational genius (Eluned uses the word genius often to describe others), or it may be that her unique talent was as a playwright. We see this most prominently as she, in her nineties, returned to scriptwriting and drama, and turned her back to an extent on traditional Welsh poetry.

In reading her long poems again, one can see that portraying characters and scenarios is an integral part of what a playwright does. A dramatised film was made of Eluned's long poem *'Clymau'* ('Bonds') but Eluned could just have easily written a comedy series in Welsh or more serious plays. One thing is certain, Eluned was not one to stay still, and when the script-writing and the poetry came to an end, she turned her hand to another kind of writing, the libretto. She stepped into that world with confidence and a new enthusiasm after reaching her three score years and ten.

Her Poetic Pilgrimage

I must be private, secret, as submerged as possible in order to write.

Virginia Woolf

It is thought, somewhat erroneously, that Eluned Phillips arrived on the National Eisteddfod stage as a crowned bard as if she had not developed any of her craft before then. Or at least, that was the impression I had when I was a young girl: that her poem was a total fluke that cut across fifteen hundred years of poetic tradition. But the truth is that she had been writing quietly from a very early age. Eluned admitted that it was mostly writing romantic stories in English that took her fancy, the kind found in the popular women's magazines of the period, and that she wrote very little poetry at the time. Eluned said that she wrote romantic novels for Mills & Boon and was given three guineas for her first attempts. There is no evidence available to prove if this was true or not.[15]

Eluned said that she wrote for different women's magazines – which were at their zenith after WWII – and wrote under a pseudonym and was given a fair wage for the work. It is possible, therefore, that it was only after coming back to Wales that the desire to write poetry developed in earnest.

The number of poems published are few, even though she admits that she wrote lyrical poems. (These I discovered after her death.) According to her testimony 'a piece of a poem would fall on to the back of an envelope or a piece of an old calendar'. Then, something happened that enthralled her – she read 'Adfeilion' ('Ruins') by

---

[15] *Ceredigion: 101 o'i Beirdd ac Emynwyr*, (ed.) Eirian Jones (Y Lolfa, 2010) p 132.

T. Glynne Davies, the winning long poem in free metres that won the Crown at the National Eisteddfod in Llanrwst in 1951. It was this winning poem that ignited the desire in her to compete. She composed a poem annually on the set topic of the Eisteddfod but without daring to post her attempts to the competition. She said that *'Ffenestri'* ('Windows') by W. J. Gruffydd, the winner in 1955, also influenced her to continue with writing poetry.

And then in 1963 she saw that for the National Eisteddfod in Llandudno the subject was *'Y Bont'* ('The Bridge'). She thought about her mother and a houseful of blue plates adorned with the willow pattern. So she wrote about the bridge of love on the 'Blue Plate' and this time she posted her attempt to the competition. Gwilym R. Jones was adjudicating and he chose five or six poems as the best of the entries. Eluned heard Nebo 'my nom de plume', in their midst, but because of my nervousness, I thought that these names were out of the competition. I felt too much shame to open the *Cyfansoddiadau* [the publication of winning compositions from the National Eisteddfod] until I got home on Sunday and saw that Nebo was one of the best'. The adjudicator said: 'Here is the surest master in all the competition at this style of paragraphing and sculpting a poem [free verse] ... some parts of the poem are untidy enough which suggest it was rushed to comply with the entry date... but I must admit that I like many of the stanzas in Nebo's work.'

According to Cynan, who put the poem far lower in order of merit:

This is a fanciful *vers libre*, but is also quite complex as it looks at the bridge on the old willow pattern plate. Even though there is an attempt at peppering the poem with old Chinese words, there is a comical mixture of contemporary Welsh words also, words such as *'jolihoitan'*, *'bitnic'*, and the poet uses the word *'bit'* (beat) to mean 'pitch'. I do not feel that the author has succeeded in conveying the overt romanticism of the traditional story depicted on the plate.

The appeal of the story lies in its simple clarity for all generations of children.

Apart from what was said on stage, Gwilym R. Jones' comments spurred the poet on as he noted that, 'Nebo relates the traditional story seen in the picture on the Chinese plate in a style that suggests the lyricism of the Far East'.

Two doves Chang and Li Chi
Crooning, crooning,

And the two-in-one heartbeats
Cavorting happily.

When I was a virginal girl

I grew beyond the fifteen rice harvests
A woman to a suckling child.

Cynan explained further:

We see here the bitterness of a young girl who has been disappointed. The bridge in the adroit poem is a bridge over the river of love. The following lines show how cleverly Nebo can use his metre:

Between a leap and a quick kiss
And a quick kiss and a leap,

Two pairs of souls danced

Over the Mandarin-devil's bridge.

And a casket that would break a miser's heart
on a bamboo pole between the two.

Eyes deep in the eyes of another
Onwards

For a thousand moons and more.

The adjudicator details the poet's craft, noting the poet's intelligence in discussing her subject:

> Nebo is a poet who has immersed himself in the tale of the Chinese plate and has blended this with Chinese poetry, and he also knows how to hit the right note in reality, as the end of the poem shows:

The Flesh is older than the bridge
Old like ancient rice,
Old like mice, and lice, and sparrows.

> And here are some of the most graphic images of real life in the Far East as if to underline the antiquity of the flesh. There are parts of the poem that are rather unpolished and suggest a poet being hurried in his writing. Indeed, it would be better to omit some of the poem in order to concentrate on its virtue. There is no need for a catalogue of lines in order to expand the poem. But I must admit that I am fond of many stanzas in Nebo's work.

That year twenty-four poets competed for the Crown, and to receive comments from the acclaimed poet Gwilym R. delighted Eluned. The comments also noted something that she would be criticised for frequently: that her work seemed rushed in parts, something that was characteristic of Eluned's style of writing. Indeed, this was not only true of her writing, for Eluned was always in a rush wherever she went, according to friends. And she admitted herself that she would consider an idea for a poem for a very long time and then rush in headlong at the last minute to try and crystalise the ideas that had been collecting in her head and heart for a long while. She was put in seventh place by Waldo Williams who says of her work:

> This is the story of the Willow Pattern told in twelve free-verse songs by the characters in the story. The poems have a *staccato* but allusive style, and succeed more in the songs where emotion is strong rather than the parts where the story is told. The structure is faulty. He writes using contemporary syntax that does not work as well in the context of a poem.

•

Less than a year later, and perhaps because she received a fairly favourable commendation from the judges, she decided to compete for the Crown at the Cardigan eisteddfod, Gŵyl Fawr Aberteifi. This was an eisteddfod considered to be one of the biggest apart from the National Eisteddfod, known by many as a 'semi-national'. Perhaps it was this that inspired her to compete again at Gŵyl Fawr Aberteifi in 1964. In her own words:

> I heard on the field that the winning poet was W. J. Gruffydd and I took myself home before listening to the adjudication. In time, the Secretary, the genial Rev. D. J. Roberts pushed the written adjudication through the letterbox, and I saw that the Rev. Eirian Davies had complimented my efforts.

She felt enough 'confidence to compete the following year'. The subject was 'Thorns where once was Grandeur', and she said her attempt was 'a necessary tribute to Dewi Emrys that won me the Crown'. In his adjudication on the poem, R. Bryn Williams wrote the following:

> This poem was written out of respect for Dewi Emrys, and it outlines the course of this highly gifted man's life. It is not the

history of just one man, but also the history of the thorns that grew in the society where he loomed large. And this competitor possesses a voice of his own, and writes in an arresting way ... he can taste the words and give us a flavour of the places that he leads us to ... This poem excels in the competition because of the originality of the vision ... possessing a craft, but ultimately as a poet. This is an affectionate poem: 'this is a poem that Gŵyl Fawr Aberteifi are honoured to be crowning the author of this year.'

The fact that Eluned kept a tidy copy of the adjudication shows clearly that she delighted in her success and it fired her desire to compete in the National. In 1965 she sent a play in metre to the National Eisteddfod in Newtown and was given a 'fair and complimentary adjudication by none other than Dr Thomas Parry', but there is more criticisism than praise given to the play, submitted under the nom de plume of Pryderi. This is what Cynan said of her attempt to write about Nest:

It is the story of Nest, the wife of Gerallt, a Norman lord in Dyfed who escapes with her young Welsh lover, Owain ap Cadwgan, and who takes her children with her. Later, she returns to her husband at the command of King Henry.

This is quite a drama to be writing about this Welsh Helen, but Pryderi doesn't have an idea how to structure a play from it. The young stranger persuades Nest to escape with him on very tenuous grounds and it is on very unpredictable grounds that the king persuades her to return. There is no plot development and the story is introduced through long speeches where nothing happens.

The play attempts to work on an overwritten metre, but the sentence is parallel to the line almost every time. There are way too many feeble lines, and muddled lines at the end of speeches without the next speaker finishing the metre.

Thomas Parry recognises the ability of the writer in his critique of Pryderi:

> This is one of Pryderi's many faults also, in his attempt at telling the story of Owain ap Cadwgan attracting Nest, the wife of Gerallt de Windsor – a story that should be told in a lively and vibrant way. The long speeches slow the pace of the drama and produce stupor in both the actor and the audience. There is room, of course, for long declamatory passages, and it is the business of the actor to know where that should happen.

Bobi Jones places Pryderi's play in the third class along with nine other plays, making a general comment about the fact that they tend to be 'romantically stereotypical and echoing'. And yet he says that 'all the plays in this class are readable and smooth'. It is likely that this would have pleased Eluned as, in the process of climbing the ladder towards creating a literature of a high standard, she would have predominantly been seeking constructive criticism.

Knowing of her fondness of sending two attempts in to each crown competition, it is highly likely that Eluned also submitted a play about the French Revolution and the execution of Queen Marie Antoinette. Cynan says about the work of Yr Allt Goch (The Red Hillside), *Gwaed y Cyfnos* (*Twilight Blood*):

> This is a three-act play in free-verse form about the Royal Court of France during the Revolution. The author has immersed himself in the history of the time and in the characterisation of the main dramatis personae. It is unlikely that two handmaidens would be so willing to divulge the Court's secrets to a strange man that they met by chance in the Versailles Gardens, in order to get their pictures in his paper.
>
> What detracts from the dramatic value of the work are the speeches in bookish and archaic language so as to suggest the eighteenth century. But the supple Welsh of Ellis Wynne would have been far closer to the life of the time and much easier for the

actors to utter. There are too many static speeches and not enough action. This is a detailed scenario towards the creation of a play, rather than the play itself.

Again, Bobi Jones places her in the third class, without referring directly to the play, but Thomas Parry mentions Yr Allt Goch's work when referring to another weakness found in some of the plays in the competition:

> Another thing that interferes with the unity of the whole is the lack of brevity, or that of rambling. This is a problem for Yr Allt Goch in his play about the Revolution in France and the execution of Queen Marie Antoinette. The execution of the Queen should be the climax at the end of the play and the author should have concentrated much more on creating imagery and developing her character in the main body of the play, rather than turning to other characters, some of whom could have easily been dispensed with.

I believe that the author of this play was Eluned Phillips because there is a notebook written in her handwriting, full of facts about Marie Antoinette and the bare bones of a play there. In her autobiography she says that once whilst at a conference she had been locked by accident in Marie Antoinette's room in Versailles when she was following a group on a visit to her palace:

> We came to Marie Antoinette's room. Now my interest ballooned. Marie had been on my mind for years. I had even written a play about her so I was determined to inspect even the molecules of dust in her room. The party was urged to move on by the guide, but I wasn't ready to go and knew that I could catch up with them. I turned the bed-cover over and looked under the bed. Finally I was satisfied and went to catch up with the others. The door was locked. I struggled and struggled with no luck. I

was locked in. I shouted and then yelled in all the languages I knew – even added some non-dictionary words too by the end! By now the lights were turned off and it was absolutely dark. I tried to take a rest on the edge of Marie's bed but her head kept rolling under my feet. At the crack of dawn, I thought I heard a cockerel crow three times but that I am convinced was my confused mind.

She was found early in the morning, as the leader of the conference noticed she was missing. A fictional tall story? Is there an element of imaginative writing here? Perhaps, but it proves the fact that she created a play about Marie Antoinette and confirms that Eluned posessed a playwright's sensibilities. A talent not fulfilled totally, even though she appreciated the honest type of adjudication given by Cynan and Thomas Parry about her shapeless, disorderly plays. Her attempts also show her interest in creating plays on subjects that belong to other cultures as well as her own – another prominent feature in her work throughout her life.

The following year, in 1966, she wrote a poem for the Aberafan National Eisteddfod on the subject of 'The Boundary'. In Caradog Prichard's adjudication, and the first in the *Cyfansoddiadau* [*Compositions and Adjudications*], he states unequivocally which poem should win, a poem written by Dafydd Jones, Ffair-rhos, and also he names three other long poems that he greatly admired. He said that he could not decide between two long poems, which were 'Y Maen Hir' ('The Menhir') and 'Ogam' ('Ogham'). And then, he says something quite unexpected as he refers in detail to Mererid's work, Eluned's nom de plume:

Who else deserves to be at the top of this list with the two poems? One, most definitely – Mererid. I have to admit that at the first reading, it did not grab me, but having heard the unanimous recommendation of the poem by my two co-adjudicators, I also became fond of its craft and facility. The boundary is a symbolic one here; it is the boundary that has riven Jerusalem in two and perhaps it is the allegorical ambiguity that meant I failed to warm to the poem at first. There is more of a quiet passion here than in any of the others, and that is expressed in memorable lines, with each word chosen carefully. This passion appears from the start in the Voice of the City or *Llais y Ddinas*:

I am called the City of Peace. I lie like a gem in the hollow between naked breasts.

All day the lascivious gaze burns me and makes the air quiver ...

The rest of the poem is in the voices of a middle-aged Jewish man, who had been fighting there; an old Arab man who finds the door to heaven closed; a young Arab man, who waits for the 'dawn or retribution'; a young Jewish man, who sees in the city the deliverance for his people and the end forever to the 'Jewish bowing down'. And it ends with Another Voice, the neutral observer who cries for the city as another cried once, and says:

The extreme of grace and tenderness was seen
in Jerusalem
but the bayonets guard the mount of Calvary.
Lord, for how long? Will she be called the City of Peace?

And the Boundary becomes very obvious in this description of the Garden:

But from afar we Welsh stood; between us and the Garden
there was the slime-trail of barbed wire with its hidden traps;
new furrows that men cultivated on such a beautiful ridge.

And these words were a flow of inspiration for Eluned to compete again, as he ended his adjudication by talking about her poem with

129

these words: 'Here is a poet who is sure of his standards and who is worthy of the National Eisteddfod's praise when he wishes. I can easily believe, indeed, that he has already worn the crown because of his maturity as a poet.'

Consider how encouraging these words were to Eluned. 'when he wishes ... I can easily believe ... that he has already worn the Crown.' Maturity? And like Caradog Prichard, Cynan also praises Mererid in these words:

> This is a long poem about Jerusalem today. The work is separated into half a dozen melodious songs between half a dozen different voices, The Voice of the City, the Voice of the Middle Aged Jew, the Voice of the Elderly Arab, the Voice of the Young Arab, the Voice of the Young Jew and the Other Voice – the poet's voice. Between them these voices form a composite unit that reveals the parlous state of a torn Jerusalem today, Jerusalem the City of Peace and the bitter hatred between Arab and Jew having torn it apart:
>
>> Bayonets taunt the mount of Calvary,
>> And the slime-trail of barbed wire around the Garden,
>> A new furrow cultivated by men on such a beautiful ridge.
>
> This is a tragic juxtaposition that Mererid saw in the life of Jerusalem; but it is a pity that he did not use the word Boundary at all in the body of the poem to bind it closer to the subject.
>
> He refers to No Man's Land in the city, as being full of filth and weeds; but this is not the same thing as saying *boundary,* as I tried to suggest on his copy.
>
> His metre and rhyming pattern is fresh and experimental.

This is an extremely warm adjudication, and Caradog Prichard closes his comments by saying: 'This is the only lyrical long poem in the competition, and I liked it greatly because of its feeling, its colour and its Eastern atmosphere. The story is frighteningly contemporary, and it is a story that has been summed up with passion and related by a poet.'

G. J. Roberts said of Mererid's attempt:

Here is a new poem, which bewitches the reader, avoiding clever turns of phrase and expressing its message in a series of gripping songs. 'Boundary' by Mererid is the separating wall that now divides Jerusalem and separates Jews from Arabs. Here is the city talking about itself before the fateful partition happens.

... Towards evening

the breeze curls down from the nearby hill
and plays with the water in my wells in uneasy squares
and shake the vines gently in my secret gardens.

He draws the reader's attention to recent history; it is 'the city in the mouth of the middle-aged Jew' who remembers the fighting between Jews and Arabs to possess the city. Then the Old Arab makes an entrance and remembers riding on a horse:

. . . Swiftly over the hillsides,
pausing among my father's silent servants who lead his wealth with endless bleating,
on a zig-zag journey.

The Young Arab comes to complain about losing his heritage in the city:

The wind gets colder as it runs from the naked land,
The old men become colder as they shiver in their tents
And the children in their angry, coughing huts.

Then the Young Jew comes to brag that his people have had

enough of grovelling and bowing down, and now that they have won their rights through force, they do not need to feel guilty:

As if the great arrival
that cannot be turned back to Israel Erets is a sin –
and comes faster than the Messiah, before God is ready.

The poem closes with the voice of a Christian visitor describing the difference he sees in the pilgrims of yesterday and today in Jerusalem. It used to be that people went there 'like God's glorious rugby scrum.' But today:

I gazed yesterday on the Mount of Olives
On its stony side, white with few trees;
I remember the prayer, the spears and the still sleepers.
But from afar, we stood, the Welsh; and between us and the garden
there was the slime-trail of barbed wire with its hidden traps;
a new furrow cultivated by men on such a beautiful ridge.

And this is what the adjudicator said to finish his comments about Mererid, before turning his gaze towards the winner:

I was mesmerised by Mererid's poem from the outset but I could not see how there was a scar on the face of Jerusalem, the crack in the gem, and the No Man's Land that runs through its centre makes a hedge/boundary. It is true that these things are real enough – but there is a difference between a separating wall and a hedge/boundary. A hedge/boundary has an innate neatness and specific features which are missing from this poem, and I am sorry for that.

A counter-argument could be made against G. J. Roberts by saying that not all hedges/boundaries are neat and that he has a very narrow interpretation of the word 'hedge/boundary'. The 'boundary hedge' and the idea of a frontier and border is just as powerful today when we think of the sadness of the situation in Jerusalem. It is also strange to see how detailed the adjudicator was in quoting extensively from the poem, especially since it's a discussion on a poem that was not going to win. But since *'Maen Hir'*, Dafydd Jones' poem, was deemed the winner, perhaps the adjudicator felt the need to draw attention to its flaws.

Eluned was placed second in G. J. Roberts' opinion and third by the other two judges, but their words of praise had given her enough enthusiasm to compete again in the National Eisteddfod in Bala the following year in 1967.

The momentum and the impetus gained from year to year shows her learning along the way from the judges' constructive criticism. Some poets might have responded to the reaction of the judges on a poem of an unfamiliar theme by deciding on a subject that was more acceptable to the literary Welsh world. It could be suggested that her long poem 'The Boundary' was depicting a world beyond the understanding of most Welsh poetry readers.

But Eluned had her own unique expansive world view and to an extent that clashed with the idea of being a poet who had to please the judges. Surely, saying something different in poetry should always be the poet's primary endeavour? If ever there was a poet within the bardic circle who was different, then Eluned was that poet. As she considered competing yet again the following year, at the Bala National Eisteddfod in 1967, she said: 'I had previously written a piece on Islam when I was in Morocco. I decided that I would write about three of the world's religions. Work hard on it, but accept that it would be a dense complex poem with an unsure style.' This is how she told the story in her autobiography:

There used to be a saying that, if you won the Cardigan Gŵyl Fawr, you would go on to win the National Eisteddfod. I didn't believe that, but it did give me confidence to send in an entry in 1967. The subject that year was *'Corlannau'* ('Sheepfolds'). I knew absolutely nothing about sheep. So that was that. Except I couldn't quite get it out of my head. Aunty Hannah was rather poorly and I needed some activity to keep me going.

One night in bed, things stirred in my head; I had recently been out in Morocco. It had been quite an experience. I had spent a lot of time in Marrakesh. I had a young guide, Hassan, son of Abdel Mahmoud, who took me to all the nooks and crannies of this fascinating Arab town ... in the Koran I found a whole new world to try and understand.

Her personal copy of the Quran was never found, as her books had been distributed to various second-hand shops in Cardigan shortly after she died, but there is no doubt that she read extensively from it. It is possible that she began writing the poem after returning home and not when she was out in Morocco:

I moved on to the Atlas mountains. I read the Koran from cover to cover. I cannot pretend to understand the Islamic faith but I found the Koran fascinating. There were phrases that I did not comprehend but which were still music to the ear. I scribbled a poem in the vastness of quietude. Too often, my scribbling poems get lost but somehow this one saved itself. I had seen it when looking for something else. I got out of bed and went for it. I decided that I had found my 'folds'. Not ever competing for winning only, I recklessly thought, let those who know their sheep get on with it. My folds would be Islam, Buddhism and Christianity.

It is difficult perhaps to accept her comment that she was not competing solely to win and yet, as somebody who did not have a mentor, had not been to college so far as I can prove, the eisteddfod was Eluned's only bardic school and the only means by which she could gain recognition for and appreciation of her work by respected poets. Perhaps these were the guiding forces that inspired Eluned to compete for one of the main prizes in the Eisteddfod.

These comments also show the dedication of a poet who is moved to write a specific poem whatever its fate might be. And even though she finished the long poem which later won, she also sent a second poem into the same competition. This is how she explains what happened in one of her notebooks:

Whilst watching over a member of the family, there came a longing to write a poem about Piaf, the lost sheep. I started around eleven that night and finished around three in the morning, tired and confused. I posted it before I had a chance to correct or change anything. I still regret doing this because I was unfair to myself and to Piaf, as I have to work hard in order to make sure a poem is fairly polished. But it was heartening to understand that Alun Llywelyn-Williams (a poet of whose work I am a great admirer) had seen poetry in it in spite of the mistakes.

The poem about Edith Piaf took second place in the competition– – she came second to herself! And the poem that she herself considered 'dark' with an uncertain style, won the Crown at the National Eisteddfod in Bala, 1967. This is what Alun Llywelyn-Williams wrote:

If the general standard of the competition was disappointing, we received some recompense with three really interesting poems. The long poems by Dans la Peau, Glyn-y-mêl, and Maen Llwyd are obviously the work of writers that feel the true mystery of the poet to the highest degree. Judging by the style and characteristics of the typewriter, Dans la Peau and Glyn-y-mêl are one and the same, and if this is correct, then we should welcome two able poets, who, even though they are different from each other, sing both with conviction and authority.

Alun Llywelyn-Williams refers to another author who is placed third and and comments, 'even though it is good, it is not as interesting and exciting as the work of Dans la Peau and Glyn-y-mêl'. It was noted that her poems had 'conviction and authority', although he did not know when writing that she was the author of both. He goes into detail about both poems:

These poems are quite unusual in their style and content. They are not easy poems. It is not that they are obscure or dark – they are two poems that leave a very definite impression on the reader, and my experience was that they not only drew my attention from the first instance but also that even on the first reading they elicit a shivering response to their atmosphere, to their rich imagery and to the dexterity of their language. What makes it difficult is that the author has been immersed so much in his subject that the references often are beyond the understanding of the reader who is not as well versed in the background. Reading Dans la Peau and Glyn-y-mêl's work is like reading the work of T. S. Eliot for the first time. In order to fully appreciate the mystery and message of these poems the reader must, obviously, read up on all the references within them, and this could seem like presumption and would be asking too much from the reader. But then the same could be said about the poetry of Ann Griffiths and William Williams Pantycelyn, and if our culture today is not broad enough to fully comprehend their theological and biblical references, then the fault lies within us and not the poets. So too with Dans la Peau and Glyn-y-mêl's poems. One thing is certain, the more one reads the poems and contemplates them, the more one sees that there is some new miracle coming to light. I do not know of a better test of the true poet.

He goes on:

[Piaf's] career was interpreted – and here is the link with the subject – as a campaign by the singer to arrive at the sanctuary of the sheepfolds of love and the recognition of society, as she had gone astray and was shunned. Through the strength of her art she was accepted and at the same time created for her audience a fold of comfort and happiness.

The last comment, about Piaf creating a place for herself whilst at the same time creating a fold of comfort and happiness, makes me feel uneasy today when we think that Eluned herself did not create a place for herself – not according to some, despite her successes.

In this respect, the portrayal of Piaf also strikes today's reader as a portrayal of Eluned herself. From her fairly stark and poor beginnings, she climbed and 'gave voice to most intense experiences of the muted masses'. Isn't this what any artist does, to sink into the lives of others through the intricacy of art? Eluned can be seen through the mirror of her words about Piaf: both were redheads, both had not known their fathers, possessed unique voices, both – though they received the praise of audiences – were amazingly lonely at times. The same adjudicator notes:

> There are many wonderful touches in this poem, in lines that are often full of perceptive imagination that is expressed in startling imagery and comparisons. Every word counts, every adjective is carefully chosen, and many of the turns of phrase stay in the memory, like 'toy prayers' and 'holding tight to faith with climbing fingers'. But Dans la Peau's language and syntax is not without its faults, and it appears to me that poet's vivacity leads him astray at times ... Dans la Peau's uncontested talent has not disciplined him to the extent that I would have expected in such a proficient poet.

About the winning poem, the adjudicator says Glyn-y-mêl's poem is more assured in its metre. He summarised the contents before talking about its merits:

> Three religous folds are the subjects of this poem, the fold of Islam, the Christian fold, and the fold of religion in China, 'the yellow

folds'. They are discussed in that order and this unusual order raises a question instantly. It is not only portraits of folds that are given but also a critical interpretation and the poet looks intently at the foundations of three whole civilizations. The suggestion given at the end of each chapter is that all the folds built by men for their souls through the centuries are falling apart in a storm of disillusion and disappointment. For example, in Islam:

A white robe sweeping under the lazy palm trees
The hem licking the threshold of tents belonging to the poor.

And in China:

... the Great Bird will come
to earth to retreat
from the moon and stars.
Tomorrow,
He will hatch iron eggs.

But the view of Christianity is more ambigious. The poet turns towards Wales at the end of the chapter and describes the powerful effect that the Revival of 1904 had on society temporarily, and then contrasts the state of the country then and today:

Today
Meaning is empty like Moriah's collection box,
And the faithful chesnut tree
waits by the Chapel House door.

And yet this fold has belief in the resurrection, and we find emotional lines following the thrilling expression of hope arising from the mystery of the empty grave:

But it is not said anywhere –
'This is where he lies.'
Two angels were called home from their three days' vigil ...

When the forest withers on the street's chimneys
Choking from the whorled gutters of the flesh
He will be a kiss on the lips
And his scarred hands shall mend the sheepfold.

He will be here and there,
His tired eyes watching the fold,
Until He washes his feet on the banks of Jordan
Pulling Charon to the land of the living after the final journey,
Leaving the boat to dance into destruction.

The section about Christianity raises questions in Alun Llywelyn-Williams' mind as he tries to understand the significance of that part of the poem:

It would be easy to quote other lines from all sections of this poem that would show the same impressionistic talent and the same depth of thought as the lines already quoted. The particular feat of this poem is how the author succeeds in expressing the very atmosphere and feel of the three civilisations. For my part, it is Glyn-y-mêl's poem that I like best in the competition. Without a doubt, there are within it some very wonderful sections. It is a better poem than Dans la Peau's because it is more stable in its structure and it is broader in its vision and, in my opinion at least, is clearer in its imagery ... I would be willing to say too that it is a more promising and exciting poem than many that have won the Eisteddfod crown for several years.

His co-adjudicator, G. J. Roberts, agrees with Alun Llywelyn-Williams, and puts Dans la Peau in second place and Glyn-y-mêl as the winner. When he comes to the poem by Glyn-y-mêl he says:

> Here is a poet who creates images through reference – colourful and effective references, but not always easy to understand. I believe that this poet is also Dans la Peau, but in this poem he has more discipline. He has chosen a wider canvas so that he does not repeat himself and, he has written better and without redundancy – indeed he has created a poem that from frequent reading conveys his vision effectively and memorably ... I must admit that I am not well-versed enough in the history of Muhammed's religion and its later developments, nor in the religion of Confucius and Buddha and the many superstitions and beliefs that have gathered around them, to understand every message given by Glyn-y-mêl, but he can discuss these religions and their adherents in a witty, perceptive and effective way. When he introduces Christianity he uses the line, 'Into the fold of Christianity ...' and strangely enough he betrays a deep lack of knowledge of the history of Christianity from the days of the early Church until the time of the Methodist Revival. But in spite of this it must be said that he discusses its roots, its historic past and its present in a masterful and skilful way, and I have no doubt that his aim is surely to show its excellence in the face of the other two religions.

In his summing up he says:

> The message of the poem, to me, is that the day will come when there will be only one fold and only one Shepherd, He will bring Charon (the representative of every other attempt at delivering souls to Paradise) to the glory of His own fold. The boat can be scuttled then because he will have arrived... There are faults in the craft of this poem that one could allude to, but, despite these, I believe that the National Eisteddfod should be proud to crown this

poet and he has expressed his vision lyrically and mesmerisingly and expressed that in a new, beautiful and effective voice.

A new voice, beautiful and effective? This 'new voice' at times can be an ambigious term. A new voice for whom? For the judges? Or was that 'new' in the sense of the work being fresh and different? Are 'new' and 'different' synonymous in poetry? What becomes clear from reading the two adjudications is that they were surprised by subjects that at first glance are seen as foreign. The poems appeared to be very international in essence in relation to the literature of Wales and in a time when writing about Wales and 'the fate of the language' filled the minds of poets, and the old nostalgic world of the Wales that had disappeared was a worrying subject. But Eluned had chosen a subject outside Wales and had not done it to surprise, but because that was the essence of her experience as a girl who had left the bank of the river Teifi, gone to London and spent time in Paris and beyond. What a disappointment it was then when the third judge, the most international in his vision about the literatures of the world, had disagreed with the other two adjudicators' opinions.

John Gwilym Jones' adjudication was discerning and powerful, and was justified to an extent by the fact that he believed that the poet, in spite of her talent, had not used allusion in the correct manner. He begins by saying:

To explain my adjudication, which happens to be different from that of my co-judges, I feel I should express my confession of poetic faith.

Every adjudication must be personal, and restrict itself to the opinion of one particular person. At the same time the opinion of worth is not a whim but is something that has been based on intense and catholic reading: not only reading original works but reading and studying the literary critics of the age in regards to the nature of poetry ... Put simply this is what poetry is for me – a picture that does not list sensory impressions of similar qualities but rather than join and tie together extremes in order to show the fundamental relationship between everything, and through expressing different truths to the truths of science, truths that are beyond facts, about the state of man in the world...

There are essential considerations too of course – the poet's mastery of words and striking concise turns of phrases, his control of the relevant rhythms, his knowledge of poetic structure and of all of these things, his talent to excite in the truth of his emotion. All these things in unity give pleasure that is literary pleasure.

I feel, as I said, that it is only fair on my part that I make this statement... What right does anybody have to speak like a Pope and claim to be the voice of any infallible authority that has trusted to him the only key that exists to the only door that exists to the only opinion that exists on a creative work? We all need a good dose of humility, and an even bigger dose of polite communal tolerance. Then it is possible to treat literature with civility and friendship. There are plenty of things in this big old world to be caustic and bitter about without being full of bile towards each other when we deal with one activity from all other activities which have sympathy and empathy as foundations to their effectiveness.

Even though I have left the third judge to last here, and not put him first as he was seen in the Compositions, John Gwilym Jones' perceptive comments make his adjudication one of note and the ending is especially pertinent in light of the winner. And even though I agree with his comment that 'There are plenty of things in this big old world to be caustic and bitter about' that are not in the field of literature, one cannot help but feel that his words were prophetic, as if he could foresee to an extent the lack of sympathy that would ensue. He could not have known that at the time, but his powers of observation are extremely revealing when we consider his sincerity in not agreeing with the other judges that Eluned should win the Crown.

When he comes to Dans la Peau, John Gwilym Jones says this:

There is no doubt of the originality of this poem. Edith Piaff [*sic*], the French singer, is the lost sheep who traces her story through poverty and illness, through prostitution and being a mother and through years of hopeless drifting without a fold to be accepted in, thanks to Cocteau and Cheralier [*sic*], to the security of sheepfold of praise and worldwide glory. There is no doubt either that the poem has 'depth' – it is a criticism of society that cannot recognise genius because it is opposite to the safe accepted morality. As I mentioned before, I do not have much to say to the view that glorifies the arrogant individuality of the artist – indeed, that goes so far as to insist on it. Nobody is a good singer because she is a prostitute – not that a prostitute (and there are many!) cannot be a good singer. But it is not the place of the judge to criticise a point of view but to try and decide whether the poetry created from it succeeds.

This is a difficult poem. Not only does it require much knowledge about Edith Piaff [*sic*] in order to respond fully to it (and the author is perfectly entitled to expect that), but it asks for an 'understanding' of the indirect, of highly succinct multi-metaphors and mixed metaphors within the poem. The poet's mastery of words must be acknowledged (and I do this gladly) even though he is often grammatically incorrect, if that is of any consequence, and has a liking for inventing bizarre words. But my feeling is that the poem is too difficult in the wrong way. The author seems to have decided, come what may, that he is not going to say anything in a simple direct way, and so small innocent things are pulled apart in order to be difficult and create inconvenience and nothing else.

The judge says that he 'acknowledge[s] the cleverness but feel[s] that it is only cleverness and it does not, even after the effort of understanding the poem, give more than the enjoyment of having solved the problem'. When he comes to Glyn-y-mêl, he says that it is a 'new poem and is even more difficult than the other one'. He hastens to say that the difficulty was not a condemnation at all.

Then, he summarises the poem and the various 'folds' in it. Acknowledging again that it is a 'referential' poem, he says:

> Without extremely detailed and esoteric knowledge the reader has no hope of understanding nor of responding to it. But, as was said previously, every author has the right to expect that. A judge cannot refuse a poem because of his own lack of knowledge. I must admit that more than half the poem is beyond me ...
>
> I am not rejecting the poem because of my failure but because I do not consider that the author has used the references in the correct manner ...
>
> In the second part, which is quite clear to me, the poet traces the growth of the Christian faith by quoting the Old Testament.
>
> ... The references are totally historical and not literary:

There was a sound of live things' wings touching each other
When the son of man opened his mouth to eat the book.

And here is Ezekiel: 3:1. 'And the sound of live things were touching each other.' 'And he said to me, son of man, eat what you have been given, eat this book ...'

It can sound quite pretty:

> The Shepherd became flesh
> Became feeble in the hay in the year of the Murder of the Innocents;
> The sparrow's breast has swollen
> And Judas' body swings like a pendulum on a tree on the common.

But pretty or not this is only quoting or half-quoting from the Bible. Without knowledge of the references, it is to all intents and purposes unintelligible. I take it for granted that if this is true of the section that I understand, then it must also be true of the two other sections. To be fair with my co-judges, I must confess to have agreed to crown

Glyn-y-mêl when we discussed the entries together. After going home and reading and contemplating the poem many times, I realised what I had tried to explain. Kindly and good-naturedly, the other two agreed to let me say my piece first. But I do not deny that Glyn-y-mêl should be given the Crown for a second – there is no doubt of his talent and his intellect and his knowledge – but for the reason that I gave; I did not feel content 'upon my conscience', to give him the Crown. Who knows, maybe my adjudication will be undone by time and opinion? But there we are!

Did any other eisteddfod poem in during the second half of the twentieth century receive such a thorough going-over? I doubt it. John Gwilym Jones asks if 'my adjudication will be undone'. In 1983, at the Anglesey National Eisteddfod, Eluned Phillips won the Crown for the second time and was applauded this time by the very judge who did not wish her crowned in Bala in 1967. But the reaction to the fact that Eluned had won her first crown in 1967 is one that deserves to be documented.

Eluned's joy at having won the Crown was soured a little because of the fact that the decision was not unanimous, and that John Gwilym Jones' comments were so substantial. But one must remember that she won in a competition where there were twenty-nine entries. The fact that she had risen to the top with two poems in itself shows her exceptional talent and that she had been recognised as a 'true poet'.

But what is the truth? And this is the question that plagued Eluned following her great success. Perhaps the comments gave some unknown people, or poets, the ammunition to suspect the authenticity of her work. How could someone without formal higher education accomplish at such a feat? Neither was she a part of a poetic coterie. And what did she know about religions and their complexities? And to cap it all she was a woman, *hen ferch*, an 'old maid', according to the spiteful term of the time. She did not have a husband who was a publisher of books and magazines, nor did she have a minister of religion as her partner. This led to unpleasant murmurings and muttered insinuations in some quarters. She seemed an unknown poet who did not belong to the Welsh-language establishment. She could not purport to belong to Dafydd ap Gwilym nor to Williams Pantycelyn. In the eyes of many, she was a 'nobody', and the common conclusion was that she must have been helped by some other person. A man of course. Dewi Emrys perhaps? But he had been buried in 1952, so why wait until 1967 before sending her poems in, if she had one in her 'bottom drawer'– a phrase of the time aimed at a woman who should collect things in preparation for getting married. Even now some say that Dewi Emrys was the author of *'Corlannau'* ('Sheepfolds') though there is no foundation to the allegation at all. This was told to me as fact by people who know nothing of the literary world. Had they read the poem? I asked kindly. No, came the answer, with the comment, 'but it's what everybody says.' And the comment made by a few has become everybody's. The story has become a legend and the legend a part of mythology. In a crueller age, Eluned Phillips would have been drowned as a witch for her talent and her imagination. Instead, the whispers became a plague throughout Wales, from Ceredigion to Anglesey, from the most ordinary of folk to the most educated amongst men.

In the haste to identify 'somebody else' as the author of *'Corlannau'*, it was forgotten that Eluned had won the Crown at the Cardigan eisteddfod, Gŵyl Fawr Aberteifi, in 1965 for her long poem, *'Mieri lle bu Mawredd'* ('Thorns Where Once was Grandeur'). She also competed the previous year in Cardigan on the subject of *'Y Syllwr'* ('The One Who Gazes/The Spectator') and had been given an encouraging adjudication by the Rev. Eirian Davies who 'praised my efforts'.

Here is the opening section of the poem 'The one who gazes' which I found in a notebook written in her handwriting. There were extensive crossings-out in the text and it was difficult to read the poem at times because of it.

A group of seats fit for riff-raff, the arse-end-of-flies,
Fools with their eyes following the rhythm of the show
No farce, no tragedy / There's a farce and a tragedy.
But before the curtains come down [?]
Back to the Gethsemane of yesterday and seeing.

Hurry:
There are a thousand eyes staring
And the front seats are heaving ready to watch the circus,
You will see under the branches of the old olive tree
The twelve amateurs and the king
In the mess of their rehearsals –
Groups zig-zagging on the set ...

In the enlightened drama of the centuries,
The main character hides his head
Like a sulking eel under the banks of sin
And the villain of the piece with his itchy feet
Trespassing over the white chalk lines
And rubbing corn oil into the hands of the Jew.

There are strong dramatic motifs in this poem and the words convey an element of drama and sweeping statements. And what is constant about Eluned Phillips' work is that when she writes long poems, she always looks outside Wales and draws upon her experiences in other countries. The poet T. H. Parry-Williams is praised for his broad-visioned poems, but for a woman to intuit faraway worlds and to write about them in Welsh was deemed a rather strange preoccupation rather than allowing the poet a sense of wonder at life beyond Wales.

Eluned calls her desire to write about things outside Wales 'the romanticism of distant calling'. The local poet, who would write about her environs, of different characters and occasions, is extending her gaze towards poetry that would allow her to cross

Wales' borders and look to the east. Even so, she knew full well that she would have to improve her grammar further, as she wrote in her notes: 'Even so, I accept Dr John Gwilym Jones' adjudication and spend the next fifteen years trying to improve my style, my language and to try and get rid of the complexities that made people complain that I wrote dark poetry.'

She is silent about the insinuations when she writes notes about her poetic life story but shows characteristic modesty in being aware of her own failings. This shows her sense of vulnerability, even though she won one of the main prizes at the National Eisteddfod. The fact that she had 'accepted' the adjudication's criticism of her grammar says everything about her desire to improve her use of language. In her autobiography she dismisses the accusations, reminiscing about her childhood need to prove her ability:

Oddly enough, many years later I would again be accused of not writing my own poems. I offered my detractors my mother's solution: I would write one under supervision. The offer was not taken up. Sadly, I lost the respect I had for those I had always admired. I have never found out whether it's redheads they don't like in Wales – or merely women who have the audacity to write poetry.

In a television programme Eluned says: 'Dilys [Cadwaladr] had warned me that I would not be accepted into the society of the Bards' – this comment suggests that there was a door, and that the door was locked, so that no woman could go through it, whatever her craft. Eluned had admitted openly 'the Eisteddfod was in my blood', and it is a shame in this case that the door to success should be closed to women. I should very much like to imagine the conversation between two female crowned bards at that time: two poets – and what a crime against women that the very word 'poet' suggests a male – ahead of their time, perhaps, the two of them being shunned to an extent by the establishment to which they tried their best to deserve to belong. Suffice it to say that the same insinuations were made of Dilys Cadwaladr's work, even though her stories had been published and praised by the noted man of letters, G. K. Chesterton.[16]

When Eluned Phillips won with her poem on the subject of 'Sheepfolds', another 'fold', the Welsh language, was endangered. Saunders Lewis, in his famous radio lecture in 1962, had predicted the death of the Welsh language before the end of the century unless efforts were made to stem the tide with civil disobedience to protect its future. This was the time of the protest songs of Dafydd Iwan and other pop groups creating a wealth of songs about Wales. It was the time of Tryweryn, and an exciting time for Cymdeithas yr Iaith (the Welsh Language Society), which was starting to use peaceful law-breaking as a tool for change. It was also the time of Gerallt Lloyd Owen's volume of poetry, *Cerddi'r Cywilydd* (*The Poems of Shame*), reflecting the zeitgeist of the younger generation.

'Corlannau' realised a very different world view that looked towards the east, along with a section about the 'square mile'. It was a new world to many, with alien religions that encompassed worlds that few people knew at the time. The adjudicators themselves confessed how ignorant they were of the subjects broached in the poem. But perhaps this is not something to do with the time; as recently as 2015 I heard an expert from China expressing the view in a documentary that the West has never attempted to understand that huge country. A cursory look at the situation of Islam today shows that the West's understanding of the positive aspects of the Muslim faith had not penetrated the mindset of the majority of people even before the recent threat from IS Islamic extremists. What hope was there for a poem that shed light on different religions of the world with Christianity merely one among the others?

---

[16] Eigra Lewis Roberts, *Merch yr Oriau Mawr* (Tŷ ar y Graig, 1981).

One of the few reactions given by the poet herself on the kind of criticism received was that the poet Dic Jones had commented that she had not adhered to the set subject, because she had not written about sheep! And with tongue in cheek, Eluned agreed that she knew very little about sheep of that kind. Another critical response was by John Roderick Rees in the poetry magazine *Barddas* who stated that '*Corlannau*' was the 'the most alien and least typical' poem and he saw the poem as one of 'atmosphere and feeling', 'one that was easier to sense than to understand'. Who knows if this poem would have had a better reception today, in a more global world where we have at least an inkling that there are other religions apart from Christianity?

After Eluned won the Crown in Bala, not much was heard from her. It is true that she made a programme called *Dal Pen Rheswm* (*Holding a Conversation*) with Dyfnallt Morgan interviewing her in October 1967, but apart from occasional programmes similar in format, Eluned did not receive as much attention as the winners of Crown and Chair at the National Eisteddfod in previous years. She herself admitted, when she won in 1983 at the National Eisteddfod in Anglesey, that she had been saddened after 1967, and had eschewed competition after that until two years before she won for the second time. Once again, her honesty comes to the fore. She admits that she got an urge to compete in 1981. That was an interval of fourteen years without competing, but she followed every ceremony faithfully in the meantime. Why did she hold back from competing? Was it because the whispers that someone else had written the work hurt her to such an extent that it made her afraid of being wounded the second time? Or had she decided, come what may, that she would go at it again to show the world that she, Eluned 'Give it your best shot, girl' Phillips, was behind her desire to prove herself worthy of winning?

When she won the second time, she noted that she was a professional writer and that she 'mostly starved'. As one of the first Welsh-language professional writers, part of the same line as

Saunders Lewis, who wrote at a time before television gave the self-employed a better life, money was very tight. What did she do, then, during the ten and more years when she did not compete? She noted that she had written three novels, two of which are in my care; they prove without doubt that she was an instinctive author, even to those who still maintain that she did not write her poems. But she entered the poetic field again in the National Eisteddfod in the Maldwyn area in 1981, and was placed in the first class by Dafydd Jones, Ffair-rhos. Her nom de plume was Banc y Brain (Crow Bank) and he placed her fourth. This is what Dafydd said:

> The poet sees the picture of the Last Supper and shows the faces of the disciples only, with the face of Christ as a shadow there. Here is a beautifully written poem that adheres closely to the story in the New Testament. Again, the poet's expression depicts a picture of the exciting story of the celebration of that first Easter, without veering far from the story, apart from perhaps giving us the story in poem form.

Banc y Brain was also placed in the first class by Gwilym R. Jones, and highly praised:

> Here is a competitor who decorated his poem with a copy of the wonderful portrait by da Vinci of the Last Supper, and the faces seen in that fresco is Banc y Brain's subject. The main achievement of this poet is to create an atmosphere. He must have steeped himself in the history of the picture and the story of that unforgettable Supper. There is subtle use of language, and he grasped the rhythms of storytelling. He made a fair effort to take us to the Upper Room but the verb-forms are quite monotonous at the beginning of the lines: 'Faces whispering ...' 'Hands preaching,' etc.
>
> One must suspect a poet who talks about 'One romantic evening' (a word that has lost some of its mystery over time), and of 'a forest of beard'. But Banc y Brain displays excellence in his

work. I liked: 'The man between two lights, with his bric-a-brac thoughts / He has licked his finger to search for the direction of the wind;' this is 'the unbelieving believer' in the midst of the disciples. It is a shame that the portrait of Iscariot is the weakest in Banc y Brain's gallery.

Gwyn Thomas placed the poem in the third class in his adjudication. This is what he said: 'Banc y Brain chose a subject that appealed to many in this competition, that is the faces in Leonardo da Vinci's famous *The Last Supper*. He created an interesting impression of characters, but did not succeed in expressing himself with an ability that would give his words a special quality.'

After receiving the adjudication on her poem, it's possible that Gwilym R's kind words urged her on further. She went on to compete in the National Eisteddfod in Swansea in 1982, where thirty competed in the Crown competition on a long poem, a sequence no longer than 300 lines on the subject *'Y Rhod'* ('The Wheel'). This is what the adjudicator Rhydwen Williams said about *'Tresi Aur'* (Golden Chain), whom he placed in the first class:

The poem has a very promising opening:

Away in the Middle East
The desert is scorched and grave
When the southwind whips showers of blood
And the pigeons coo drunkenly in the heat.

Then we have a poem under the name of *'Abdwla'* ('Abdula') and no one would be considered at fault for presuming that we are in the midst of Eastern wonders, but we come back soon enough and unceremoniously to home turf and to:

152

Wil Ffynnon Garreg
Engineer B.Sc. (Aber)
The Blue Bulls' prop – a tornado on the rugby field.

It is true that this poet cannot avoid the appeal of the east:

Allah's blessing
On the boardroom table's capitalism in OPEC's chambers.
Again tomorrow
The man who sells camel dung to the poor
shoots across the world
in the belly of the Great Concorde.
Everything has changed
Apart from the Quran's cry in the soul, and the thrill of the flesh
in the harem.

The story is a little unmanageable perhaps, even though the poet
worked hard to keep it under control.

Eluned was given fourth place by J. Eirian Davies in the same
Eisteddfod. Here are his comments about Tresi Aur:

Here is an extremely original sequence of poems that talk about a
young Welshman (a man of letters) out in the Middle East. It must
be admitted that it is an exception to find such a competitor as this
– a poet of sunshine with a poem about oil – slumming it in the
mud in our Literature Tent. It was refreshing to receive this
sequence of poems in the bundle that came to hand.

And Tresi Aur is a poet. He has his own notable way of
compressing an extensive comment into the scope of one or two
words. It could be called subtlety. I enjoyed reading the work. But
conversely, I do not believe that it is a great poem. Indeed, this
poem is shallow, with intriguing poetry more than anything else.

No comment was made by the other judge, Bobi Jones, on Tresi Aur's work. Rather, he looked at the craftwork and technique of the four poems he put in the first class; he did not place Tresi Aur there. Eirwyn George won that year, with a poem about places in Pembrokeshire.

I am certain that Eluned was also Cwrt y Graban (Corn Marigold Court), as seen in some pages in her papers. These poems are placed in the second class by Rhydwen Williams. He quotes from the poem:

> In the stillness of the researchers I read
> about my stubborn ancestor
> Dragged from Aberelwyn in the Year of Election.

The adjudicator says further:

> Here's a beginning! Tracing the whole story then, 'The Wheel', 'The Mill', 'The Fellowship', 'The Farm', 'The Mother'; this is the pattern and it is a tale that's worth telling.

> The night song
> Excites the blood ...

> It is possible that Cwrt y Graban does not give his vision fair play.

These poems are seen in her collection *Cerddi Glyn-y-mêl* (pp. 46–58) about her native land: 'The Land', 'The Mill', 'The Fellowship', 'The Farm', 'The Mother'. It is possible that she wrote the finished poems for that collection.

She was given third place by J. Eirian Davies, following Tresi Aur in the order of comments, saying:

> Here without a doubt is the most balanced poem in the competition. Between the prologue and epilogue there are four

poems under the headings of 'The Mill', 'The Fellowship', 'The Farm', 'The Mother'. But the poet does linger three times over on the same ground. As sure as the clock ticks, Cwrt y Graban moves his finger on through the times, following the fashions and styles of the day. It is direct, imaginative and wide-awake all the way. I feel however, that the poet lets go in certain parts, and satisfies himself with some clauses that do not rise above the ease of prose.

In one of her notebooks, Eluned can be seen reworking her poems constantly and planning them like this:

Long poem plan: The Wheel, Yesterday, Today, Tomorrow, etc. Notes on the Middle East and Muslim religion/customs.

Far far
In Arabia where there is no drink
The pigeons complain
Drunk in the heat;
the wind whips the crabby sand into a shower of blood [?]
and the prayers of the locals choke the sky
like the sound of bees druming on a heavy summer's day:
Allah the Merciful! Allah the Compassionate!
The eternal wheel of the digger is
here,
where Fate is a dictator still turning
empty pitchers ... and scatters
without the comfort of water and the
donkey with his legs... [?]

Then, she writes her notes in English: Plan: 'The Wheel'. "The wheel turns to no avail" is written in English, and it notes the steps to be taken in order to write the poem. She has a comical shorthand, and writes short comments like 'Yanks on scene', 'Welsh workers treated like second-class citizens', 'the spend, spend, spend syndrome', 'the *rhod* (wheel) has stopped except for townies with guile?' And strangely enough, she says that the Arabs are different: 'the Arabs – poor peasants praying for the engineer's wheel to turn for water treat Wil Penlandraw and his Welsh crew like gods'. Then, water – a tear of water from a barren land.

In her trajectory written in Welsh there is a hopeful message and even though the son leaves to go and teach beyond Offa's Dyke, his grandson comes back to the area, buys the mill, rebuilds the place and the mill-wheel turns again. The young man leads his grandfather, who is blind, down to the mill: 'I hear the wheel turning. It sings joyfully.'

What these notes show is that Eluned possessed a technique that facilitated the process of composing her long or extended poems. They were not created accidentally; her poems were structured and considered carefully from beginning to end. Even though she said that her best way of working was last-minute, these sketches show that she would think deeply about the framework of poems, even if she raced to get them finished towards the end. They show also how she would swing smoothly from Welsh to English. It is almost as if she is not aware of the difference between them as she puts ideas down on paper. She was equally at home in both languages, with the English perhaps constantly pushing to the fore. There is evidence of script structuring in the notes too; she seems also to swing between drama and poetry. But the core of the poems that come from the planning are wholly in Welsh, not just in language but in their texture. Her sensibilitiy towards the change happening in rural Wales is a clear message in the poem mentioned previously. Perhaps she adapted some of these ideas about belonging and landscape as she set about writing again for the National Eisteddfod in Anglesey in 1983. The main feature in these plans shows that she has the sensibilites of a playwright – she sees the need to create a narrative with elements of tension and change and a dramatic cycle.

She was placed high up in the competition in 1982, and it is no surprise therefore that it spurred her on to compete the following year. The judges were Jâms Nicholas, Nesta Wyn Jones and Dr John Gwilym Jones. The subject given was *'Clymau'* ('Knots or Ties') for a long poem. This time there would be another rule that the poets had to adhere to: that was the poem, in metre and rhyme, was not to use *cynghanedd* and not be more than three hundred lines long.

It is worth noting the three judges' comments, in order to show unanimity in the opinion on the merits of Pant Glas' (Green Valley's) poem. Jâms Nicholas' comments appear first in the *Cyfansoddiadau*:

> Pant Glas gives us a short story in metre and rhyme. A feat of subtlety characterises the style. The poet devised a story using the tragic history of our viewpoint as Welsh people and the human race; through telling the story a great irony comes to the fore. There is also a deep meditation on the subject: ties to land and place, ties to a piece of land and all that this entails in this story, ties to a country and nation, ties to a state with the restrictive, compulsory elements until death, the ties of human love, the ties that bind, the ties that free, and all brought together in one whole tapestry. The poet is an artist in the way that he introduces all the complexities of the ties in simple pictures.
>
> This is the subject; what about the execution? The poet uses metres usually used with *cynghanedd* but without using *cynghanedd* ... At the first reading I must admit that I found this difficult ... But after several readings I overcame this obstacle ... Pant Glas has therefore created a unique new poem using metre and rhyme. The expression throughout is direct and economical. The poet does not waste words, there is special skill in the subtlety of his images and he succeeds time after time in suggesting much more than what he says. It is no surprise that verses in the form of an *englyn milwr* [a poem of three monorhymed lines of seven syllables each] are some of the best poetry (and according to *Cerdd Dafo*d, there are early examples of the *englyn* without *cynghanedd* in them)

Leaving the mountains atlantic,
Leaving a cabin that was an altar,

Leaving a girl at the bottom of the sea.

Longing ties the heart
For the beauty among the seaweed,
Missing eyes: missing her.

Here is poetry of the highest order. And one could continue to quote but everybody will get the chance to read the poem in its entirety. I am certain that this is a poet who shows the signs of discipline in the strict-metre rhyming poetry of *cynghanedd* over a long period. Here are ties of naked thrilling imagery, brought together to create a piece of work that is a contemporary tragedy.

And to conclude, Jâms Nicholas says that, if some were to believe this competiton to be a weak one:

This has been a notable competition, as many of the competitors deserved the Crown. I agree with my co-judges that Pant Glas has the most mature and polished poem in its craft and language; this is the most complete poem, a poem with a chilling and shattering message in the midst of the inanity of the times we live in today. Eric Gill said: 'All art is propaganda;' Siôn Cent said: 'It is the state of the poet to be studying the world,' and Pant Glas is in the Siôn Cent tradition. Pant Glas truly deserves the Eisteddfod Crown and it is an honour to crown him.

Nesta Wyn Jones's comments are just as vibrantly complimentary:

My question often when reading poems sent in to competition is: 'Would this poem have come into existence otherwise?' 'A song is born often in words and in metre,' said T. H. Parry-Williams. So Pant

Glas' poem appears to me. Here is inspiration ... It was high time that somebody declared the Welsh nation's feeling towards the unecessary Malvinas War, and this poem does that, subtly, in an incusive way through creating a story that juxtaposes two periods. In 1865, Pant Glas' farmer is hounded from his smalholding by the landlord and crosses to Patagonia on the *Mimosa*.

They lost a girl in their hardship;
her golden locks given to the deep,
and the sea closes around her.

Pant Glas is a *cynghanedd* poet – or the *cynghanedd* metres at least were what he used, rather than the convention of metre and rhyme, but without the *cynghanedd*. (There will be much discussion on this!)

It is totally obvious that here is a craftsman who is sure of his journey, because he succeeded in creating a suggestive poem without any redundancy. He is a poet who possesses a lively imagination, he possesses patience that enables him to rein in this imagination for a purpose. It is not everyone who can describe modern combat as he did, even though we have all seen some skirmishes on the television. Throughout the poem, every line is full to the brim of meaning – and yet as clear as crystal. Pant Glas, without a doubt, is the champion of this interesting competition this year.

Here are two of the judges emphasising the craft of the poem and the attention of the 'craftsman who is sure of his journey' – surely a prize as finely wrought as the crown that she would receive. But there was one other judge who made Eluned's heart sing; John Gwilym Jones, the judge who did not wish to award her the Crown for the poem in Bala in 1967, was as sure in his opinion as the other two.

This is his opinion of Pant Glas:

It is a satisfying and delightful experience, having read, in this context, twenty-two long poems – and some of them of an excellent standard – that one is quietly certain from the beginning as to which has excited one emotionally and intellectually. This was my experience this time. But one had to justify the conviction in a coolly rational way. The first justification is that it is a contemporary long poem, that belongs so closely to our times that it could not have been written before this year. Its subject and content is the sad and futile Malvinas War. The plan, once it has been revealed, is so obvious that one asks, 'How on earth did anybody else not think of this?' As it happens, it was this particular author who had the vision. It begins in 1865 with the departure of the Pant Glas family, because of oppression, to Patagonia;

O'r niwlen daeth sŵn mudo ym Mhant Glas
A llef gwraig yn wylo.
Yna mudandod cofio –
A llidiart ffald o dan glo.

Through the mist sounds of moving at Pant Glas
and a woman wailing;
the muteness of remembering;
a locked gate a final sting

A child is lost on the way:

Losing a daughter their adversity,
the golden tresses to the ocean
and the sea closing around her.

Arriving after suffering, building a house
Planning a home,
A second Pant Glas
A miracle, ashes of nightmares

Then, we jump to 1982. The Pant Glas of today devastatingly portrayed as a place without any roots or heritage. The son of the contemporary Pant Glas has lost the ties that bind, and joins the army without once imagining what will befall him. The war against Argentina starts and he finds himself on board the *Sir Galahad*:

Sir Galahad is a ball of fire
bundles of khaki writhe in water
to escape the lips of hellish fire

Having been injured, in his torment the soldier remembers his homeland:

With sightless eyes he sees a meadow thrilling with lambs
and the face of a mother whom he will see no more

Somebody from Cwm Hyfryd, Patagonia, comes to his bedside, and although the comunication is limited, 'the ties are stronger than any injury'. The son of Pant Glas is left in his loneliness to die:

The definitive fragile bond
for a son deprived of summer

The author chose to write using the old measures – but all without *cynghanedd*. A very wise choice, because *cynghanedd* does not have metre – it has variable metric rhythms. On top of this he succeeds in tieing the present with the traditional – an extremely sly symbolic tie. The tone changes often; sometimes it hurts, sometimes it is heroic, cutting, painful or exceedingly sad; and these qualities succeed in generalising and widening the picture to represent oppression and sadness and the wastefulness of all wars through the ages and the suffering of men who are prey to its greed. And the great virtue is that this is done in a critical, cold, clinical way without the author once intruding personally; he just tells the story factually and objectively.

> Just like W. H. Auden during the Spanish War who felt a need to express himself politically, this author also feels that he cannot stand aside. He must condemn what all his emotions and reason, his humanity and his social conscience see as arrogant insolence and as irresponsible and sad. But it is not a political essay that he composed, rather earth-shattering poetry. The three of us all conclude that it is a privilege to give the Crown at the Llangefni National Eisteddfod to him.

After a long period of silence of fourteen years from the poet from Cenarth, once again she received praise and honour from the National Eisteddfod. It could be said that winning again should have silenced the unpleasant gossip about the authorship and authenticity of her work. If she had been considered a poet 'on her own', then that also is what faced Eluned after winning so resoundingly in the Anglesey National Eisteddfod in 1983. Who would have thought that the nasty rumour-mongering would have followed her again, for seven months after winning her second crown? In 1984 she had to face a new storm about the authorship of her poems. Was there ever a journey with as many trials as the one that this once carefree girl from Cenarth had to face?

The Lonely Pilgrimage

I think that it will only be poetry which will make me so sensitive
to criticism ... perhaps because nobody is very willing to accept a
female poet.

[from Eluned Phillips' papers, late 1960s]

I have become drunk on the metre of the poem without
cynghanedd, and I hope I never get sober.

[Eluned's words in her handwriting
at the end of a copy of her poem *'Clymau'*]

It was only the white Gorsedd robe that made Eluned seem the
same as the rest of the chaired and crowned bards at the National
Eisteddfod every year. Usually she could be seen in the front row
of the Gorsedd in the main ceremonies, seated directly behind the
Archdruid and the Gorsedd officials, her curly red hair and wide
smile catching the camera lens. However, it's fair to say that her
presence at these events was the only lead role given to her by the
society of the Gorsedd, other than occasionally greeting the
crowned or chaired bard, and leading him or her to the stage – that,
and occasionally representing the Gorsedd in other Celtic festivals.
She was never invited to adjudicate the Crown competition,
though she won it twice. Why was that?[17]

In her autobiography, *The Reluctant Redhead*, Eluned's feelings
regarding the poetry community in Wales are kept hidden, except

---

[17] In this instance, she was treated differently from Dilys Cadwaladr, who was
invited to adjudicate the Crown competition at the Bro Dwyfor National
Eisteddfod in 1975.

for a few comments which slip out, such as : 'Oddly enough, many years later, I would be again accused of not writing my own poems.'

There is a history behind that word 'again', for she is referring to the second crown she won at the National Eisteddfod, in Anglesey in 1983. The comment reveals how she had long been accustomed to hearing accusations that she was not the author of her own poems, even after she had won her first crown in Bala in 1967. Now, having read through her work – published and as yet unpublished – I can categorically state that Eluned Phillips is the author of all the winning poems. Moreover, she was also a close contender for winning the Crown on other occasions.

Discovering how this amazing girl became a poet in the first instance is a useful place to start in considering her career as a poet. Her unusual upbringing has already been mentioned and the lively home in which she was raised, gave her the confidence to develop and venture into different fields. In an introduction for a radio programme entitled *Y Llwybrau Gynt* (*The Trodden Paths*), Eluned had this to say about her life and the process of writing:

> I'm not very good at looking back. Perhaps because I never had the luxury to ponder. My story was one of a mad rush to live life at full tilt and reach every milestone, breathless. One thing is certain, that I was born an absolute optimist, and although I have now been wandering for half a century more or less, it's the dazzling horizons which stay in my mind, not the steep hills, though there have been plenty of those. Somebody said that one could never be a true poet unless one suffers months of depression (or get the blues as we would say in Cardiganshire). I know better than anybody what it feels like to experience melancholy having finished writing a long poem, or a story, or a play, or even a short poem sometimes, but it would not be long before I would shake off the mood – usually before the sun got the chance to go to his bed again. I do not know if this is significant – maybe it shows a lack of depth of character perhaps – it is possible.

This piece does not do the author justice but it is characteristic of her way of looking at life and confirms the fact that she was ultimately a modest and humble person. Who else would declare publicly, in front of the whole nation, that she might not possess depth of character? And yet I almost believe that she was protecting herself by saying these things in order to mitigate any hurt that might come her way and indeed, did come her way. She opens a previous draft of the same script in a very different way:

> I must admit that Mrs Lorraine Davies's invitation to write my autobiography for the radio came like a bolt from the blue. I had not stopped to think backwards. And suddenly here I was, having to face the fact that around a half a century had disappeared somewhere. Where to, I do not know. Following every pathway at full speed, I shouldn't wonder, and arriving at every milestone out of breath, no doubt, the temptation when looking backwards, more than likely, would be to romanticise in the classical sense; to turn every small cloud into a dark hatred, and every glimmer of sunlight into an everlasting Riviera of pleasure. It is so much easier to sound prettily poetic than to stick to bald facts. One poetic genius once said to me that I would never be a poet if I could not disappear into depression for a long time. I would arrive at melancholia after writing a piece of poetry, a script or a play ... but the blues would be short-lived ... *mini* not *maxi*. I have little to say to the *maxi* ... neither clothing nor time. A lack of depth in character perhaps, but I have always been one of Rabbi Ben Ezra's disciples, and that is what I wish to be ... 'Grow old along with me / The best is yet to be'.
>
> But one thing that is fairly clear (totally clear) as I look back, clinically like this ... that I was born an absolute optimist.

These changes are small variations from one draft to the final version. But it is possible to see the thought and style being distilled as she edits her written work, deleting things that would most likely reveal too much about her. For example, she changed the words 'poetic genius' to 'somebody'. Anonymising and impersonal. Also, even though she mentioned the blues in both paragraphs, she pooh-poohs the condition in a few words in the revised version rather than lingering with the mini and maxi. But the most revealing sentences that were totally changed were the ones containing the comment, 'to turn every small cloud into a dark hatred'.

It would be easy to compare the two paragraphs and to look for the personality hidden within the changes she made in order to crystallise her thought, or fine-tune it. Certainly the comment, 'to turn every small cloud into a dark hatred' sounds very strange when we remember how joyful Eluned was as a person and that she lived good-naturedly and graciously.

Even so, there is an apologetic tone to some of the comments Eluned makes about her work as a poet and in the middle of a pile of unpublished material there are notes by her in her own handwriting trying to explain her way of writing – or rather she explains why she had not published more between 1967 and 1983. She says:

> I wrote occasional poems after 1967, but I did not publish any apart from one or two for the radio. The one reason, I suppose again, was that nobody asked me to publish a book. I am not an organised person and the poems are usually written on the backs of old envelopes and wait somewhere in the house to be rescued. I must admit that long poems appeal most to me. Since there is an obvious desire, after winning in Llangefni, that I should publish a volume, then maybe I shall. The draw towards competition for me is that I get an honest adjudication, without a hint of the kind of patronising that can happen when a Welshman knows/recognises a Welshman. We are, worse luck, living in a small country where literary critics trample on each other's feet.

But was this true? One could argue that her statement about getting an honest adjudication stirred up more turmoil in the wake of her success. 'Without a hint of the kind of patronising that can happen when a Welshman knows/recognises a Welshman?' Do these words hide another emotion here, in that what she means is the hint of the kind of patronising when a Welshman recognises it as the work of a Welshwoman? Hiding the identity of one's sex can be advantageous sometimes, but it is fair to note that she became a figure of ridicule after she won, as this *englyn* shows; its authorship is hidden behind an anonymous collective identity:

> There was talk amongst the Bala foals
> There was fun, there were doubts.
> Was the stuff of this long poem
> The same style as the old stallion's?
>
> 'Say no more' (The Pentre Arms Poets)

The two most revealing words in the *englyn* are the words 'fun' and 'doubts' which indicate that she was the topic of conversation and distrust in the wake of her success. Also the word 'stuff' is a derogatory one. But it is the last line that drives the message home and takes aim straight at another poet 'The same style as the old stallion's?' Was this a shot at another crowned poet? Whatever the sub-text, Eluned must have been aware of the fact that she was the target of ridicule. Could it have been the poets of Cardiganshire who were the most vindictive towards her, since the Pentre Arms was located in Llangrannog where local poets met, often to spar with one another through poetry? Was there a geographical as well as a literary jealousy in that she trod on their toes? But this sentiment was not only confined to Cardiganshire for a similar reaction was expressed elsewhere since the story spread like wildfire through Wales.

After she won fot the first time in the National Eisteddfod in Bala in 1967, the immediate reaction was at best lukewarm. The rumours spread about her work disappointed her, and after that she was never properly considered as a poet for sixteen years. Apart from unpleasant tittle-tattle about the authorship of 'Corlannau', comments were made which undermined the poem totally.

In its 7 September 1967 edition, the 'Led-led Cymru', 'Throughout Wales', column of *Baner ac Amserau Cymru*, a weekly Welsh-language newspaper, made an attempt to compare the two long poems that came close to winning: the winning crown poem and the one placed third. The fact that Eluned's poem on Edith Piaf was placed runner-up was duly forgotten. Instead, comments were made comparing the winning poem by Eluned and Mathonwy Hughes' 'Corlannau':

> By now, I have had more of a chance to read Eluned Phillips' *pryddest* (long poem) and also Mathonwy Hughes', and I must admit that I appreciated my colleague's poem more than Miss Phillips' allusive poem.
>
> Neither I, nor many of its readers, can fathom how relevant the quotes given by the crowned-girl of Bala regarding the philosophy of Eastern religions are, but we can weigh up in detail the picture she gives of the Christian faith, and one is sorely disappointed by this part of the poem. It is nothing like the Christianity of the New Testament; it is full of symbols and the philosophy of the Old Testament, Judaism! It is fair to ask: are the images Eluned Phillips creates of Hinduism and the religion of China more accurate than this? If they are not, then I wonder if our faith in her as a poet is shaken. I know that we do not expect to be given concrete pictures of the philosophy of any religion by a poet, but she invited an interpretation of the subject by talking about the three religious 'folds'.
>
> And what about Mathonwy Hughes' poem? He kept his feet firmly on the ground and gave us the essence of the old shepherding life that he knows so well; he makes the stones sing – literally so. There is great mastery with the subtle use of *cynghanedd* and the *triban* metre [a triplet] as used by the poet. I am surprised by the fact that the three judges did not give the Crown to the

poem by the deputy editor of *Y Faner*. But maybe my blood is not cold enough in the matter of this discussion to judge fairly.

It is fitting that he concludes with this last sentence. But as if this was not enough to denigrate Eluned's winning poem, yet another review appears on page six of the same paper a fortnight later. This time it was by the crowned bard Dafydd Owen, a poet from the same geographical area as Mathonwy, offering his adjudication on the poem:

I received great delight from reading the adjudications for the Crown and Chair. Even though, like D. E. T., I was amazed to see land between two rivers. In Rhoslan, I am astounded at the acuity of John Gwilym Jones' contribution to literary criticism. And yet again, here is a wonderful adjudication by him. I may be old-fashioned but I cannot understand what right anybody has to adjudicate the Crown and Chair competition if they themselves have not won either prize or contributed greatly to literary criticism, however suspect the standards. Having read the poem, I was tickled by G. J. Roberts' mention of a 'lame line' and of the colourful and effective reference that is not always understandable and clear. Surely, the understatement of the year! I would be willing to forget the lame line if G. J. R. could explain even a quarter of the references to me!

I know that we constantly talk of excellence in poetry but the problem is that so much of it is borrowed excellence. It is strange that the accuracy of John Gwilym Jones' adjudication was not accepted . Perhaps I should explain that I did not compete, so that I am not accused of prejudice! ... And there is certainly a plan to the poem ... But there are far too many literal references here. More than half the section on Christianity is quotations. And if it is so in this 'fold', then it would be interesting to inspect the other folds. Here is page 62 in the *Cyfansoddiadau* which notes the borrowing. (Some were obvious – plenty of them – so one can surmise that if one searched harder many more could be found.)

The breasts were dry – Exodus 2:9
In the fullness of time of our Fate – Exodus 8:3
The dust of lice – Exodus 8:16
River of blood – Exodus 7:19
Horses and camels – Exodus 9:3
Fire walked – Exodus 9:23
He destroyed the locusts – Exodus 10:115
And there was night – Exodus 10:22
Before the lamb – Exodus 12:5
The bread was like hoar frost – Exodus 16:14
There was the sound of wings – Ezekiel 3:13
When the son of God opened – Ezekiel 3:1 a 2
The eagle came –Ezekiel 7:3
And the willow grew – Ezekiel 17:6
Who judges? – Ezekiel 31:20
Offering a young bull – Ezekiel 46:6
Turning an animal from king – Daniel 4:25
The lion with wings – Daniel 7:4
The Old Doom/Death – Daniel 7:9
The flies came – Ecclesiastes 10:1
The Sword of the Lord – Isaiah 14:6
He was fattened – Isaiah 14:6
The Valley was filled – Isaiah 34:11
In the early hours – Ezekiel 23:3
He travelled – Isaiah 23:20
The beast travelled – Daniel 7:7. and 23
He became flesh – Luke 2:7 and Matthew 2:16
He swelled – Matthew 10:29
The hen collected – Matthew 23:37
From the hawk [*sic*] no reference given by the critic

Even though Glyn-y-mêl is a good poet, having recognised all the scriptural references here I'm drawn back constantly to the sensuous and well-crafted poem by Maen Llwyd (Mathonwy Hughes).

170

One could have responded by drawing attention to other poets' use of Biblical imagery in their poetry. Suffice to say that some of these references are so short for the criticism to border on the ridiculous.

Nearly twenty years later and three years after she won her second Crown in the Anglesey National Eisteddfod, 1983, Alan Llwyd in his book *Barddoniaeth y Chwedegau* (*Poetry of the Sixties*) makes a similar claim:

> Eluned Phillips' winning poem was full of references, but as John Gwilym Jones said, it is historical rather than literary referencing that appears in the poem. The poem discusses three religious 'folds' of the world: the religions of Islam, Christianity and Chinese Buddhism. It is an esoteric poem in essence and a stillborn poem, unfortunately; it did not ring true at the time and it did not survive. The first half was recreating and rewording parts of the Quran, and the Old Testament and New Testament in the second half, and not creative referential writing. John Gwilym Jones said that he read a tome on Mahometism in an attempt to solve the mystery of the first part of Eluned's poem but only partly succeeded. The truth is that the key to the mystery of the section about the religion of Islam is in the Quran and in the stories about Mohammed, as they appear in the two following lines in her '*Corlannau*':

> In the Beginning
> Allah created man from a clot of blood.

According to tradition Mohammed, the founder of the Islamic religion, had removed himself to a cave in Ramadhan around the year 610, and the angel Gabriel came to him, when Mohammed was sleeping and said, 'Speak ... Speak in the name of your Lord and create man from blood clots'.

It is direct literal reference here and not a literary recreation that appears in these two lines. Here are two more lines from the poem:

171

Did you see Allah flooring the Elephant's master.
And the lumps of mud on the donkeys' tails?

These two lines are completely impenetrable without knowing the source. They refer to these lines from the Quran:

Did you not consider the way that Allah defeated the Army of the Elephant
Did he not defeat their plans and send
Scores of birds against them and hurled
Clay stones towards them until they were as plants
Trampled and eaten by cows.

It is true that there is eloquence in the poem, but it is borrowed eloquence, as discovered in the literal references rather than meaningful and effective literary references. It is not that the winning poet is without talent, but rather she has misdirected her undoubted talent, at least in 1967.[18]

After criticising the poem, it must be said that Alan Llwyd accepts that Eluned is not bereft of talent. Commendable indeed! But in his next paragraph we get to understand the subtext to the unfolding events, as he refers to a poem that came close to winning:

But in truth a chance was missed in Bala. *'Corlannau'* by Mathonwy Hughes is far superior to the *pryddest* by Eluned Phillips, and Mathonwy Hughes suffered because of the fashion of the age and because of the emphasis put on the obscure and the allusive, on quirky poetry that is written in a contrived and different way. Mathonwy Hughes' poem is subtle, bold, memorable

---

[18] Alan Llwyd, *Barddoniaeth y Chwedegau* (Cyhoeddiadau Barddas, 1986) pp. 234–6.

in places, subtle and bold like the *englynion* [four lined verses in metre and *cynghanedd*] of the *Hen Ganiad*.

And here we get to the crux of the matter. Here is the literary tradition in its entrenched way protecting and upholding the 'tradition' and extending the continuation of that type of poetry and claiming the supremacy of poetry of this nature. What right did anybody have to write in a 'contrived and different way' and to be 'quirky', let alone be 'obscure'?

He goes on:

There are also many vibrant descriptions of the old shearers and the old shepherds that congregated by these mountain folds at shearing and marking time.

Short on patience, (frequently spitting)
Was old Pyrs, and a thorn for everybody
The old rascal saw in the white woolly shearings
The comforts of a wealthy man.

In the three verses that Alan Llwyd quoted, the word 'old' appears three times, a word that is often used in Welsh poetry through the ages and one that engenders certain emotions. It is interesting that he did not mention the second poem which came close to the winning poem, Eluned's poem about Edith Piaf written under the nom de plume Dans la Peau. Rather, he goes on to applaud Mathonwy Hughes' poem:

There is no doubt that Mathonwy Hughes suffered a great injustice at the 1967 Eisteddfod. The brightly coloured, multi-textured thin shawls were favoured rather than the simple, plain but hardwearing Welsh flannel; distance was favoured over familiarity and the exotic over the indigenous, and that was a great loss, in 1967 at least.

The language of the criticism itself borders on being sexist – even though I do not believe that the author intended that for a moment – but the imagery is remarkable. Would it not be a girl who chooses colourful, light clothes and would a man, especially men from years ago, not favour a shirt of Welsh flannel – simple and hardwearing – rather than some skimpy material? As far as 'distance and familiarity' goes, Eluned took us to places that were beyond our understanding at that time. If the poem had competed in 2017, no doubt the judges would have been more aware of, would have better understanding the world's other religions. But there is another way of looking at the 'indigenous' and the 'exotic'. Eluned Phillips was a foreigner in the poetic world, while Mathonwy Hughes was well-known to the literary Welsh press, as a poet and a journalist. Eluned, if anybody knew her at all, was seen as a nascent poet and *persona non grata* by some in the wake of her friendship with the poets of the fringes, including Dewi Emrys. As for Mathonwy Hughes, he was highly regarded in literary circles and was seen as one of the mainstays of Welsh language society and the literary establishment. Did he suffer such a great loss? Mathonwy Hughes was already a chaired eisteddfod poet when he won the Chair at the Aberdare National Eisteddfod in 1956 on the subject of 'Gwraig' ('Woman'). But as for loss, I believe that the poet from Cenarth suffered much more, as she was shunned by the kind of poetic society she craved. Furthermore, she lost her good name and was defamed as a 'fraud'. To my mind, this is a 'great loss', especially since she was undeniably a poet who spent her life unable to fight against what we might now call 'fake news'. And even though the force of the tide of opinion was against Eluned, Mathonwy Hughes, himself, one of her co-competitors, in the 24 August 1967 issue of *Y Faner* said: 'I enjoyed the winning poem very much and I agree with the adjudication given by the three of them. If I had been a judge myself, my adjudication would have been exactly the same.'

•

After Eluned had won at the National Eisteddfod on Anglesey in 1983, the reviews of the poems had been quite favourable but Dylan Iorwerth drew attention in *Y Faner* (19 August 1983) to the fact that she had not succeeded in explaining the way she had gone about creating the poem. He said:

> For some reason or other, Eluned Phillips could not give us a credible impression of what the impetus was behind the poem nor how she went about it with bricks and mortar. The windows were opened on the two brothers from Flint, too, without us being invited into the house. Tudor Wilson talked more about sitting on his father's knee listening to the novels of Daniel Owen, and Einion Evans was able at least to scratch the surface of the pain that went into his elegaic poem of rememberance for his daughter, Ennis.

This draws attention to a time when there was an expectation that the poet would express himself in public and pour forth his technique as if it were as transparent as water from a well. For a poet to explain the workings of a poem is a difficult endeavour. Denise Levertov once said that she would often tell people that she could not explain how a poem had been created but that the only thing she could do was to talk around that poem. To her, the poem was like a musical score, and in the sound of the music the poem came alive.

Vaughan Hughes suggested, in the same issue of *Y Faner*, under the title 'The Disappointment of the Pryddest', that the poem's style drew attention to itself – even though he also praised it. But the reactions to *'Clymau'* were pretty lukewarm. I remember listening to the late Professor Hywel Teifi Edwards interviewing Eluned in the Literary Tent at the National Eisteddfod and throwing a jokey question her way, something about whether there had been any 'doctoring' done to the poem. I remember that word as I did not at that time know what such a comment meant. It was, after all, a suggestion that somebody else had been its author or at least had made significant input. Maybe Eluned knew what was being suggested, and she closed up like an oyster in seaweed.

In her own style again, in an unpublished essay, she says this:

> There were a plethora of reasons, rather than one, why I chose the old strict metres without *cynghanedd* for the poem *'Clymau'*. I was fed up with reading free metre poetic forms which included *cynghanedd*; I thought that I should rather like to hit back. The main reason certainly was that I had lost myself in the history of the Celts and because most of the early poetry was written without *cynghanedd*, I felt a frisson in setting out to use the old forms.

'I remember too,' she said later, 'at the time of the announcement in Llangefni that Vaughan Hughes, when he saw the list of competitions and their subjects, had cursed "metre and rhyme" and had prophesied that they would get a loadful of *"Nant y Mynydd"* as a result of restricting the poets. And I felt quite jealous that the *awdl*, the long poem in strict metre, had the twenty-four metres of Dafydd Nanmor.'

Eluned went on to explain her choice of forms like this:

> Experimenting, and finding that there was enjoyment and satisfaction to be had in the pattern of the non-*cynghanedd*, and realising straight away that this was the best way of saying what was on my mind, in a subtle and epigrammatic way, I came to the conclusion that I had the right to take the *cynghanedd* out of the strict metre forms if writing *cynghanedd* in the free metres was acceptable.
>
> I know that Dewi Emrys' proof of good poetry was that it was melodious. I have already heard *'Clymau'* being sung skillfully to with the harp. I also heard the poem being read by an experienced elecutionist, and both forms were totally acceptable to the audience

at the celebratory event. I had indeed not considered so much the responses of the judges to the '*pryddest–awdl*' poem, but the thrill of composing overcame any of the competition's requirements. I got the chance to rhyme monosyllables with multi-syllable words, a monopoly owned by the strict-metre poets for centuries. Perhaps I also smashed the stricture of Sir John Morris Jones (*Cerdd Dafod*), by using names such as Buenos Aires, San Carlos, Casa Rosada, or even '*tiwnig a chlogyn*' [tunic and cloak], but I felt that the old metres complemented what I had to say succinctly.

It appears that Eluned had the means to express things on the page far better than she did verbally in the Literary Tent. It must be remembered that even though she was an extrovert when young and created sketches and sang to the soldiers that came back from the war, in other ways she was a shy and private person when she wasn't hiding behind another persona. It is possible to see the Literary Tent at the time as some kind of lion's den, and no doubt she would have been aware that the experimentation with poetic form that she undertook would have been anathema to some. Not only that, but she would have been self-conscious when facing an audience that was already suspicious of her because of the sly accusations thrown at her in 1967. It is easy to understand, therefore, why she would not want to open the floodgates to comments such as those made above in public.

In other notes written as if prepared for a friendly literary society meeting she mentions that she gained confidence in competing, something which eluded her at the thought of writing a book.

She says: 'Lack of self-confidence, it seems, is why I have never published a book of poetry. Perhaps too, that is the reason why I swing back and forth instead of not finishing one of the three novels that have been in the making for a long time. I'm quite happy to move from one novel to the other; for me, it's like going on holiday.' When she wrote her notes about what spurred her to write '*Clymau*', she said:

177

I have already explained how an Eisteddfod conversation instigated research into the history of the Celts, and in the end had forced me into writing about the Falklands. The Falklands War and the connection between us and Patagonia has worried me a great deal. My intention at the beginning was to discuss the problems in a play. Then, all of a sudden one night, the obstacles faced by my forefathers – so that they were forced to emigrate to America – stayed strongly in my mind, and I could not escape the ties between Patagonia and Wales. Losing the friendship of those who were previously our fellow Celts hurt deeply and I felt a need at the same time to show that all war was a waste and so vainglorious. Again the inspiration came to join the time of the 'Mimosa' with the Falklands; the ideas begged to be tied together in a poem. The ties insisted on making themselves known, and I did not feel it a strain to write upon the subject. If there is excellence in the poem, perhaps that is its strength.

In an article in *Carmarthenshire Life* in December 2005 Eluned explains clearly in English the genesis of her poem *'Clymau'* ('Ties'):

I had been listening to a great friend of mine, Owen, a surgeon from Bangor, talking about the Celts at the Swansea Eisteddfod. I listened for about three hours – I'm a great Celt, always have been.

Anyway, another friend of mine, Dr John Owen from Porthcawl, got frustrated because I wasn't paying attention to him. We started talking about the Falklands War. This was '82. When we'd finished talking about it John told me: 'Go home and write a play about it.' And that was that.

When the subject for the poem for Llangefni crown came out it was *'Clymau'*. At first I thought to myself, 'I'll write about the Celts – the bonds of the Celts'.

I got about twenty books on the Celts, read them all, and now I was prepared to write a poem about the bonds of the Celts. When I sat down I had about twenty poems to think of not one. So I gave up.

Then in bed one night I suddenly remembered my talk with John Owen about the Falklands, and it became quite clear to me that I wanted to write about the bond between our young boys and the Patagonians. We were going to fight our own kith and kin.

I was very worried over that war. One of the casualties was from my next village, Llechryd, and he was the grandson of the man who looked after me all my life to keep me out of mischief, the man who once saved me from choking when I stuck my head in a cask of tar. The boy killed on the 'Sir Galahad' was his grandson. I was very affected by it because it made me remember the old boy. So I decided to write about the links between Wales and the Patagonians. That was it. That was the Crown poem.

I cannot remember if Eluned told this story in its entirety in the Literary Tent that afternoon on Anglesey. I have a feeling that she either did not get the chance, or that she had been reticent in sharing a story that was so personally intense in front of a multitude of people. In their midst, many who had doubted her since 1967. And we return again to the fact that she was weighing up her words. Was it shyness? Or was she too frightened?

In one of her notebooks, there are succinct and clear notes:

You ask if there is any difference between the '67 Eluned Phillips and the '83 version. It's likely that there is. My life was more itinerant in '67; because of family reasons, I am now more willing to live an everyday life at home. The faraway used to appeal more than the familiar, and now, after growing out of my 'sulking' period, I am willing to accept that this was the main reason for being accused of writing 'dark' poetry. I had not been totally saved until this year; I took myself away to Florence and Italy in 'Wynebau' ('Faces') and to Saudi Arabia in 'Rhod' ('The Wheel') ... I tasted the words rather than the substance. I am not sure yet whether I can choose between the poems of Bala and Llangefni. I am happy that *'Clymau'* ('Ties') was so acceptable to ordinary people, but *'Corlannau'* ('Folds') is still very close to my heart. Perhaps I did not succeed in making the meaning in that poem clear, but there was a message in it: the difference was that I framed the poem in a foreign context. Reading Dr John Gwilym Jones' totally fair adjudication of '*Corlannau*' certainly led me to try and improve my craft this time. I shall treasure the three judges' adjudications this year, and certainly when inspiration comes to write new poems there will be a renewed sheen on them because of their sensible and fair appraisal of my work. Even though I shall not be eligible to try for the Crown again – I am still a pupil, I am still learning – no, I do not have *cynghanedd* in me, I adhere to the pattern!

Her confession as a poet is a modest one, is it not? She sees herself still as learning her craft. How I wish she could have shared this confession with the nation. Tecwyn Lloyd, the editor of *Taliesin* (a literary Welsh language periodical) in issue 47 (December 1983) raises another question when he says in his editorial:

The decision of the literature committee at the Llangefni Eisteddfod this year to insist on a *pryddest* without *cynghanedd* in metre and rhyme was a success and I hope an example to follow. As I mentioned in another place, we had too much material in *vers libre*, without form and with sloppy syntax, giving the title of crowned bard to someone and then seeing very little (writing) by them after that. But of all the small mysteries that tickle one's curiosity, why is it that a poetess as accomplished, polished and multi-faceted in her style as Eluned Phillips has not published a volume of poetry by now; nor published, as far as we know any poetic piece in this magazine or any other Welsh-language periodical. Between 1967, when she won the Crown in Bala and this year, sixteen years slipped by under the bridge in Cenarth. But Miss Phillips must have continued to compose during that time, otherwise she would not have been able to show such poetic mastery as was witnessed in the *pryddest* this year. Because her art of poetry is like *cerdd dant* [a form of singing with a harp] and all other arts of poetry and music require frequent and diligent practice to reach excellence; and certainly, the expression in *'Clymau'* is the work of a master, even though the story of this poem is not unexpected. I understand also that the poetess writes many short stories and novels for English and American magazines and publishers. It would be good to receive a bibliography of these works, as surely studying them would be of assistance to some of our young novelists and storywriters, who often complain that they do not have Literary Guidelines or Good Working Practices to adhere to. This would be a wonderful chance to offer assistance to the uninitiated in the kingdom of our literature.

It is difficult to measure whether these words are a challenge or chastisement but the magnifying glass was certainly placed to look more closely at the poet from Cenarth. It could be said that other crowned poets since 1983 who have won the Crown at the National have not published much poetry. What is obvious here is that the comments have been aimed squarely at Eluned's forehead. These words are designed to urge and inspire nevertheless, and they must have spurred Eluned to send a long poem, *'Y Rhod'* ('The Wheel') to him at the beginning of the year, but he returned it with the comment that the poem was too long to publish in *Taliesin*. And so Eluned wrote again in March 1984, with the following comments:

Glyn-y-mêl
Cenarth

Dear Editor,

Thank you for sending the poem 'Y Rhod' back to me. I did doubt whether you would be able to make use of it in *Taliesin*, but the S4C correspondent had been most insistent that I should send the long poem to you. I must admit that I do not understand the connection between S4C and *Taliesin*, and I am not happy with that. I found it disappointing that the BBC News correspondents had corrupted the truth so much that they misled me about Sir Thomas Parry's letter in *Y Cymro* [a weekly Welsh-language newspaper] and the matter is now in the hands of my solicitors. I am willing to accept criticism but not slander.

I had read your article in the Christmas edition of *Taliesin*. I had been meaning to get in touch at the time, but I am careless with correspondence even if I am constantly misquoted.

But I take your point that not very much of my work has seen the light of day and that I should have done something about the matter. This never crossed my mind and, as I have already explained, I have not published a single thing without been given a definite invitation to do so.

For me, writing poetry is an exceedingly personal thing. My only reason for competing was to get an adjudication and through that to improve my work. I did not think that I was going to win in Llangefni, and certainly did not foresee the wonderful adjudication. I was fairly certain that the poem would be thrown out because I had dared trample on the feet of the *cynganeddwyr* and I'm still not sure whether some of them are still baying for my blood.

It took fifteen years for me to feel confident enough to compete after the literary criticism given in Bala, and during these fifteen years I concentrated on refining the language and simplifying my ideas. I worked hard on 'Clymau', to hone it to its final shape. I was lucky in the subject, and more than anything, possibly, lucky about the metre I chose, the *awdl* without *cynghanedd*. I learnt one astounding thing, that writing in this style helps me write more correctly, simply, and more concisely. I feel now that this is the pattern that suits me. I felt this time that I received some kind of inspiration. I do not know whether you, as an experienced literary critic and adjudicator feel that there is such a thing? I did not before now, and I have been writing and composing some sort of poetry since the first piece

Studio photograph from the 1950s

Crowning ceremony from the 1967
National Eisteddfod, Bala

Eluned and her crown
after the ceremony

Cenarth welcomes home the victorious winner of the National Eisteddfod
Crown, Bala, 1967. The horse and cart were organised by Wyn Jenkins,
Penwern Farm, and Mr Williams, Gorslas.

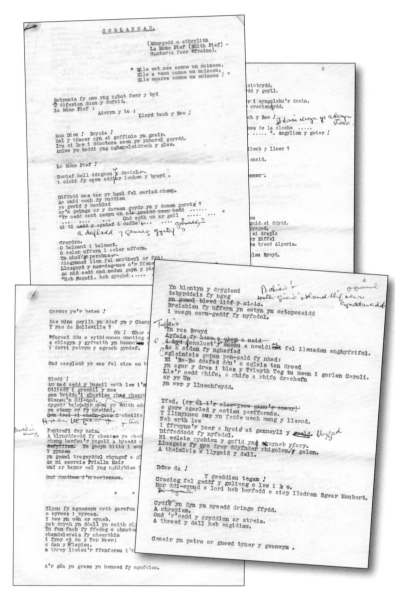

Annotated typescripts for the *pryddest* 'Edith Piaf', which
came second in the 1967 National Eisteddfod at Bala.

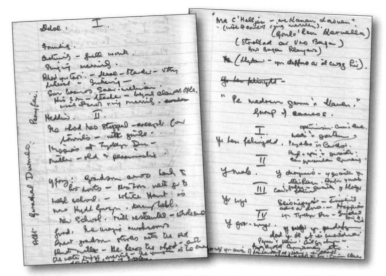

Notes from Eluned's red notebook for the single poem 'Y Fro'
which was published in the 1985 collection 'Cerddi Glyn-y-mêl',
her sole published volume of poetry.

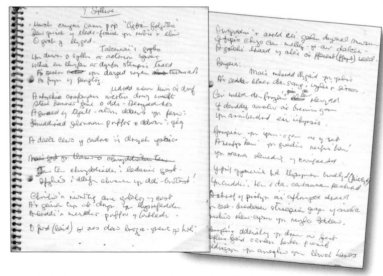

Early drafts from the sequence of poems, 'Y Syllwr', in competition at the
1965 Cardigan National Eisteddfod and for which she received an
encouraging critique – as written in her blue Wellbeck notebook

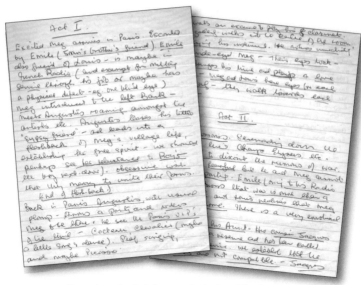

Notes for a play which didn't see the light of day, but was used as the basis for Ewart Alexander's script for 'Rhith y Lloer'

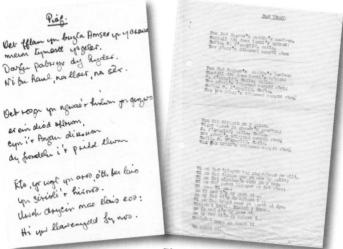

Handwritten copy of the poem 'Edith Piaf'

Eluned's typed copy of 'Daw Yfory'

Eluned at a homecoming celebration after winning her second
crown at the 1983 National Eisteddfod in Llangefni

Eluned holding her two crowns – 'two crowns,
one head' as she said in her memoir

Eluned with a coracle on her back

Glyn-y-mêl – Eluned's house on the road out of Glanymor

A gifted storyteller to the end…

published of my work when I was seven years old. I was brought up by Mam to write under the nose of the doubter. A prejudice against women who write poetry? I do not know.

I have a lecture 'A few footprints in concrete'. If you had had the chance to hear me, perhaps that would have helped you understand a little more about me. There are lyrical poems, sonnets, around twelve long poems (*pryddestau*), as well as a play in metre that was given quite a good adjudication by the chief adjudicator, Sir Thomas Parry, somewhere in this house... I have never had a system and it is too late to change that. Here are one or two individual poems written this week. I must admit that it is the long poem that appeals to me the most, perhaps because I have spent years writing dramatic scripts for the BBC and so forth.

If I get time to collect and create a little, perhaps I will bring a volume of poetry out at last.

Eluned

It appears that Eluned kept a copy of this letter, typed and corrected before sending it to him. One can sense her disappointment as she pours out her feelings to the editor: that 'personal thing'. What other winning poet would expose their failings in front of another as well as hint at the suggestion that she had been doubted as being the author of her work at seven years of age? And in this letter we have evidence of one of the few times that Eluned suggests that perhaps there was a prejudice against her because she was a woman. Why did D. Tecwyn Lloyd not jump at the scoop and ask to publish her lecture? Would that not have contributed towards showing her validity as a poet? Was this, one wonders, what she really hoped would happen?

It is difficult to know if the rumours had reached Tecwyn Lloyd's ear when he said in his editorial, 'of all the small mysteries that tickle one's curiosity'. Whatever the truth of the matter, Eluned received a warm and courteous response from him noting that he had received the short poems in the place of the long 'Y Rhod':

Maes yr Onnen

Maerdy Corwen

Clwyd

June 5 1984

Dear Eluned Phillips,

Thank you very much for your three poems. This is the kind of material I welcome in *Taliesin* – not long pieces. I shall use them, one in the next issue. And from that issue onwards, one issue comes out quarterly and so, one will appear in the autumn and I shall keep another of your poems for that issue.

I enjoyed the discussion in your letter. T. S. Eliot has a sentence somewhere that says the zenith of the spiritual research for a poet (similar to a craftsman) is the 'complete simplicity that costs not less than everything'. It is, I believe, a good definition.

Indeed, you must publish a volume of poetry.

Sincerely, and with thanks,

D. Tecwyn Lloyd

A warm and encouraging letter and one of the few in her correspondence collection. Her volume of poetry, *Cerddi Glyn-y-mêl* (*Glyn-y-mêl Poems*) appeared the following year, 1985, from Gomer Press. There is little doubt that Tecwyn Lloyd's letter and his kind encouragement to publish her work had a great influence on her. Did he sympathise with the backlash that she faced from the eisteddfodic establishment as far back as 1967? Or did he know in December 1983 that there was another storm brewing and that a letter was about to appear in *Y Cymro* [a weekly Welsh-language newspaper] in March 1984, from the hand of none other than Sir Thomas Parry? His letter was positioned on the left-hand side of the paper's front page. The title was in capital letters:

AN APPEAL FOR AUTHENTICITY (20 March 1984)

It is time to send in the compositions for the National Eisteddfod, and I am certain that I express the feeling of hundreds of my countrymen when I say that I hope that no one will send compositions in the name of another, so that person, were they to win, should get undeserved fame and attention, as happened in Llangefni last year, and at least at one other time before that.

Bangor, Thomas Parry.

The feeling of hundreds? Who were these hundreds? And "at least at one other time before that"? These are the insinuations and libellous accusations that had followed Eluned since 1967 raising their heads yet again, and this time from one the highest echelons of the world of the Welsh eisteddfod. What drew Sir Thomas Parry to raise the matter at all, considering his difficulty in the Aberafan National Eisteddfod in 1932 as he competed in the *awdl* [the long poem in *cynghanedd*] competition even though he knew that his cousin was one of the judges: 'Those who sow brambles should not walk barefoot!'

Even though Eluned had ignored the rumours about her for a decade and more she showed this time that she was tough, and willing to stand her ground and defend her authenticity openly. Here is a letter that appeared the following week in *Y Cymro*, on 27 March 1984 – it was not given space on the front page but appeared on page six:

As one who has been a great admirer of Sir Thomas Parry, it is obvious that somebody has misled him with slanderous rumours. What causes me concern is the fact that *Y Cymro* (the nation's only Welsh language newspaper) has published a letter based on insinuations.

According to BBC correspondents (and again, they emphasise they are working on nothing but rumours), the suggestion is that

185

the poem *'Clymau'* is a collaborative plot as a joke against the establishment.

I feel that this not only degrades a poem that received high praise in the adjudication and was written by me without aiming to be political or anti-establishment, but was created from my deep feelings about what had happened to my family, to the family of a neighbour of mine, and to my fellow Welshmen in Patagonia, and it also degrades the rumour-mongers as (if they have read the poem) they are devoid of feeling, unable to appreciate poetry or deliberately malicious.

Unfortunately, rumours will spread; they are dirty and unhealthy. Is it too much to expect Wales to be rid of its plague of fleas before the illness kills the nation that I have, until now, been so proud to belong to?

Glyn-y-mêl,
Eluned Phillips

Eluned Phillips was not the only one who reacted to the letter from Sir Thomas Parry. As could be expected, the chaired bard Einion Evans also wrote a letter in reaction under the title 'The Truth Against', and I assume that he was angry considering that his winning poem that year had been a touching and elegiac poem about losing Ennis Evans, his only daughter, a talented young writer. Einion insisted that Sir Thomas Parry had besmirched all the winners of the Eisteddfod with his unexpected letter, a sign perhaps that there were not 'hundreds' behind his letter as he claimed. Einion's brother, T. Wilson Evans, the winner of the Literature Medal that year also sent a letter to challenge Thomas Parry to name those who supported him and he gave the title 'Thomas Parry is not a coward' to his contribution.

The letter-writing continued, with Eluned Phillips sending another letter to *Y Cymro* on 3 April 1984, this time using satire:

A Sponge without Spice

Fame at last!

Having reached 'Rock Bottom'. I enjoy a joke – even by now, the Llangefni big joke. It's a shame, though, that Radio Cymru spoiled a wonderful programme by forgetting to include the most important element in their sponge, that it was the BBC's correspondents who were responsible for saying that Sir Thomas Parry published his letter in *Y Cymro* based on rumours.

As *Y Cymro* is late arriving in this area, and as there had been no chance to read the letter, nor hear its contents being read as it appears that the S4C News Department are too poor to employ someone to answer the correspondents' phone – one journalist called here at lunchtime and one had to listen helplessly to what was suggested.

Is it a paucity of programmes that causes such extremes?

But as the matter is now in the hands of solicitors, then it is time to stop.

But a sponge without any spice pleases no one.

Eluned Phillips,

Cenarth

Who would not have reacted in such a manner to the accusation that *'Clymau'*, a poem of such magnificence, was not her own work, and the original accusation by Sir Thomas Parry throws a shadow and suspicion over *'Corlannau'* the poem that won in 1967 too. When reading the words: 'one had to listen helplessly to what was suggested' in her letter, it is easy to feel the hurt she felt. Any other winning poet condemned in such a way would no doubt have taken comfort from fellow-poets, or compatriots within the bardic circle. There would be strong rebukes, quite a furore by defenders of the poet. With that in mind, it could be argued that such a letter would not have appeared at all. But instead, Eluned herself responded, and against learned men of influence who held positions of status and importance. Who was this Eluned after all? To them, it was an amusing scenario, and Eluned became a comical figure worthy of ridicule, and because of that they believed she had undermined the whole ethos and history of the National Eisteddfod.

'But as the matter is now in the hands of solicitors, then it is time to stop.' That was Eluned's last comment and realising that she had to seek legal help from strangers in relation to literary concerns in order to deal with the matter emphasises the hurt and anguish she faced. It also demonstrates the sexism of Welsh-speaking Wales in the early eighties; it was possible to make such attacks on the work of a woman in the light of 'slanderous murmurings'. Would Sir Thomas Parry have been as ready to challenge a man if he thought he'd been given 'a helping hand' by one of his compatriots? In *ysgolion barddol*, poetry schools, and in creative writing departments in colleges, the mentoring of work by emerging writers is a given. But for Eluned, receiving an impartial adjudication on her work under a nom de plume was the only mentoring available. Her aloofness made her an easy target.

I should like to imagine that such a thing would not happen today, but in 2014, the centenary year of Eluned's birth, the issue raised its head again. In a biography of Thomas Parry, *Y Brenhinbren* (*The Majestic Oak*), the whole saga was recounted by the biographer Derec Llwyd Morgan, who said that Thomas Parry had opened a can of worms following his letter in *Y Cymro*. He noted how there had been opposition to the letter from the poet Einion Evans for his winning poem, 'Yr Ynys' ('The Island'), and he mentions also how T. Wilson Evans also had maintained that 'Y Pabi Coch' ('The Red Poppy') was innocent, 'assuring ordinary folk that his volume was nothing to do with any accusation of any wrongdoing'. Derec Llwyd Morgan said of Eluned:

As for the third, Eluned Phillips, the winner of the Crown: directly after the publication of the *Y Cymro* where Thomas Parry's letter was printed, the BBC correspondents were on her doorstep quizzing her about it even though 'they only had whispers to work on'. Even though nobody was named in the original letter, it was

Eluned who was under suspicion, by everybody. Indeed, there had been doubt about the authorship of her long poems ever since she won the Crown at the National Eisteddfod in Bala in 1967. The whole country suspected that another winning poet had written her work for her or at least had improved her work for her.

In her anguished letter to the Editor of *Y Cymro*, on 27 March, Eluned Phillips said (correctly) that Thomas Parry's original letter was 'based on insinuations', that 'degraded a poem that was given high praise in the adjudication' (correct again), and degraded her feelings as they were expressed in her poem. But another letter was published at the top of the front page in that issue of *Y Cymro*, from the Reverend W. J. Gruffydd (Elerydd), who won the Crowns in Pwllheli 1955, and Cardiff in 1960. He wrote from his home in Bro Dawel, Tregaron:

Dear Sir,

Because my name has been vilified as a result of Sir Thomas Parry's letter, I make this statement: Apart from the lines in 'Ffenestri' ('Windows') and 'Unigedd' ('Loneliness') I have not written, changed, nor edited any lines that appear in the Crown competition. Over to Sir Thomas Parry, a man I respect greatly.

Tregaron, W. J. Gruffydd (Elerydd)

It can only be surmised, given the way the story is reported, that it was the subject of great amusement among the intelligensia that prompted the discussion. This hilarity continues as his biographer refers to Sir Thomas Parry's reaction to the furore:

The instigator of the saga reacted with a straighter-than-straight poker-face. I do not know, he said, how Miss Phillips, Mr Einion Evans, Mr Wilson Evans and especially the Reverend W. J. Gruffydd could react in such a way to the story, for I did not mention a single one of their names ... and why would they protest so vehemently, more than any of the other 104 people who won for original compositions in the Llangefni Eisteddfod? Miss Phillips has said that the matter was now in the hands of solicitors, but of course, because Thomas Parry had not named her, nothing came of it.

When reading the comments above, I cannot help but feel for those that were drawn into the drama that set out to defame just one person. More than anything, perhaps, I feel the lack of sensitivity as he notes the 'straighter-than-straight poker-face'. After all, not only did he infuriate Eluned, but Sir Thomas Parry also succeeded in distressing Einion Evans who created a poem in remembrance of his only daughter, Ennis. Suffice it to say that the 104 others winners of literary competitions were hardly in the firing line. After all, 'fame' was mentioned, and it is unlikely that winning on the sonnet or *englyn* would be deemed as 'fame' by anyone. How I wish I could have omitted the following comments, which appear as a footnote on page 362 of *Y Brenhinbren,* the title of Morgan's biography. I read with incredulity:

> One of the adjudicators for the Crown in 1983 was John Gwilym Jones. A few days before the Eisteddfod he asked me – as I was the Chairman of the local Executive Committee – whether I know who the winner was. Although I should not have told him, I did so. His reaction was, 'Is it too late for me to change my mind, boy?'

I was astounded by those words. In the first place John Gwilym Jones, the adjudicator, was – and still is – widely regarded as one of the most formidable critics of Welsh literature, one whose perspicacity is unrivalled, and his influence continues to this day. Secondly, he was an amiable person as well as a stellar critic. But the cat is out of the bag. The most damaging part of this is that John Gwilym Jones' personal comment was repeated, thus debasing both John Gwilym Jones and Eluned. This, even though he praised her work as being groundbreaking in the *Cyfansoddiadau* and from the stage on the day of the crowning. This is what she said about that experience: 'I must admit that I seemed to be under the influence of a wizard, as if I had escaped into the land of magic having listened to the masterful, wonderful adjudication, and for me, totally unexpectedly ... from Dr John Gwilym Jones ... one of the treasured great experiences of my life.'

I hope that the adjudication given by John Gwilym Jones still stands despite the comments made by him in a private and perhaps jocular conversation.

•

2014 was the centenary year of Eluned's birth, and yet nobody thought it appropriate to celebrate her century in any way, particularly any kind of Gorsedd or eisteddfod event. She appeared on the television days before the National Eisteddfod in Llanelli. She was seen on the screen, wearing a pair of large spectacles, sitting neatly if a little uncomfortably, in a television studio. It wasn't Eluned, of course, rather it was Eluned in the person of the actress Sharon Morgan playing her part. But wait. This was not a programme about Eluned at all, and her reason for being there was not to be interviewed about her work either. She was a guest, and had been invited to talk about Dewi Emrys. But think about this again. It wasn't the centenary of that old reprobate's birth nor was it his birthday, but it was deemed appropriate to air a programme about him, using Eluned as the person who was his friend – an ironic situation at that.

During her life Eluned was seen as an impostor, a charlatan, by an anonymous and critical bardic group, and here she was on screen after her death being impersonated by a professional actress. This would be almost sitcom material if it were not so sad. Keeping her character company in the programme was another woman poet: Dilys Cadwaladr, played by Judith

Humphreys, who had lived with Dewi and who was the mother of his child, Dwynwen. As the programme alternated between Dilys and Eluned, the impression given was that the two were his lovers. This was conveyed through insinuation, of course, but it was obvious from the subliminal messages that this was at the heart of these portrayals. How would the ordinary viewer not come to this conclusion, given a scenario that juxtaposed Dilys enjoying the fact that he lifted her over the river with him then doing exactly the same for Eluned? In spite of this, Eluned was portrayed well, as a person who was mesmerised by him as a poet. As somebody who wrote a biography of him it was natural that she should have been a part of the programme, and her most revealing comment, when answering the interviewer was that there was 'no such thing as a comprehensive biography.'

Another guest on the programme was Emyr Llewelyn, son of T. Llew Jones, a contemporary of Eluned, who stated that Eluned did not know Dewi as well as she asserted – or that was what his father had told him, as recalled by the Cilie Poets (an influential family of poets from the Cilie farm in Ceredigion). Emyr Llewelyn must have been a young boy himself when Dewi Emrys died in 1952, and so he was merely echoing what he had heard. He repeated the old refrain that some notable poets from the patriarchy kept trotting out about women: 'What does she know?' Wasn't she some kind of groupie, tagging behind him? Or at least that was the impression given. The fact that Eluned inherited Dewi Emrys' literary works proves clearly that she was a true friend to him. Indeed, letters between Eluned and Dewi's daughter show that there was a close friendship between the two women, before and after Dewi died, as noted previously.

A few other letters exist between them which testify to their healthy and friendly relationship, as expressed by Eluned's idiosyncratic way of sending word to Dwynwen:

Dear Dwynwen,

Goodness gracious – my days fly by like … sandals!

I went away into the Continent and have only just touched down again in this … Thanks awfully for the detailed p.m. – it was kind and I readily accept the contents.

This is merely a note to say that I have read the news safely. I shall write to you again and enclose the manuscript as soon as I have had a breathing space. I shall certainly delete the reminders about – and the clauses. It was never about to cast a reflection of selfishness on you in any way – rethinking it…

Eluned

These letters show that she and Dwynwen were friends, and when discussing literary matters in a letter to Tecwyn Lloyd she says:

I am looking forward eagerly to reading your comments on WJG in the series *Writers of Wales*. I had quite a bit of fun discovering the distinction of style (?) whilst researching the life and times of Dewi. The English-language series is well-known and the one most known to the English is Saunders Lewis, according to Dwynwen (Dewi's daughter).

Warmest wishes, Eluned

•

Apart from a few warm friendly letters between Tecwyn Lloyd and Eluned, the spirit of friendship and brotherhood was not extended towards her. It was unusual for women during this time to be honoured by becoming members of the Welsh Academy; an author would have to be invited to be a member, and even then only a handful of women attended the Academy's meetings. Though the Barddas society (the Art of Poetry Society) enlivened the Welsh bardic tradition through the unstinting efforts of Alan Llwyd, thus creating a place for poetry and a new excitement in strict metre *cynghanedd* poetry, the opportunities were few and far between for somebody like Eluned Phillips to feel a modicum of poetic cameraderie. During Dewi Emrys' time, Eluned could enjoy being a member of *Forddolion Ceredigion*, or Wayfarers, a literary society and, in time, became their secretary, but the society was disbanded after Dewi's death leaving Eluned once again feeling like a pilgrim in the desert.

Is it any wonder that Eluned, at the end of the eighties and beginning of the nineties, seemed to have had enough of the prejudice against her? Happily, a new poetic deliverance came her way from America. Her readings brought light to their societies and concerts and these people delighted in her company. She was invited to visit whenever she wished and she spent time in their midst in California, where she was given a warm Welsh welcome. She made a new career for herself, or rather she reconnected with her writing, working with the composer Michael J. Lewis. In a way this was a return to her first talent, writing words for songs, to be sung by the South Wales Male Voice Choir. In her nineties, she was still creating and composing verses but she did not dare share anything with the literary Welsh-language world. She retreated, and who can blame her?

Yet, she was faithful to the National Eisteddfod, even if she was never invited to adjudicate the Crown competition, a competition that she won twice. I have wondered often, as I write this book, how she felt when she saw other women, myself included, being given the honour to be chosen as a judge in that competition. How did it feel to see our backs on stage as she sat, dignified and demure, onstage in the front row of the Gorsedd? As I write this chapter, the Rhestr Testunau Eisteddfod Genedlaethol Mynwy a'r Cylch 2016 (Competition List for the Monmouth National Eisteddfod 2016) has appeared, and it notes that the Eisteddfod was entrusting the adjudication of the Crown, on the subject *'Llwybrau'* ('Pathways'), to three women. Shouldn't Eluned of all people have been chosen as a judge during her lifetime? A reminder again that she was ahead of her time, or of the fact that other women were now standing tall on her broad shoulders.

In October 1985 a few reviews appeared in the magazine *Barddas* (Number 102), by Wendy Lloyd Jones who frequently expressed the kind of opinion promulgated at that time. Discussing the volume *Hel Dail Gwyrdd* (*Collecting Green Leaves*) that I edited she notes:

> I feel that it would not be a good idea to publish another book like this as women now have the same opportunities as men to write creatively in schools and colleges; from now on, women should compete for their place using the same level playing-field as men when it comes to books. This is more natural and is fairer in the long run because above all else, adhering to a high standard in language and literature is what is important, and if one day anybody wanted to research the literature of the end of the twentieth century, they would have to search in various anthologies of poetry for the works of men and women.

These words suggest a healthy optimism, the idea that women would be given equal opportunities to men in the poetry world. It could be referring to a poem by Eluned Phillips in that anthology which was an exception, content-wise, in contrast to the number of anthologies where not a single poem of hers appeared.

Another example of such absence was the definitive anthology of Welsh language poetry that appeared two years later in 1987, *Blodeugerdd yr Ugeinfed Ganrif* (*An Anthology of the Twentieth Century*), edited by Alan Llwyd and Gwynn ap Gwilym. Again, not a single poem of Eluned's appeared in that collection, even though she had won two crowns and made history by being the only female poet to have done so in the twentieth century. If *'Corlannau'* did not fit the bill – and it was a complex referenced poem – why could *'Clymau'* not have been included, having received such plaudits and having recorded the story of one of the most futile wars in history?

The Foreword states:

> Welsh twentieth-century poetry is criticised frequently for failing
> to react to the present-day situations facing society. This anthology
> shows that this is untrue. The poets have written about the effects
> of the century's great events – the First World War, the Depression
> in the thirties, the Second World War, the national resurgence in
> the sixties and the general crisis of civilisation. These things caused
> the vast majority of them to return to their roots as Welsh people
> and back to the canons of the Christian Faith.[19]

Be that as it may about the 'canons of the Christian Faith', wouldn't
a poem or an excerpt of *'Clymau'* about the lunacy of the Falklands
war, a few years before the anthology's publication, have been
eligible, and extremely contemporary? Once again, what
explanation can there be for the fact that Eluned's work was not
included? Could it be that it was the poet herself who was the
stumbling-block?

Since Eluned was excluded from the book, it is very strange to
see her contemporaries, born in the same year, being included: D.
Gwyn Evans, 1914; J. Arnold Jones, 1914; John Penry Jones, 1914;
D. Tecwyn Lloyd, 1914; W. R. Nicholas, 1914. I dare not say that
these poets did not deserve their place, but how could it be possible
to justify omitting a poet like Eluned, who succeeded in working
within the bardic structures? I remember feeling a pang of
disappointment that I was not included in the anthology. I had
four volumes of poetry under my belt at that point, but I realise
how foolish that was considering the massive absence of somebody
like Eluned, who had in winning two crowns achieved a bigger feat
than I had. I was not shrewd enough at the time to see or to
understand quite how much of a disservice this was to her. These

---

[19] Gwynn ap Gwilym, Alan Llwyd (eds) *Blodeugerdd o Farddoniaeth Gymraeg yr
Ugeinfed Ganrif* (Cyhoeddiadau Barddas, 1987) p. xlvii.

poets – her contemporaries – only have a few *englynion* in the anthology, so perhaps there was no room to include even an excerpt of her work. Yet D. Tecwyn Lloyd has two poems in the collection, one in *vers libre*: his winning poem from the Maldwyn Eisteddfod in 1981.

I have already demonstrated the way that humour was used occasionally as a way of disparaging someone, with the example of 'a straighter than straight poker-face', and it happened again at Eluned's funeral. The eulogy was given by the late former Archdruid and bard, Dic Jones, who praised her work and her personality. There to assist him was the Archdruid T. James Jones. In his autobiography, *Jim Parc Nest*,[20] Jim tells the story of seeing the coffin being carried, and placed upon it were the two crowns.

Dic made a comment to Jim that he was glad that she did not win a Chair! An innocent enough joke between two friends to break the sadness of the event. But a tasteless story to note in an autobiography. Nevertheless, one remembers how Eluned was treated by the Establishment and the doubts of others that plagued her when she won those crowns. Yet the image is poignant. Against all ridicule, even at her funeral, the two objects that proved that she was indeed a poet, were emphasised and recognised. There is little doubt that she paid a high price for winning the crowns. It should also have been announced in eisteddfod style, 'Is there peace?' So that the crowd could answer: 'Yes, peace at last, for Eluned's good name!'

There is one last comment that summarises, if not crowns, the kinds of insulting comments made in a jovial way, be it derisive laughter or tongue in cheek. It is made by Rhydwen Williams in an article in the magazine *Barn* under the title *'Gorau Barn, Gorau Chwedl'* ('The Best Opinion, the Best Story') in September 1983 following the Eisteddfod: 'It was strange to see the crowned poet, a small frail woman, extremely modest-looking, walking the Eisteddfod field between half a dozen muscular policemen, with

---

[20] T. James Jones, *Jim Parc Nest* (Cyhoeddiadau Barddas, 2014) p. 58–9.

her crown firmly in the fist of one of them. Is there no end to the lengths certain creatures will go to get their hands on a crown?' It is possible to read this last comment in various ways. The image of the policemen helping and protecting Eluned as she walks from the field is a colourful one, but one can read the last comment about the policeman as a wily one. Indeed, the comment itself is a ruse and the rhetorical question loaded: 'a small, frail woman'. Once again, it is extremely presumptuous to describe Eluned as 'frail'. 'Tough' would have been closer to the truth. I shy away from being too critical of Rhydwen as he stands up for her to an extent later in the same piece:

> But as happens every time without fail, the poet and the judges promptly come under fire. We read about the meeting in the Literature Tent where Eluned was reproached for failing to answer satisfactorily some questions pertaining to the *pryddest*. No one who is human should be surprised by this. The surprise is that we would think that anybody could be quizzed and interrogated in the heat of such an exciting hour in their lives. We have an obsession with pulling things apart, dissecting things instead of accepting something as it is and being willing to sit back and enjoy it.

And so, here I must confess also, because I threw a similar allegation at her as did others in the closing lines of my review of her poem in *Y Faner*, 26 August, 1983:

> In conclusion, I cannot but turn back to the poet. To the power of her poem. I wonder at the fact that she has kept the sum of her work for the purpose of competition. Eluned Phillips is not typical of the women who write in Wales today. And yet it is she who is crowned.
>
> She would be doing us a good turn therefore if we were to see more of her work in the near future...

At the time that I wrote these lines, I was also aware of the literati and the chattering classes' opinion and their doubts about her work's authenticity. I am ashamed that I should have made such a comment. The lack of sincerity from her detractors was one of the constants that Eluned had to fight against throughout her life, yet she did this in a quiet and candid way. This was true to the nature of her personality. Jon Meirion Jones states in a tribute to her after her death, under the title of *'Y Ddau Felyn mewn un Wy: Sylwadau ar Fywyd a Gwaith Eluned Phillips'* ('Two Yolks in One Egg: Comments on the Life and Work of Eluned Phillips'):

> She admitted to me that she was suspicious of taking part in an interview and of talking into a recording machine microphone. Her 'unofficial' words (off-the-record) were used in the context of her many escapades that caused her much embarrassment from time to time, as the gentlemen of the press had quoted her out of context. She was scammed on several occasions by the press, as they took advantage of a woman and gave assurances that these were not comments to be used publicly. Suspicion continued to be a feature of her relationship with the press generally throughout her life. And yet she was very willing to turn things to her own advantage occasionally.
>
> After the experience of sharing two-and-a-half hours in her company and receiving a warm and courteous welcome, I promised that I would show her the final copy before submitting it. I received a phone call from her congratulating me about the accuracy of my recollections and the fairness of my comments regarding her motives and vision: 'You are one of the rare ones who have quoted me correctly. The people of the press are bastards!'

To be fair to the press, they were only going after the trail of a red fox or, in this case, the redheaded poetess... And they were trying to capture all the bile that had been directed towards her. But, as she had been charged by her grandmother, 'If ever you're cornered, don't back down, stand your ground.' She did have to stand her ground many times, including standing twice to the short-lived ovation of the bardic world. Then she was given a haven and an escape to America at a time when she became totally exhausted by being torn apart in Wales.

Without realising it, I gave Eluned another chance to show the narrow bardic world what kind of reception she was getting outside Wales. In a satirical article in the 226 issue of *Barddas* in 1996, *'Beirdd y Tafodau Fforchog'* ('The Bards with Forked Tongues'), I asked a question that had vexed me about the dangers of composing in English. The reason for my angst was that my first volume of poetry in translation, *Eucalyptus*, had just appeared with Gwasg Gomer in 1995. It came into being in the wake of receiving many invitations to read my work in other countries and I saw that this development could lead in due course to writing in the two languages of Welsh and English. This, to me, was a stumbling-block that could damage the Welsh language in the long run. My fears were unfounded given the arrival of the younger generation who received a bilingual education and who would be able to write fluently in both languages. But, at the time, adhering to my mother tongue was a part of my desire and my mission; Welsh was the only language of my imagination and vision.

The editor, Alan Llwyd, asked several authors for their reaction to the challenging questions that I had asked, wanting to stir things up a little. Three questions were posed to several people, including Eluned Phillips:

Many of the Society's members had expressed an opinion on the matter and had discussed subjects like this:

Does this latest shift prove that we are at a linguistic crossroads and that Wales' poets have started to turn towards English?

Are Wales' poets turning towards English because of a lack of audience generally, like the Gaelic poets in Scotland?

Is translating from Welsh into English a good thing?

And the responses were interesting. 'A stain upon my teeth,' was Emyr Hywel's response, quoting Saunders Lewis' comment about the translations of his own plays. 'It is the privilege of the Welsh poet to be communicating with his people,' was Gwynn ap Gwilym's reply, giving a sideswipe to some Welsh authors who had been seen on English programmes! 'The second language can undermine the mother tongue,' was W. J. Arwyn Evans' response. W. R. P. George thought that it was 'A natural development to be welcomed.' Alan Pinch believed that there was 'No support for the poets of Wales.' But the best reply was given by Eluned Phillips because she chose to write from personal experience about the welcome and the chances she received through her use of the English language.

Indeed, it is a revealing essay on this subject. And I include it here in the knowledge that I instigated her response and I'm glad that I gave her a golden opportunity to kick back at the small narrow world that excluded her throughout her life:

I think very highly of Menna Elfyn, but I must disagree with her viewpoint that there is a danger in writing poetry in English. In my opinion, the biggest peril for poetry in Welsh is parochialism, and the over-production of the sheer amount of poetry in Welsh, like a sausage factory. I feel like shouting 'Hurrah' when I see young poets of the calibre of Gwyneth Lewis, Einir Jones, Huw Jones and the like writing bilingually... The poems in English will reach a wider audience and through doing so will focus more attention on the Welsh language. Ostriches must take their heads out of the sand sometimes if they are to continue to live.

Maybe this is the main reason why the keen-eyed Scot writes in both languages frequently – because he is drawing attention to Gaelic in the long-run? I shouldn't wonder. We also need to use every tool available in Wales to broaden horizons.

I had years more distrust of translation than Gerallt Jones had at one time. That it was some kind of rehash – even though that could be pleasing according to some. But having been given an invitation to discuss Welsh-language poetry outside Wales, at the Purcell Hall, London, under the auspices of the Arts Council of India, or across America, and on the radio there, or indeed in Wales where the audience is often three-quarters monolingual English, I realised that translating from Welsh into English was not only beneficial but totally essential if we are to be noticed and if we are have an intelligent discussion. I am also convinced by now that self-translation is a bonus, as it is the poet who best knows about the impetus that drew him to write the original. I come out of these sessions feeling stronger, prouder and more confident that poetry in Welsh will survive any experimentation. Without the translations of works by poets from Germany, Russia, China and other countries, I, and others like me, would be as lifeless as an anorexic mouse. I have a question – was it wise to translate the Jewish Psalms into other languages, Welsh being among them?

This last comment shows how Eluned, in her casual way, could introduce an argument and win it. But what we also get in her response is her chance to undermine the questions. Having started out in a courteous praiseworthy manner, she shows the *Barddas* literary audience how her mind was changed by being able to read outside Wales and to see her work in a new light with an audience that knew nothing about the haranguing she received from several directions. And I delight in the one sentence in particular, that says of reading her work in translation, 'I come out of these sessions feeling stronger, prouder and more confident that poetry in Welsh will survive any experimentation.' But in reality it is she who feels better, because her self-image is stronger, having been treated with respect and admiration.

I smile when I think I engendered this response and now I would concur with her and admire her for pioneering and for standing her ground, as mentioned in this piece. More than that, she showed the literary bards that she was being appreciated for her poetry.

202

I have searched diligently for writings on her work, or even for essays on her as a poet. But apart from whimsical stories about meeting some of the most famous artists of the twentieth century, there is scant discussion of her work. In the September 1983 issue of *Barn*, a few weeks after she had won the Crown at the National Eisteddfod in Anglesey, 1983, Rhydwen Williams in his editorial column notes the following when referring to the Eisteddfod:

> We take this opportunity to congratulate some of our friends: the brothers from Pen-y-ffordd, Einion and Tudor Wilson Evans on their great achievement in the Anglesey Eisteddfod and for such notable works from the two. Stuart Burrows for his concert held on the stage that is closest to his heart; Dr Terry James for returning and taking his place in our midst once again; Dr Kate Roberts for the tribute given to her, and Kyffin Williams for his exceptional portrait of her, Manon Rhys for many reasons; David Bowen George for being appointed the solicitor for the Union of Welsh Independents; Hywel Teifi Edwards for his accomplished lecture on Llew Llwyfo; and our literary friend, Elerydd, the Reverend W. J. Gruffydd, for being appointed the Archdruid of the Gorsedd of Bards and for resolving to inject humour into the life of the Eisteddfod's Gorsedd and into the nation.

Friends were mentioned; feats were talked about. Two brothers congratulated: one, Einion Evans, for winning the Chair and the other, T. Wilson Evans, winning the Literature Medal. But as for the winner of the Crown, there was not one mention of her. Once again, she was excommunicated from the inner circle; not a single word was said about Eluned Phillips' feat. She was omitted from the list in a similar way to the day when she won her first crown in 1967. Why?

It must have disappointed her to be left out, since she noted her admiration of Rhydwen Williams' work and his *pryddest* 'Ffynhonnau' ('The Wells') as the kind of poetry she endeavoured

203

to write herself. She called herself an 'absolute optimist'. Was this comment, made several times, an attempt at being hopeful, in spite of everything and everybody? Was she trying to lift her spirits above disappointment and to live out her grandmother's comment that she should stand her ground and not back down?

And how strange – yet perhaps it is not so strange – that her lonely pilgrimage would have therefore been an independent one and that Eluned should have retreated from view apart from enjoying the company of those who believed in her ability and in her sincerity as a poet. She admits in her notes her complex thoughts:

> I would stay awake to write for some Eisteddfod or other. It was not possible to do it earlier. The thrill did not happen until the eleventh hour. The same is true today. Writing is a night of wild pain, even though the subject, possibly, had been churning in my subconscious for a long time, until possibly, the taste has soured ... Strangely, this did not happen when I wrote series and stories in English ... I have never been able to reason with myself about the difference. Perhaps I feel that the writing in Welsh is a bit of an Eisteddfod hobby.

Did the taste of writing in Welsh turn sour before the end of her days? If it did, who could blame her for she was, after all, castigated publicly. She got a second chance in America, but in a sad comment made at the end of her life, she reflects on herself and her sister, Madge:

> Today Madge is married to an Englishman, and lives in Staffordshire; she preaches in English, and rarely hears Welsh. I am back in Wales, having been conditioned by England's education to think in English first and then translate my thoughts into Welsh and even though the old country has bewitched me totally, I find it difficult to write in Welsh because of my early exile over Offa's Dyke.

Was it really the considerable time she spent over the border that made it more difficult for her to write in Welsh, or could it have been that the wind was taken from her sails? Was it the lack of motivation? She could not under the rules of the Eisteddfod compete again for the Crown, having won it twice. Did that fact silence her desire to write in Welsh? Or did she feel closer to England and America towards the end of her life? Whatever the truth of the matter, Eluned held her ground and sat in the front row of the Gorsedd year after year, and showed that a cheerful countenance trumped bitterness, and that graciousness can beat jealousy. Nevertheless, her enjoyment of the Eisteddfod per se did not cease, as she says in an unpublished essay, under the title *Eisteddfod y Wladfa* (*The Patagonian Eisteddfod*). It starts like this:

'That girl would go to the ends of the earth in order to go to an Eisteddfod.' How many times did I hear Mam trying to explain my rush in trying to catch some Eisteddfod or other. Of course, I'm pretty certain that Mam's version of 'the ends of the earth' would have been somewhere in Wales. Well, I had to admit that I was a fervent Eisteddfod-goer from the first moment I blurted out a four-line poem on a stage when I was two and a half, apparently. It is half a century since I missed my last National Eisteddfod, and by now I have been given the honour of representing the Gorsedd in Scotland, Ireland, Brittany and Cornwall. These were integral experiences that colour my memories ... the 'Fiddlers' rally in Motherwell; the bubbling conversation of the man in the flea-market in Glasgow; the old woman in Dublin giving a rendition of folk music as if it was straight out of Celtic times. My memories are brimful of Eisteddfod treasures. And now I have one more Eisteddfod to be given a prominent place on my treasure-shelf. Little did Mam think that I would travel outside Wales and that I would literally be in an Eisteddfod at the end of the earth ... eight thousand miles and more from little Wales, in the Eisteddfod in Patagonia.

If she was a lonely pilgrim in Wales one gets the impression that she enjoyed visiting Patagonia, and that she was appreciated there as a poet of note. She had a new lease of life and was given the opportunity to greet the eisteddfod there with these lovely verses:

Patagonia
(greetings on her visit in 1988)
A childhood fairy tale – you embraced
The sun on a flower;
And the passion, a fever,
My thirst for stories forever.

Following the frisson of arriving – a desolate place
And a wild desert looming,
To live through a sea not expecting
A Patagonia made of husks – and nothing.

We wide-eyed today's gazers – see the vastness
Of nature's colours;
Was it the tears of the pioneers
Who irrigated the green pastures?

How proud the kin of their homeland – they treasure
The memory of the landing;
Through the boldness of believing
The harvests that those seeds would bring.

This is such a beautiful poem about Patagonia, serious and yet exultant. It is also the exact form used in her long poem *'Clymau'*, which proves the fact that she enjoyed rhyming in epigrammatic form and that she could easily create a mood and beauty within this form. One senses too that 'praise' is one of the constant themes that inspires her, as a local poet or as a poet whose sights are set far beyond Wales.

John Adams from Cwmbrân came to record her reading twenty-eight of her poems. Once again this was a non-Welsh-speaker taking an interest in her achievements as a poet. But Eluned laughs at herself saying that the sound in the recording makes her sound as if she was sitting in Dan yr Ogof caves, where the stalactites hang like tongues. Again, her imagination comes to the fore in explaining why the recording is less than clear. Unfortunately, it was not possible to find those tapes even though I found several tapes of her talking privately with others. But as she talks about the recording experience, she admits something else about her doubt regarding the quality of her compostitions:

> Surprisingly, those select persons who have listened to the effort have responded with enthusiasm, clamouring for more. I may just agree to that, if time permits. It really was a boost. I have never been good at discussing poetry publicly, having always thought that prayer and poems are personal and private.

And here is another reason for her exile from literature discussion programmes: she felt inadequate when she tried to explain her writing. After all, who can explain a prayer? Isn't that something that happens between a person and some external power? Eluned understood this and kept her poetic door under lock and key once again. Even though she closes by saying, 'such responses, along with my commitment to working bilingually in America, have given me such joy'. This shows that Eluned found a totally new and welcoming reception on her lonely pilgrimage in a place as far away as the west coast of America. Before the end of her days she was drawn to a new family on the other side of the world.

I should like to share a poem seen in a file of poems left by her. The poem is pure satire but also reinforces the fact that the form of the *englyn* without *cynghanedd* she adopted suited her. She made it her own and no other poet as yet has adopted a similar style. Intriguingly, the title of the poem is 'Gorseddgawl' ('Gorsedd Soup/Mess'):

The great critics believed fully
That my poems were dense and misty,
Turned to Betjeman for some balming
And me on a job that is worthy.

I marched from the darkness- wrote
simply to seek blessedness;
In a world of fair play for poets' muse
I'd have help to lift me from the floor – unaccused.

On her throne was our Lizzy; and Maggie
An uncompromising lady;
Isn't it somehow a pity
That I wasn't made laureate from Cymru?

But no it was Ted Hughes who could boast
A long poem at his baptism
Him, Chief Poet of her royalty
And his poems more difficult than mine/me.

There's no fairness for women poets – it's the men
Who've led the way through the ages,
Shoving me with the relics, to spool
In a far corner with my knitting wool.

In the poem, Eluned turns to satire as a powerful tool, berating male poets. As she says: 'There is no fairness for poetesses.' She shared her fears once with a neighbour that the press was hounding her whenever it was time to elect a new Archdruid and the question thrown at her – would she accept the challenge? 'A woman will be Archdruid one day, but I'm too old now to consider it … perhaps if I were younger.' It is unlikely that she would have succeeded had she been nominated; indeed, the likelihood is that she would have been the subject of jokes and tittle-tattle once again and not only from the Gorsedd Circle but from an even smaller circle. In the 1984 issue of *Lol*, there is a picture of Eluned on the Eisteddfod stage with the crown on her head and above her the words, 'Behind every great poet there's another great poet ...' – an acerbic comment indeed when one remembers that the comment was used to refer to wives who supported their husbands.

But there seems to have been a shift in the bardic world too, and I am confident that she would have delighted in seeing Christine James as Archdruid, a woman being exalted to high office. It is regrettable that the opportunity was lost for a female Archdruid to recognise Eluned's contribution to the Eisteddfod and the Gorsedd from the National Eisteddfod stage during the centenary of her birth in 2014. This was surely a further sign of her absence from the Establishment that she served so honourably for seventy years. But since she was scarcely noticed during her lifetime why should she be remembered after leaving this world? How different it was for that poet from Swansea, Dylan Thomas, who was the same age as her, to the day, and who was given extraordinary attention for his centenary celebrations. Her centenary passed by without a murmur, confirming her insignificance for the last time.

This truly was a lonely pilgrimage. It is strange to compare the difference with the justified celebrations that happened when Mererid Hopwood won the Chair in 2001, thereby achieving a significant historical feat. How different it was when Eluned won her first crown, and even her second, continuing the suspicion that dogged her throughout her life. The millennium brought with it a new age, and an awareness of women's status in our society. Eluned says this about the ceremonies in the Eisteddfod:

A few women have complained to me that everything in the bardic ceremonies leans towards the men – even the song to greet the Crowned poet that was composed last year. I have never worried about this, neither have I felt inferior to the men. Even so, I admit that the poets' view of women who dare to compete is chauvinistic.

There is an element of contradiction in these words, even if Eluned was not one to struggle against tradition. Rather, she tried her best to conform – even if her closing comments suggest an alternative viewpoint. Surely, the word 'chauvinistic' indicates politically unaware thinking and stereotypical phraseology and is a word that feminists denounce as it is loaded with empty emotions.

Even though she was included in the *Cydymaith i Lenyddiaeth Cymru* (*Companion to the Literature of Wales*), the attention given to her is scant. There is a note in the *Gwyddoniadur* (*The Welsh Encyclopedia*) when referring to the connections between Wales and Patagonia and to the futility of wars in the eyes of many: 'Eluned Phillips (b. 1915) [*sic*] expresses feelings like these in *"Clymau"*, the long poem that won her the National Eisteddfod crown in 1983; the people who remember her poetry are few and far between.'

When I told some people that I was working on this book, the reactions were interesting: 'She was the one who had a fling with Dewi Emrys'; 'Dewi Emrys wrote her poetry, didn't he?'; 'Picasso's mistress'; 'Wasn't she with Cynan, am I right now?' Or, 'Edith Piaf's best friend'.

'They've called me a lot of things,' said Eluned on tape with David Fielding, the editor of *Carmarthenshire Life*, who wrote several articles about her. 'Even been called a lesbian!' She can be heard laughing uproariously at such an insinuation.

Eluned was an unconventional person in every aspect of her life, which gave a false impression of her. She dressed differently. According to one of her friends, she cultivated an airhead image of herself, and suggested for the cover of *The Reluctant Redhead*: 'What about me wearing leathers and on a motor bike?' In the end, it was one of the ugliest covers ever created – a picture of a mirror with some necklaces hanging on it and a bottle of perfume close by – the antithesis of the likeable, daring image that most people associated with her. It is a picture of some kind of small, dull room, like a bordello somewhere, and is not compatible with this woman who lived a carefree but decent life.

This is a poem typed by her but not published, which was her reaction to the prejudice against her – once again she uses the *englyn* without *cynghanedd* as her form:

Them
Mockery not satire is rampant
in our small island;
critics like a defiled machine
spreading dung everywhere.

Losers, not learning how to lose,
insist on hitting unrelenting;
sick patients without medicine
like snakes spitting venom.

The strange learned ones – masters
on every small matter.
They seem to know all the answers
and everyone's secrets.

Ego scratching ego – a group
with a group conspiring;
and their prey – fleeing
for safety to a door – unlocked.

A lonely pilgrimage? The reason behind the writing of this book was to ensure that Eluned's name is not forgotten and her work left out of the canon of twentieth-century Welsh literature. My wish was for her not to be one of the disappeared in the literary world, until some other writer 'discovers' her work in decades to come. To unearth her innovative writing about striking subjects in another era would be a travesty. Yet, at times, I found it difficult to carry on with this book without feeling some dismay, and compunction at the way she was overlooked. But she would not have wished me to view her as a victim. She fought her corner in her congenial way and was accepted by an eager and supportive audience, across the pond at least.

After Eluned's lukewarm reception in Wales, a new dawn arrived with Mererid Hopwood winning her place in the National Eisteddfod. It is fitting that this chapter should close therefore with a warmhearted *englyn* written by Mererid for the remembrance garden to Eluned in Cenarth.

Eluned gave light – a melody
Gave sun as company,
Gave magic mischievously,
A golden smile sang with glee.

The Librettist

Despite her having won the Crown for the second time in the Anglesey National Eisteddfod in 1983, not much of Eluned's poetic work was published other than when she accepted the occasional invitation to contribute a poem – for example 'Y Llygoden' ('The Mouse'), written for the anthology *Cerddi'r Troad: Barddoniaeth Newyddi'r Mileniwm* (*Poems of the Turning: New Poetry for the Millennium*), edited by Dafydd Rowlands, and published by Gomer in 2000. But it is misleading to believe that she gave up writing and working with words, and it is possible that she wrote her richest work in the last decades of her life, work that hasn't yet been fully appreciated. After all, 'composing' is multi-faceted and within the word is the musical element that is key to our historical understanding of Welsh poetry. This is the kind of composing that Eluned relished in her final years, when she enjoyed writing libretti.

The composer, Michael J. Lewis, asked her to write the words for some of his compositions, her first foray into 'composing', creating a partnership that flourished for several years. Michael J. Lewis hails from Aberystwyth and as well as a composer he was once the conductor of the Welsh Choir of South California in Los Angeles. Among his compositions are the scores for films such as *Julius Caesar* (with John Gielgud), *The Madwoman of Chaillot* (with Katharine Hepburn and Danny Kaye) and *The Medusa Touch* (with Richard Burton). He sent Eluned a tape of his work in 1997, but because of two serious road accidents she could not reply to him at the time. Later, she met him in person when she visited America.

Following their meeting, Michael Lewis wrote the music for 'Llwyd Bach y Baw' ('Little Sparrow'). That was followed by music for a song called 'True Love'. Eluned loved the fact that this song was a favourite with some people for weddings and similar occasions. There was also a Welsh-language version under the title 'Cariad Pur'. Eluned worked with gusto, and when Michael called it would usually be a last-minute commission that would mean Eluned would have to catch the bus to Cardigan to her friend Jackie's hair salon in order to send a fax to the composer. This was in the days before email and electronic attachments. Here is an example of her ability to compose poetry in English:

True Love
Our life's a map of varied shades,
of sun and clouds and nights of fears.
And trees shed leaves like crying babes.
True Love will wipe away our tears.
We sow and reap and get our dues
in black and white and colours bright.
When life is low and spirits bruise,
True Love will set the balance right.
When hail of winters chill the air
and songs of birds no longer thrill.
And dreams are nightmares and claws tear,
True Love shall conquer with God's will.

Did the new medium give her the impetus to pour out her emotions in a way that did not happen in her Welsh poetry, apart from the praise poems to relations and occasionally in *'Clymau'*? Another of her songs has a nostalgic tone. Could it be that she was thinking of the love that was not to be between herself and Per when writing such a deeply personal poem as *'Rhamant Dau'*?

Young Love or Romantic Tryst
Walking on the banks of Rheidol,
ever keeping lovers' trysts,
drinking wine with lips of passion,
the sun kissing clear the mists.

Listening to the pebbles' motions,
love of two hearts to be won,
little stream to be ocean –
my dearest one.

Seeing needles on the blackthorn
on the bank, a fair display,
watching our two hearts imploring
to be one in love, one day.

In our arms in nights of dreaming
faces in the pool, we spy,
as we float on life's love river
the moon's ballet smiling high.

Walking on the banks of Rheidol
two hearts one, forever more,
the sky rainbowing a pattern
of our paradise in store.

Listening to the pebbles' motions,
love of two hearts having won.
Our stream now and ocean –
my darling one.

Another libretto written at Michael J. Lewis' request was 'Cenarth',
sung by the Welsh Choir of South California at various events in
California and beyond. However, it was a thrill for her to hear the

choir perform in the Methodist chapel in Cenarth, with the local tenor Washington James entertaining the Californians with a specially-written aria. This event was organised by Eluned when the choir was on tour in Wales:

Cenarth
Creator through time
of all things sublime,
his true caring ways
enhancing our days.

God's faith we adore
and praise evermore;
let's sing in accord
our thanks to our Lord.

We'll all voice our love
to Heaven above,
again and again
a glorious refrain.

Hearts afire, we sing
Hosanna our King.
Hosanna to Heaven,
Amen and Amen.

Eluned's work wasn't just admired by the choir from California. The South Wales Male Voice Choir was also enthusiastic in its appreciation of some of her songs and included her work as part of concert *repertoires*. What is interesting is that during the last twenty years of her life she continued to write lyrics to be sung, as if she trusted the power of the libretto more than that of a lyrical poem. It gave her joy to collaborate with an eminent composer and see the work performed on stage or with an accompanying orchestra.

In her collection of unpublished works, there is a treasure-trove of material showing the essential attributes of a librettist at work: the talents of a playwright, her lyrical use of language, her ability to create a scene along with colourful characters.

I mentioned that radio, television and stage directors – apart from one director friend – missed the chance to use this marvellously rich work written by a poet of note. It is our loss that we failed to take advantage of her brilliance. She wrote libretti until her death in 2009.

Her first publication, originally written when she was twelve years old, was later published by Gomer Press as *Caneuon i Blant* (*Songs for Children*); the music by Pencerddes Emlyn (The 'Musician of Emlyn'), words by Luned Teifi (Eluned's bardic name). It was published in 1936, the same year that Eluned, at twenty-two, was accepted into the Gorsedd of Bards, using words she had written when she was being given piano lessons from the Pencerddes[21]. This was the beginning of Eluned's musical career which blossomed through the kindness of Rita Evans, Pencerddes Emlyn. The songs have simple words, as they were intended to be used daily in schools.

Yr Hydref (Autumn)

Autumn comes full of hustle and bustle
Collecting fruit with busy hands
That he hides from winter's sights
Safe in his barns, the harvest of the lands.

The farmer, see him tirelessly working
In his fields of corn nearby;
He has golden crops aplenty
To use in winter by and by.

---

[21] Pencerddes = female musician

The way she was bewitched by words is evident in the way she used them, even in these simple verses created when she was twelve years old. The desire to learn the piano and buy a guitar was also a sign that Eluned leant towards music. How strange that six decades should pass before she reconnected with her talent to create words to be sung. In turning towards libretti, Eluned showed a desire to immerse herself in another artistic style, to develop new forms of writing. Dana Gioia, the poet and author from America, in an interview with Lequita Vance-Watkins in *Acumen*, September 1999 says:

> In Shakespeare's time, poets took for granted that they could work in all three basic forms – the lyric, narrative and drama. But nowadays poets are supposed to settle down and just write short lyric utterances. I want to try the larger forms of poetry that are now mostly neglected – the narrative and dramatic forms. There are some things a writer can only do in drama
>
> ... opera allows a writer to explore all sorts of material that doesn't easily work in other forms.

This interview might also encapsulate Eluned's feelings. When referring to the difference between a libretto and a poem, the collaborative nature of the work is emphasised. A libretto is not intended to stand on its own literary merits; rather it should exist to inspire a composer to create a powerful musical drama. This highlights again the fact that Eluned was more comfortable with commissions of all sorts than submitting work unsolicited. That, as well as the fact that others acknowledged and appreciated the worth of her words.

Certainly she benefitted from the opportunity opened up by those who were not a part of the Welsh world. After all, wasn't Eluned a member of a multicultural world, given that she had escaped to London and then to Paris? And here she was, in her eighties, besotted by the wide horizons of America and being given the honour of promulgating her love of the Welsh language and of

Welsh culture. Now she was being honoured by the descendants of Wales who felt a longing for the old country. Perhaps she longed for the vibrant extended family that she came from and the kind of Welsh community that was the essence of her upbringing? By this time she was travelling to the USA four times a year, each visit lasting a month. Perhaps it made her heart ache to see rural life at home and the community she loved disintegrating?

Indeed, she could easily have embarked on a new career as a librettist in Wales; she could write in English just as well as in Welsh, a talent that not many Welsh-language poets at that time possessed. Her work was appreciated by one of the most successful choirs in Wales, the South Wales Male Voice Choir. It is worth noting that many members of the choir were not Welsh speakers, nevertheless here we see Eluned again being appreciated and seen as a queen in their midst. One of the most astounding experiences of her life was to sit in the Royal Box at the Albert Hall and listen to her words being sung by the choir. She pretended that the experience had been unique for her, but according to her friend, Trixie, her companion at the concert, 'she was quite used to such royal treatment!'

Being acknowledged and praised obviously meant a lot to Eluned, particularly by those fellow artists appreciative of her talents. Even in the autumn of her years, she had plans and aspirations to see her work being accepted by a composer and performed on stage. She sent a libretto about the historical character, Nest, to the choir's secretary. In her letter she says:

Dear Phil,

I am sending you *Nest* which was an impudent impromptu suggestion on my part but I always value your reactions. If you can find time to read it through I would really like to know if you think it would be of interest as a Musical. I have never written one, but have always wanted to, so I have no judgment.

The theme was 'True Love'. It started because a Los Angeles Director came to one of Michael's concerts, heard 'True Love' being sung and approached Michael and myself with a suggestion that we should write a musical. I had always intended to write up my childhood fairy Princess Nest so tried to combine both. It's a very first draft, composed on to the computer without a break, so of course, will need a lot of adjustment … It just occurred to me that the new Millennium Centre in Cardiff would be ideal for a Princess of Wales production.

It was meant for Broadway New York, but Sept 11th has rather damped that idea.

Now that you are a man of leisure, I wish you would start an Agency for Musicians, Writers, etc … It is very much needed and you would be ideal, for you know and have an easy way with a varied number of media people etc. Just a thought – but I for one would be delighted if you would consider it.

Please don't hesitate to tell me that poor Nest is rubbish – I would welcome the truth.

Eluned

At the bottom of the letter there is a rushed handwritten note stating that she is in a hurry to get to a dentist's appointment, thus combining the 'business' element with her busy daily life. Another feature seen throughout the correspondence between Eluned and friends is her haste and last minute rush for everything. There was no pausing or wondering about things; such introspection was not a part of her personality.

The letter is revealing in that it demonstrates that she is an author eager to succeed despite her self-effacement. Note her way of adding caveats: it is the first draft, that she had composed it straight through without a revision, the realisation that there would have to be some changes and adaptation, as well as the warning to be honest and the request to say outright whether it was worthless. On the other hand, the fact that she had written it in the first place, in her late eighties, shows extraordinary determination and energy. There was no stopping her either from dreaming that it might be suitable for

Broadway or for the opening of the Millennium Centre in Cardiff. Once again, I feel a little sad on her behalf, as I was commissioned to write the words to Karl Jenkins' music for the opening of the Millennium Centre. Again, an opportunity was missed to acknowledge Eluned and to give her recognition of another kind.

Here is a little of her musical drama *Nest*, and the words from the first page of the opening scene. The whole of the work comprises 72 pages, but the style and tone of the story can be heard in the voice of the Druid who tells the story and events intermittently through the drama:

Blind Barac, in Druid robes, peeps around the corner of the Curtain, hands uplifted in sympathy with the plight of the young couple, and shaking his head, mutters

Barac:
The paths along the road of love
are seldom without rubble;

and our Princesses of Wales
are seldom without trouble.

Barac shakes off his mood and comes centre Stage in front of the Curtain.

Barac:
I'm blind Barac, bard and soothsayer
to the family of Rhys ap Tewdwr,

the Prince who rules his kingdom Dyfed
from his Castle at Dinefwr,

in the country known as Wales
but to the native Welsh as Cymru.

So sit in comfort and listen to the story.

We bards are littered throughout Wales –
some call us scandalmongers.

We aim to bring you vibrant tales
to satisfy all hungers.
So,
climb with us the mountains,
walk the dales

and maybe you will understand
a little more about our Wales –
the country next to England.

Today (tonight) it is the story
of Nest, Princess of Wales –
a Cleopatra of her race.

Embracing, brave, intelligent, beautiful and ...
alright, alright, if you insist. I'll say it ...
beautiful and ... seductive ...

but always in true love with Owain
and her country,

with a burning wish to free it from
the Normans.

But the in-fighting of her kith and kin,
who, instead of slaughtering the enemy,
still slaughter one another,

thus taking centuries, if ever, to win ...

As ever, the paths of love and war are never smooth and easy. So, why not stay around until the end of this near true story and find if true love does exist and ever ends in glory?

CURTAIN.

Another unpublished work that was never performed publicly as an oratorio was 'Moliant i Ddewi Sant' ('A Song of Praise to Saint David'). Once again, the work shows her amazing ability to understand the structure and technique required for an oratorio with a large cast of characters. There are Angels, a Chorus, Patrick, Saint David, Non, the Voice, Voices, Satan, Blind Paul, the Choir, and even a Dove. I experienced an unusual thrill reading it. Here is a brief extract of the work, displaying her ability in musical composition. The following words are both timeless and contemporary:

(Appropriate instrumental music leading to Non's solos)

NON
Nine months have gone, the birth is now on me.
I'm like a rudderless ship, blown out to sea.
O,Holy Mary, in my pain give succour,
dark clouds above look down on me in anger.
Envy is all around, and Herod, sadly,
is stomping through our land, his one aim, madly
to murder my baby boy who's known to be
the future Patron Saint to save our country.
My God Almighty, give me a sign to know
that you have forgiven me my fall so low.
You know my willing promise to refrain
from sexual approaches to man again.
I'll live my life on bread and water only,
and sing full praises to you night and daily.
Satan's serpents still lurk in grasses, spitting,

and a storm of thunder is fast approaching.
Long knives of hate threaten the pregnant mother.
Almighty God, let my small son have cover.
I promise Lord, I will repay with goodness.
The miracle of birth is now upon us.
There's evil in the bushes, and all over,
but I salute you, Lord, as my Redeemer.
I crave, dear Lord, for that sign of forgiveness,
and the heavenly peace that comes with your nearness.

(Special effects of thunderstorm)

NON
The sign reached me brightly, a bouquet of beauty.
My heaviness I lay, on a stone by the way.
O, Thank You. O, Thank You, my Lord.
The huge stone split in two, my Lord God, I thank you.
One half showed the marking of pain in birth-giving,
the other a cover to protect the shy mother.
O, Thank You. O,Thank You, my Lord.
And now the baby is born, the pride of Cymru,
and Non they'll remember, and treasure forever.
O, Thank You. O, Thank You, my Lord.
A Church will now flourish, on the site of my anguish.
I Thank You. I Thank You, my Lord.

The use of repetition is a perfect fit to the composer's rhythm.
These may be the longest lines in the work and there are other
sections which have the conciseness of strict-metre poetry. These
extracts were chosen because they convey Eluned's understanding
of motherhood under difficult circumstances and the promise that
Non made to praise God throughout her life. It is right to assume,
in the piece full of the dangers of Satan's snakes, that Eluned truly
felt the words as she identified totally with the experience.

•

But if there is one theme that is constant in Eluned's musical works, it is the 'romantic aspect' in which the pain and the ecstasy of love constantly change places. Was it in these works, where she perfectly fuses music with words, that she too felt the unity of love and disappointment, the light and shade melding together to create a sense of wholeness?

I am confident that the works that have been, thus far, hidden in a box, will be an eye-opener to those who doubt the nature of her abilities. She was able to turn her hand to different genres of writing through sheer perseverance. Yet she longed for friendship and artistic collaboration, eventually finding them in that harmonious partnership with Michael J Lewis. Collaboration invariably means that compromise must be part of a librettist's stock-in-trade, Eluned's personality was such that she was successful in working with others as she had done throughout her time at the BBC, and as part of a family where cooperation was a way of life.

I borrowed Waldo Williams' words 'Merch Perygl' ('Daughter of Danger') as the title for one of my poetry collections, I believe that the sonnet expresses perfectly the way that Eluned was perceived by others.[22] It is fitting therefore to note the words that best describe her and the portrait of her given to me time after time by her friends and family:

> She is the daughter of danger. The wind whips her path,
> Her foot where she loses heart, where she falls, those from the sky below.
> Until now, she has seen her way clearer than the prophets.
> She will be forever young and so full of mischief.

---

[22] Waldo Williams, 'Cymru a Chymraeg', *Dail Pren* (Gwasg Gomer, 1956), p. 100

Friends United

... hold fast to what you have, so that nobody steals your crown.

Revelations 3:11

Eluned dedicated her autobiography, *The Reluctant Redhead*, to three choirs: the Welsh Choir of South California; Llandybïe Ladies' Choir; and the South Wales Male Voice Choir, as well as to her friend Eira Thomas. She must have been proud of her close relationship with these societies. These were the people who showed her respect and felt honoured to travel with her to places far and wide. They were her kindred spirits. She trusted them and shared with them the kind of delightful company that she experienced at home with her family. To an extent, she saw them as her extended family and they looked upon her as a renowned poet and friend, playful and serious in equal measure. One mentioned to me at a remembrance concert in her name that she was the The South Wales Male Voice choir's mascot. She was also vice-president of the same choir, a rare and unusual honour, perhaps, for a woman from rural Wales. She read her work at their concerts and took centre stage at their events.

But the invitations to speak at literary events were few, apart from the occasional ceremony at the National Eisteddfod, or representing the Gorsedd in festivals in other Celtic countries. Sometimes she would be sent an invitation from local cultural societies to read her work. She appeared for the last time, a few years before she died, on a panel of poets who had won the main prizes at the National Eisteddfod at an event at Tŷ Newydd. One of her fellow poets gave a wry smile when he told me about some of the stories with which she regaled her audience. I knew that he was sceptical of how true they were. I did not at that time know myself whether the stories were true or false. Yet I sympathised with Eluned, because she was elderly and a woman, and perhaps therefore seen as unreliable.

In the final years of her life, Eluned perhaps felt a sense of affinity with three groups of people. The first were her neighbours and acquaintances, those born and raised within her own community of Cenarth. They knew her and were aware especially of her family's generosity towards villagers and people who were considered colourful characters. These were her trusted friends, the people who knew her as a delightful, likeable and generous person. Amongst these people were blood relatives, hailing from Aberystwyth to Pembrokeshire, who acknowledged the family ties and who were thankful and proud that I was writing her biography. 'She was so lovely,' was the cry I heard time and again as I spoke to members of her family. Eluned insisted on going to every funeral and every family event. Ann Morgan Evans, a relative from Aberystwyth, said about her: 'She would be extremely happy to know that you were organising her work and life into a book and shining a bright light on such a dear, clever person, who was full of life, modest and also so talented.'

Another group of people that she was drawn to were the ones who got to know her through cultural events: the choirs already mentioned and some members of the media, especially Gareth Rowlands, who made several programmes about and with her. Thirdly, there were those who came to respect her in the last decades of her life when she visited them in America on her extended trips. She would take only a small bag with her to the United States as she had left an entire wardrobe of clothes there, a clear sign that she considered the country a kind of second home. It appears that the US became a much-needed sanctuary for her.

As for the neighbours who were friends, there is real warmth in the way she talks about them in her autobiography – one or the other calling to see her regularly, who were more than willing to go the extra mile for her. Rhiannon Lewis, a music teacher at Ysgol y Preseli until her retirement, was one, along with her husband, Jeff, from Cenarth, who had been the head of the primary school at Newcastle Emlyn; they were close neighbours and called in frequently to see if Eluned was well. Others, like Tim and Hettie Jones, took her to hospital appointments when the need arose. Eluned suffered two serious accidents during her later years and she had to visit hospitals regularly because of the resulting injuries. Monty, the Italian ex-prisoner of war who made his home in Cenarth, was also ready to help; he would faithfully drive Eluned to different places throughout the years.

Andrew Gilbert, a neighbour, was also a willing assistant, doing Eluned a multitude of favours, especially during her last decade when she needed to get to London or Manchester to catch a plane to America. This shows that she built a community around her, many of whom were returning the favours following her generosity towards them over the years. Andrew still remembers Eluned fondly, so much so that he created a Facebook page in her memory, and by so doing, keeping the knowledge of her valuable contribution to Wales and the world alive. Even though she died in 2009, Eluned is remembered through the medium of technology; given her fondness for her computer in the last decade of her life this seems wonderfully appropriate.

Another faithful friend was Jackie Edwards, the owner of a hairdressing salon in Cardigan, who cut and styled Eluned's hair and would also counsel her on many other things. Eluned would ask Jackie frequently to comment on what she was wearing as she was somebody who loved dressing fashionably. Many remembered Eluned's leather bomber-jacket, worn with pride. Jackie remembers how Eluned came to the launch of her memoir *The Reluctant Redhead* in a neat black trouser suit, a brightly coloured scarf slung around her neck, looking like a teenager. Jackie also remembered her asking advice about the type of picture that should be used in conjunction with a record she cut, using her poem 'Cenarth', in

America. She chose a picture of herself in leather gear on the back of a motorbike. According to Eluned, this was the picture that should have gone on the cover, but between Jackie and her daughter Sara they managed to persuade her to use a picture of her with a coracle on her back. It's an iconic picture and shows Eluned in her local habitat with the traditional coracle safely on her shoulders. Perfect.

When I asked Jackie about Eluned, I was asked to sit on the very chair that she had sat on at the hairdressers when she visited. Often she would ask if Jackie was busy and then ask for a seat so that she could rest and do some writing. There she would sit making notes in a book or asking for a piece of scrap paper to write on. I have already mentioned how Get, when cleaning and tidying the house, would move – or worse still – lose the very pieces of paper that Eluned needed. Typically, Eluned would forget the date of her hair appointments and call in on the wrong day. This is another example of her disorganised nature, a trait which might also explain why more of her work was not published during her lifetime.

Her friends from chapel were also important to her. Chapel was the centre of her life in Cenarth and she was a faithful member of Bryn Seion chapel, Pontseli. Every Sunday without fail when she was home, she would be taken by June Gray in the car to chapel, a place of worship that meant the world to her. She was the one who read aloud the hymns to the congregation every Sunday, partly because the minister, the Reverend Dr Wynford Thomas, played the organ as well as delivering the sermon. The minister would have interesting conversations with Eluned and he mentioned that she had a ready laugh. According to another member of the congregation, she came to chapel in her leather jacket, which would squeak every time she stood to announce the hymn. June and Eluned worshipped together, and when there was no morning service, they would go out for Sunday lunch. June remembers once that they saw the minister drive past them, and Eluned exclaimed as she imagined his face having seen them heading for the pub, and then broke into a fit of laughter. Eluned had the utmost respect for the role of the minister and she admired him greatly. This is reflected in her autobiography, as she included pictures of previous ministers like, Herbert Evans, Gwallter Ddu and the minister at the time, the Reverend Dr Wynford Thomas, in her memoir. She shared her philosophy of her life with him, a philosophy that allowed her to look in an enlightened way at life and realise that it is too short to wallow in envy. Today, there is a picture of Eluned hanging in pride of place in the vestry at Bryn Seion.

When I asked one of the younger villagers in Cenarth how he remembered her, his first comment was that she was an 'ordinary woman'. Then, realising that I might misconstrue his comment, he added, 'What I mean is that she didn't have airs and graces, she was just like everybody else.' No airs, perhaps, even though she reached the high ground with her work, but I dare say that she really was not like anybody else either!

Trixie Smith knew her well over the decades and was a companion at Eisteddfodau. She would stay with Eluned for periods of time whenever the need arose. Every Eisteddfod, they would organise a stay at the same hotel and enjoy going to events in the evening: concerts and other entertainment. What made Trixie's company so good was the fact that the two had such fun together, and laughter is a word that many who knew Eluned would use in describing her. Another friend whose company was so valuable to Eluned was Eira Thomas, Telynores Dinefwr (the Dinefwr Harpist) and conductor of the Llandybïe Ladies' Choir. Eira travelled with Eluned as a close friend. The two travelled with the South Wales Male Voice Choir to Canada and other countries, with Eira as the accompanist for the choir. When Eira died suddenly in 2002, Eluned expressed grief at the loss of her company. In a letter to another friend, she says: 'Thank you so much for Eira's philosophy … I came back late last night from America – and hell, the gap is already horrendous … I am finding her absence difficult to accept.'

It appears that losing such a close friend had left a void that could not be filled. It was with Eira that Eluned visited Per for the last time in Santa Monica, and Eira said nothing about Eluned's relationship with him. This surely shows the depth of their friendship.

Phil Howells, a member of the South Wales Male Voice Choir, from Llansadwrn, was the one who received the letter from Eluned about the musical play *Nest*, says: 'Just reading the prologue just makes Eluned come back to life – her sense of fun, touched with a bit of naughtiness (even wickedness perhaps!), in the context of the history of Wales.' He noted that Eluned had walked across Sydney Harbour Bridge when the choir was on tour in Australia – twice!

I received a note from Haydn James from the South Wales Male Voice Choir saying, 'Eluned was a great supporter of the choir and during the five-year period when I was its conductor we shared many a laugh at concerts and on tour.'

Wyn Calvin and his wife Carole said similar things, as they remembered the journeys with Eluned to far-flung places where Eluned would take part in the choir's evenings. They recalled the great fun that came from being in Eluned's company. She would visit them often at their home in Cardiff and whenever she did so, laughter was sure to fill the house.

Sadly, some of her friends in America had died by the time of writing or were too old for me to interview them. But I had enjoyable conversations with many who were in contact with Eluned during the nineties and in the first decade of this century. Dafydd and Olive (Olivia) Evans from Manhattan Beach offered her an open invitation to stay with them. Eluned said of that house that it was 'a place that has become subsequently my second home'. Eluned says in her autobiography that their house was also a second home to many people; Dafydd had been trained as a tenor and his late wife, Olive, was an author and storyteller. Eluned could not have chosen a better combination as friends, and in the section where she thanks people in the autobiography, Eluned acknowledges Olive's good deed in helping get the book published: 'For saving the draft, editing it, and urging its publication, I am grateful to Olive Evans, one well used to drawing her expert editorial toothcomb through the work of seasoned authors.'

Here is the testimony of another friend, Caroline Roper-Deyo from California, who once again distills into words the *joie de vivre* that Eluned embodied:

> During each of the concerts Eluned was introduced to the audience and she absolutely enchanted them. She may have been a woman in her eighties but she had the spirit of an ageless soul and the performance savvy of a seasoned performer. She told them how happy she was to be with them in spite of the harrowing ten-hour plane trip ... in the post 9/11 age she, at 86, had been suspected by the security forces of being a terrorist. Somehow in spite of these crazy challenges, she was able to make it all very funny. That was another of her gifts. Making mischief.

This is a facet of her personality that is mentioned often by friends: her mischievousness and her enjoyment of all kinds of entertainment. Another characteristic was her persistence. Another friend says:

> One of the most important lessons I learned from Eluned was to do what you love to do and never allow your age or your circumstances to deter you from your course. In her eighties and nineties, Eluned was still writing and composing poems. When under a looming deadline for an upcoming concert, she would often compose ten or twenty drafts of a poem for our demanding music director at the cost of no sleep. She didn't seem to mind and in fact did it quite cheerfully.

This is the energy that is seen in her work and the material that is unpublished. Perhaps the commissions to write songs that she received in her last decades gave her purpose and enjoyment, and were given to her by people who were not a part of any bardic

232

establishment and therefore totally unaware of the unpleasant rumours that surrounded her Crown-winning work.

Eluned also forged a close friendship with Myra Lawrence Thomas, a kindred spirit who, as a Welsh-speaker embraced her company and ensured that her travels to America were never lonely or sad.

As Eluned got to know composer Michael J. Lewis he also became a friend, and the mutual admiration became a lifeline for her work. This had also happened when she worked alongside Roy Evans, the court clerk, during the war. In the same way, she trusted John Griffiths, the BBC producer, and he in turn respected her ability to deliver lively scripts. Once she trusted people, Eluned's patience with them would be unstinting and she would do her utmost to realise their every wish. Who else in their nineties would bother to narrate words down the phone-line after having heard the rhythm patterns used by the composer? Every time Eluned was in Los Angeles, the choir would sing two or three of her songs or hymns. Each concert would begin with 'Cenarth'. They would also sing 'True Love' and 'Let all things now living'. In the concerts organised to celebrate her ninetieth birthday, the choir sang four of her songs; 'Cenarth', 'Myra (God is Love)', 'La Môme Piaf' and 'True Love'.

•

What does the fact that Eluned wrote mostly in English towards the end of her life tell us? Perhaps her proximity to non-Welsh-speaking friends was a part of the process of moving closer to English in her writing. Her notebooks show how adept she was at writing in both languages. And it is unusual to see someone of her generation, raised in a monolingual Welsh-speaking family, write English in such a masterly way.

What other poet in Wales has been given not one but three concerts to celebrate their ninetieth birthday, in California of all places? Eluned notes in her autobiography that the first of the concerts was held in St Paul's Cathedral in San Diego, the second at the Presbyterian chapel on Wiltshire Street, Los Angeles. Another concert was organised in San Fransisco, at the Grace Cathedral. Eluned's own little chapel, Bryn Seion, Pontseli, would have fitted easily into a corner of one of these enormous buildings.

In Los Angeles, S4C filmed and then broadcast a programme marking her ninetieth birthday. Is it not ironic that one would have to travel all the way to America, some six thousand miles, to praise a poet who hailed from Cenarth? Accompanying her in her celebrations was another trusted friend, Gwenno Dafydd, one who also delighted in the songs of Edith Piaf. Caroline Roper-Deyo, a member of the choir in California said:

> When the Welsh choir from south California went on tour to Wales for two weeks in the summer of 2003, Eluned accompanied us the entire time. In addition to being our own poet laureate, she was also an informal teacher advising us of Welsh history and culture as we travelled along the way. We walked all over Cenarth with her, saw the coracle (*cwrwgl*) she liked to ride in, and gave an impromptu concert at her local church. She never tired of educating or inspiring us.

But apart from praising her talents, Caroline also mentions the way that Eluned could empathise fully with people's pain. As Caroline faced divorce and sadness at being discarded, the wise woman from Cenarth merely said: 'You have not been discarded. You have been delivered. Trust me. It will all come to good.'

We can imagine Eluned's grandmother saying similar things to some of the local girls and to members of her own family, when romantic matters went awry. Eluned could soothe worries with a few words, with the Solomon-like wisdom that she once attributed to her grandmother. Her wise words were uplifting, Caroline said:

Those words pierced my soul, made it easier to surrender the self-pity I was feeling, and strengthened me to face my future. I know now that her words were effective because Eluned did not have an easy life. During her life she faced many difficulties and disappointments but she never allowed them to warp her basic joyful view of life. She never allowed these caustic events to make her bitter or angry. She found incredible spiritual strength in music … Painful events never interfered with Eluned's ability to find joy in life. And she was determined to the end of her days to teach others how to be happy.

Another friend said that there were three words that came to mind when remembering her: *enthusiastic*, *enchanting* and *energetic*. How remarkable that every word begins with an 'e'. She was given the right name after all.

Eluned was so appreciative of the welcome she received from the Welsh away from home that she wrote verses for the St David's Day celebrations in America that she read out alongside another expat from Ceredigion.

In the city of angels how lovely
To be amongst companions;
Sharing a thrill from each heart
In tasting this concert.

To meet and greet the birth of our saint
The venerable David;
Gladly we bring to you 'Cymru'
And greetings from two Cardis.

One happy audience who remember
Their roots and upbringing;
Past their horizon, the sun of their faith
Is shining through their mirth.

She built a church here – to celebrate
All those miles from Gwalia,
Let her be a haven for all
good traditions, large or small.

Her American friends were all important to her during the last two decades of her life. This is how Dafydd Evans wrote about her in issue 34 of *Ninnau* (January/February 2009): 'Eluned Phillips, an icon of Welsh literature and culture, has died after a short illness. Eluned was one of the most learned and well-travelled people one could ever meet. She was an intellectual without being pompous, a brilliant poet, public speaker, music lyricist, hymn writer and raconteur.'

This list might sound unfamiliar to much of the Welsh-speaking population. Few, if any, heard her speaking to large audiences, let alone sharing her stories, apart from the snippets seen on television programmes or when she greeted a winning poet on the National Eisteddfod stage. There is no doubt that Welsh-speaking Wales missed out on the vivacity and wit of this woman because of the lies told about her, which poisoned minds against her. I heard one friend of mine saying that she had suggested Eluned's name as a guest speaker for an event in order to raise money for a charity, only to experience a deafening silence after she uttered the name. Another name was put forward quickly and the first name was duly forgotten. 'Ah! Eluned! She liked the men,' said another, but as she did not know Eluned she admitted that she did not understand why people had formed such an opinion. And when I was interviewing many of her friends, mostly women, not one of them raised the idea that Eluned was in any relationships with men. A male friend from America said that Eluned hated the idea that people believed her to be a woman of loose morals: 'She was deeply religious and was offended by that.'

Was it her familiarity with Dewi Emrys that was responsible for this: a man who was known as a womaniser and hence a case of guilt by association? Or was it the fact that she was a single woman who was able to come and go as she pleased and gallivant across the country and the world without a consort?

One characteristic that made her self-conscious and sensitive was the redness of her hair. At least a half a dozen times she comments in her autobiography how her flame-red hair reflected her impulsiveness and her temper. This is one of the last things she says in the book when she is thanking people:

> As a topsy-turvy person, I hope for forgiveness. What is more, I urge all the redheaded readers out there, stay true to yourselves and remember the magic of tinting is gloriously acceptable. Today, you will find men with rainbow coloured hair sitting next to you on the bus!

Once again, beneath the humour there lies the fact that the redness of her hair, and its associations, was a burden to her at times. I was told by one of her neighbours that she returned from London in the forties with green hair. No doubt such behaviour at that time would have been seen as unconventional and scandalous.

Did she fill a sense of emptiness by forging intimate friendships? It appears that throughout her life she had only had one lifelong love who was ever present even in his absence. Per won her heart and she continued to long for him until the end, without revealing to her closest friends the secret of their relationship. Though there was no legal marriage to bind them, the image of him remained her ideal. And yet she closed the door on their love affair and the tribulations that followed. Nor did she reveal to anyone I interviewed the reason why they did not rekindle their relationship, other than the explanation that prison had had an adverse effect on his health. Maybe the belief that is easy to pick up where you left off in a relationship is a myth.

Dafydd Evans says:

Eluned travelled the world on one-woman expeditions. Her recounting of her travels was interesting and uproariously funny. She got into jams but, through her charm and wit, would find her way out of all predicaments. Her favourite country to visit was the USA where she found the people to be open, friendly and generous with their time and encouragement. In the USA she loved Southern California which she considered 'her second home'.

These words sum up her personality succinctly: 'Eluned Phillips was a patriotic Welsh woman who loved people from all countries, races, religions, and social structure. Her loss is deeply felt by all who knew her.' This crystallises her secret in a few comments – the fact that she loved people of all kinds – the 'social structure'. To an extent she lived as an independent, strong woman. She lived like one who could control her own destiny without the help of another soul. She was satisfied with living life on her own terms. In that respect, she was not so different to her mother and grandmother, bold women whose lives were full of work and vivacity. Eluned herself could not sit still for a minute; she had to be doing something, be it mowing the lawn or writing a poem.

When she had an hour of leisure, she liked nothing better than being in the midst of friends. She loved all her acquaintances. It seems to me, as a researcher into her life, that she adopted friends along the way and that they in turn became her family. She used to meet monthly with Rosemary Beard in a cafe in Carmarthen, though they'd met originally at the Los Angeles Hotel, in Southern California, when Eluned went out there for the first time, for St David's Day, in 1990. They would speak weekly on the phone every Sunday night. She kept in touch with her by sending postcards from wherever she went, opening her message in typical fashion: 'Christmastime is hard labour. Don't think I'll ever finish. I'm all over the place at the moment but hope to give you a call before going to Shrewsbury. Roll on New York and a little time to have a little gossip.'

Another time, 'Living it up here in Dublin,' or, 'I have been away from home for days and now have to cope with mowing grass'. Or the note that shows her longing for America: 'The weeks are speeding past and I hardly have time to breathe. I do miss the Californian sun and all the *croeso* I receive from you all. Hurry up and come to Wales again soon. Next time I hope to be in residence in my little bungalow.'

These throwaway messages to Rosemary Beard demonstrate Eluned's serene personality. One without rancour or bitterness of any kind. She loved being with people. This had been the way she lived her life throughout her days, whether she was at home or on her many travels. I sat in Starbucks, Minneapolis, once and who did I see walking along the broad street at a pace as if she were late catching a train or bus but Eluned Phillips. She, like me, had been invited to the Gymanfa Fawr Festival in America. I lost another chance to be in her company, that time in 2001 – a loss that I still regret.

It appears that it was an inner circle that came closest to knowing Eluned, if indeed anybody succeeded in knowing her at all. A good friend, the actress Gwenno Dafydd, saw her as a mentor as she turned to writing. Gwenno showed Eluned her work which Eluned edited carefully. She kept in touch with Eluned and every time she visited Pembrokeshire, the area where she had been born, she called to see her. Gwenno received postcards from Eluned whenever she travelled. Again, this small act shows that Eluned would remember friends even when she was far away. It is Gwenno who sang at an event held in Cenarth arranged by Andrew Gilbert to celebrate the centenary of Eluned's birth in 2014. Eluned mentions her warmly in a letter to a friend shortly after having heard from her for the first time in May 1987: 'I have just heard from Gwenno Dafydd ... that there's to be a show on at the Sherman shortly, based on the life of Piaf – in English – Gwenno is portraying Piaf. She's calling here next week to have a chat. Interesting! She suggests that I should write the Welsh version for them.'

Despite Eluned's wide circle of friends from Cenarth to California, it was ultimately her family that was her anchor, and she delighted in it. Ann Evans, her niece, was not only the executor of her will but also a friend and companion on several foreign trips and she assisted her with research on esoteric subjects. Eluned called at their home and would stay overnight on her way, according to Ann, always to somewhere else. Ann remembers that she stayed with her and Bryan, her husband, once for more than the usual one-night stay. When I asked about the time when this happened, I realised that it was around the time of the hullabaloo with Thomas Parry. This suggests that she wanted to escape Wales and the journalists who would be on her doorstep asking question after question about the debacle. Eluned knew full well that she would be given refuge by her family, the ones that never questioned her as a poet. How wonderful that she could turn to her family for quiet support far away from the fracas. She faced many battles, and occasionally she alludes obliquely to this in letters: 'I'm still alive – but only just. Nobody has physically attacked me yet, but it's been a close run thing.' To close the door was her defence mechanism. It is enough to state here that I got quite close to the 'broken soul' as mentioned in a letter. But Eluned's personality was so tenacious that she could overcome any difficulty with a dose of humour, rising above the 'clouds of time'. At the end of another letter she writes 'life is still worth living'.

Eluned had a full and rewarding life. There will never be another Eluned like her. I hope that there will not be another case of a woman questioned as to the authenticity of her work as she was, because now we women in the twenty-first century can claim our rightful place. And voice. As I write this book, I note with pride the poets laureate in these isles: Carol Ann Duffy, Jackie Kay in Scotland and Sinead Morrissey from Northern Ireland, all women. Oh, how the literary tables have turned. The #metoo campaign current at the time of translation of this biography has ensured that women need not suffer discrimination or harassment in silence.

At Eluned's funeral, the subject of the eulogy given by the minister was a verse from the *Book of Revelations* 2:10:

'Be faithful until death and I shall give you the crown of life'.

Yes, as her minister said on the day of her funeral, in truth Eluned received three crowns.

Journey's End, but the Storm Lives On

When I heard about Eluned Phillips' death, I said to a friend, 'I wonder if we'll ever get to know the truth now?' Was she a poet or was she an impostor? Did she get help from another winning poet – as was widely thought? Would the rumours become accepted as mythology for generations to come? Was she a shining genius of a poet or a poet who duped the nation and dragged the oldest Welsh establishment into disrepute? When I heard of her death it never crossed my mind to wonder who had inherited her literary estate.

I did not mean her material inheritance but the legacy or proof that would be a testament to her life as a poet and author. Who would organise her papers or sift through the pages of notebooks and personal letters? If any existed, of course. There are enough examples of people who have chosen to burn their papers for whatever reason. Had Eluned done so in order to put an end to others investigating her work?

There is something perverse in sifting through the detritus of the departed. It can be seen as the behaviour of a vulture enjoying the prey left behind. Little did I think at the time that the task would fall to me. It happened in the most unexpected way. In retrospect, I can see that I was one of the few poets from my generation who knew of the doubts that befell Eluned when embarking on a career as a poet. To other younger female poets, she was perhaps a hazy figure, a beautiful elderly woman who would always be sitting in the front row of the Gorsedd, either because she was so petite, so that she could see the ceremony, or perhaps so that the audience could see that there were indeed some women permitted centre stage. I was astounded that there were those who did not know about her travails, because, thankfully, they had not heard the rumours. Others did not understand the controversy, as to them Eluned was a druid in the Gorsedd and therefore must deserve to be there. They were totally right in that respect. Eluned stood her ground and smiled at the world, and that is what the younger generation remember of her. Eluned certainly knew the art of smiling. She could have competed on that front with the author D. J. Williams and his beatific smile, 'the smile that did not dim with time', according to Dafydd Iwan. But it could be said that he, apart from one uneasy period when he spent some time at His Majesty's pleasure, had more reasons for smiling. He had been elevated to the status of Welsh icon, a hero amongst the ranks of Cymdeithas yr Iaith (the Welsh Language Society) and a generous benefactor to Plaid Cymru. Compared with D. J. Williams Eluned was given very little iconic treatment, for she experienced a different kind of incarceration... Not in a cell, but being locked out of the Welsh-language literary world all the same. Perhaps a kind of imposed exile. In the book *Cymru 2000* (*Wales 2000*) by R. Merfyn Jones, published by University of Wales Press in 1999, the only woman with the surname Phillips mentioned by the author was the actress, Siân Phillips. Not that this remarkable lady does not deserve her place but it demonstrates how insignificant the recognition is for a woman like Eluned, a twentieth-century woman who achieved something truly amazing.

I have not explained how her papers found their way into my hands. It started with a phone call one night, though I tend not to answer the phone late at night. I am even more suspicious on hearing an unfamiliar voice asking for me. But I need not have worried. The voice explained that he was a good friend of Eluned's and that he was the one who used to drive her to the airport when she flew to America. 'She was like a mother to me,' then, correcting himself, 'or grandmother. I learnt so many things from her.' In order to thank her for being who she was, he wanted to build a memorial garden to her. He mourned her loss as Eluned had told him that she had wanted to live until she was a hundred, a sign of her zest for living life to the full. She had been on a walking holiday when she was ninety-one.

But the main purpose of his phone call was to ask whether I would be able to take part in a memorial event for her. The South Wales Male Voice Choir would be coming to Rhosygilwen to sing with other artists, including Gwenno Dafydd who would be singing some of Eluned's songs; he also said that Tom Jones would also be there to say a few words. (I understood later that it was the former Archdruid T. James Jones who was that particular Tom!) His request was such an earnest one that I found myself accepting the invitation without considering what would be asked of me, namely to read out Eluned's work. I looked at the two winning long poems the following day and I became spellbound once again.

I read a section of the long poem *'Clymau'* at the memorial event and felt moved by the two contingents present: there were the inhabitants of Cenarth; and also members of the South Wales Male Voice Choir. Many of the choir members were tearful when they talked in English about the loss of Eluned. To them she was 'our Eluned'. Their mascot. On one hand, there were people from her own 'square mile' of Cenarth and Ceredigion whose roots were deep in the rural community, and on the other hand, there were people present who could not read Eluned's poetry in Welsh and yet they held her in high regard. She had written many songs for the choir to sing in places across the world and in America. I met a few newcomers to the area who seemed to have been in awe of her, and I went home with conflicting thoughts. I read Andrew Gilbert's words again, as they had made such an impression on me:

In Celebration of the Life and Work of Eluned Phillips
1914–2009
In recent months, whilst organising this concert and gathering support from a variety of sources, I have been asked many times for the reasons behind my efforts to celebrate the Life and Works of Eluned Phillips.

Like many other people who came into contact with Eluned, I had a deep affection and respect for her, and am very grateful for the help and friendship she gave me and my family over the years. I acted as her driver and chaperone when she travelled around west Wales and further afield, as she attended a wide range of events and gatherings. And, on those trips, I witnessed the warm and cordial reception she received wherever she went. Through her frequent trips to North America, she became one of Wales' best unofficial ambassadors at all sorts of events from *Gymanfa Ganu* to local eisteddfodau. The respect and affection felt for her in the States is evidenced by the fact that a similar tribute to her is being organised this year in California.

Eluned was not only a very good friend to myself and many others, but someone whom I found inspirational because of her energy, enthusiasm and her interest in, and appreciation of, all with whom she came into contact.

He ends his tribute by saying that he had organised the concert, 'in recognition of the remarkable contribution to Welsh cultural life by one of life's truly original characters, the unique, Sara Adeline Eluned Phillips, poet'.

After that evening, Andrew Gilbert contacted me again, this time encouraging me to help establish a writing competition in Eluned's name. The title would be the Eluned Phillips Prize, and it would be open to those writing in Welsh or English, living in Wales or descendants of Welsh heritage living in America. I tried to attract interest from a few organisations, setting out the rules of the competition, but to no avail. I realised that the main problem with such a prize was that it would be in the name of Eluned Phillips. The email I wrote to Andrew Gilbert was an exceedingly difficult one: I told him that I had made attempts at fulfilling his wish but that all had ended in failure.

But, when the door closed on that idea, another door opened and from an unexpected place. Eluned's niece, Ann Evans, her executor, contacted me. I apologised profusely for not having succeeded in my endeavour to set up a prize in the poet's name.

This initial contact turned into a correspondence by email, and I was invited to her Dorchester home to talk more about her Aunt 'Lyn'. She handed me a box which contained some of Eluned's work, and I started to wonder whether or not I should do something with the material offered to me. Ann mentioned that she had given a box of her aunt's scripts to the National Library of Wales in Aberystwyth. It was there that I started to read some of them and I was bowled over by how rich and original they were. Then I approached one of Eluned's closest friends who was delighted to hand over to me more of Eluned's work. By now, my kitchen was full to the brim of boxes, all containing unpublished works: letters, synopses of work to be completed in the future. Some of her most ambitious projects were drafted when she was well into her nineties. At times I found it difficult to transcribe some of these things, as her handwriting was almost illegible. I realised that in the first instance I would need to give the material an archival order, organise and transcribe what I could from her numerous coloured notebooks.

I began work in 2014, the year of the many celebrations in remembrance of the poet Dylan Thomas, born on the very same day as Eluned. It seemed timely, then, that a reassessment be made of the life and work of Eluned Phillips who, unlike her birthday twin, had been forgotten. There is no indication from her childhood that Eluned was a quiet person or that she followed Telemachus' advice in the *Odysseia*, that it is men who have the gift of speech and oratory as he sent Penelope to her room to spin. But in essence, this is exactly what Eluned did: she spun words, she created tapestries of vibrant and exotic poems. Often, she wrote when she was sitting at the bedside of an ailing family member. She wrote in the small hours when she would not be disturbed by family duties. And she had grandiose ideas as she travelled in places like Morocco or when travelling on a raft in Chile.

My journey writing about Eluned started with her friend and neighbour Andrew Gilbert, as he is the perfect embodiment of the tenet in Michael Ignatieff book, *The Need for Strangers*. It is Andrew who finally succeeded in the task of funding a prize in her name in 2014, receiving assistance from an unexpected source, David Llewellyn, an associate at the Curtis Brown agency in London. The winner of the prize was Rhian E. Jones, and the bursary allowed her to follow an online writing course on how to write a novel. Over a hundred people entered the competition whose rules included: 'Writers either born in Wales or currently residing in the country to submit the first 3,000 words of their novel, along with a one-page synopsis, from which a winner will be chosen.'

When this novel comes to fruition and hopefully is published, Eluned's name will have been a conduit for a young writer to begin the journey as an emerging writer. That this competition for Welsh writing in English was administered from London is regrettable but commendable at the same time. It is strange, is it not, that those who could not read and appreciate Eluned's work in Welsh were those who were the most eager to promote and remember her as a poet?

And, unlike Rhian E. Jones, Eluned did not have a mentor as a sounding board. 'She had no one to support her,' was what one neighbour told me. There were many factors that made it difficult for her to succeed as a poet. She was a woman born at a time when women had little status, and did not even have the vote. Secondly, she was unmarried and therefore drew suspicion from the conservative society of the time. Eluned was a free spirit able to spend time in London, France and beyond (while other women were tied to their domestic duties), in that sense, she followed the honourable tradition of male Welsh poets who travelled, such as T. H. Parry-Williams or T. Gwynn Jones. But how much more outlandish was it for a woman to travel alone, in the early decades of the twentieth century?

It could be viewed as a fairy story. Here is a woman who rose from a poor family, and through her own sheer will-power went on to achieve her deepest desires. She did everything with brio, be it readings in chapel or weekend concerts for the returning troops.

She made her audiences laugh at a time during the war when there few opportunities for laughter. With her BBC scripts and later her poetry, she managed to hone her writing in Welsh. She made true friends throughout her life and was genial, dignified and kind, even to strangers. If she suffered disappointment, it was kept hidden. When I asked many non-Welsh-speakers why, in their opinion, she was not received more graciously by the Welsh-speaking world their answer without fail was that it was 'because she spoke English to journalists after winning the Crown'. I did not tell them that the story was far more complex than that. Perhaps this is how Eluned avoided having to pour out her heart. It would have been an inventive way of stopping the conversation in its tracks. And since the Eisteddfod has a Welsh-only rule, it was a slick answer that would not raise any more ghosts. And the biggest spectre of them all was this; who in reality was the true author of the winning poems?

I have not mentioned a host of supporters and facilitators of Eluned's attempts to be an author. There are producers who loved her work, people such as Lorraine Davies, Eleri Hopcyn and others who made sure that her work was heard on the radio. During the time Jennie Eirian Davies was editor of *Y Faner*, pioneering woman that she was, she would insist on contributions from Eluned; Jennie Eirian herself did not receive the acknowledgement that she deserved for encouraging many women to contribute to the paper. One of Eluned's failings was that she used programmes and columns to write about subjects such as Piaf, rather than assert her own authority over literature. Her article *'Nabod Piaf'* ('Knowing Piaf') in issue 23 March 1979 of *Y Faner* displays this deferential tendency. Eluned's correspondence is full of a sense of self-deprecating flattery towards other artists and her self-effacing nature is at times at odds with her otherwise plucky character.

She should have challenged the establishment's attempt to dishonour her, yet it is easy for the author of this book to berate her. This was not the kind of behaviour expected of or accepted from a woman during the first half of the last century.

And now I come to what I did not know as I started this book. Would I be disappointed or cheered by the truth? The true poet. Eluned did fight for '*y gwir yn erbyn y byd*' ('the truth against the world') for decades without being given '*heddwch*' or 'peace' apart from the inner peace of knowing that she was the rightful author of her prize-winning poems '*Corlannau*' ('Folds') and '*Clymau*' ('Ties'). And so much more. Her coping strategy was much wiser. If she felt rejected, then to carry on regardless was her way of dealing with injustice.

Her graceful manner always won through.

•

I made one final journey to Cenarth before finishing this book. A way of paying my last respects, perhaps, before saying goodbye to someone who has been so much part of my life for nearly two years. She travelled everywhere with me. When I went to places as far away as Hong Kong she was there, and in the States I walked the streets imagining the freedom and relief she felt having left her square mile. I spoke about her constantly with friends until I would see them becoming bored. She became the topic of conversation at home and with any stranger who asked me what my latest project was. I went into bursts of enthusiasm far too often when I talked about this wonderful woman in English, so much so that I was encouraged to write the book in English. Some even told me in no uncertain terms that the book would be better received in English, and that Eluned Phillips would join the multitude of women who had been treated badly by literary traditions over the ages. I retaliated by saying that I wanted to write about her in Welsh, as it was through the Welsh language that she was traduced and subjected to ridicule. The Welsh-speaking audience deserved to know her true story, I answered. It would serve them right that those who had doubted her would hopefully have to change their minds about her talent.

In a book with the title *Women in Dark Times* the author Jaqueline Rose says:

> One reason women are so often hated, I would suggest, is because of their inability to force to the surface of the everyday parts of their inner life – its visceral reality, its stubborn unruliness – which in the normal course of our exchanges we like to think we have subdued. For me this is also their gift.[23]

And maybe the term 'hated' or hatred is too strong a word to convey feelings and attitudes towards Eluned. Perhaps some feared her: her humour, her warmth, her jocular, friendly attitude. I began my journey by looking for Eluned's spirit and found it to be one of tolerance and compassion, even when she knew full well the amusement won at her expense. If the ones who were responsible for the initial murmurings had exercised restraint and a certain sense of fairness, perhaps they would have realised the efforts Eluned had made, from cradle to grave, to find her voice and be taken seriously. She could easily have turned to write only in English, but it was our good fortune that she wrote mainly in Welsh. She kept the faith, a stoic to the end.

In his essay of reminiscences of Eluned in *Barn* in February 2009, Lyn Ebenezer enthuses about his affection for her and how he identified with every aspect of her personality: 'She stared deep into the eyes of anybody who stopped to talk to her ... The description in our area of that kind of woman typifies her perfectly; she was a "*tipyn o haden*" – "a real character". This woman's playful nature and her vibrant behaviour was an integral part of her personality. If there were such a thing as reincarnation, I should expect Eluned to come back as a butterfly.' Dic Jones said of her in

---

[23] Jaqueline Rose, *Women in Dark Times* (Bloomsbury, 2014), p. 5.

the eulogy given at her funeral, which was published in the February 2009 issue of the *Gambo*, the local community monthly paper, 'there was something outside of time that belonged to her. Some mysticism at the same time as a companionable closeness. It was as if she had existed forever – nobody now remembers Cenarth without Eluned ... I would go so far as to state that the fact that she had been raised with her feet almost in the waters of the river Teifi had formed her very character. She possessed a kind of magic and romanticism ... It is unlikely that we shall ever see her kind again.' Lyn Ebenezer concludes: 'And yes, she was bohemian by nature, and totally eccentric. And like all true eccentrics, she never realised that. And if some people found it difficult to swallow some of her stories without a pinch of salt, Eluned herself believed them. And that's good enough for me.' These are beautiful tributes from two people who knew her well.

Another poet from Ceredigion who wrote a tribute to her in *englyn* form in 2009 was Idris Reynolds:

> Between the river and the waves – in the water
> There was a story of colours
> And between the true and the false Teifi
> There was an Atlantic of words.

•

I am sitting once again on the bench commissioned and given by the local people in her memory and the river Teifi flows quietly behind me. I know nothing about fishing, nor do I know about trout or salmon. But for the sewin, there is something special about that fish and I'm sure that Eluned had learnt its quirks.

There is a saying in Ceredigion about somebody who stretches a story, that they are '*canu ar y mesur hir*' ('singing in the long metre') – this is a perfect turn of phrase to describe Eluned's talent of entertaining people with her experiences, but also the perfect description of one who could write such dazzling poetry, she definitely did sing in the long metre.

Will there be an end to the rumours, I wonder? This book is an attempt to redeem the wrong perpetrated on one of the most interesting literary personalities of the twentieth century. She was a poet of the first order – but not recognised as such in her day. Having read her letters, her notebooks and her works, I have no doubt that she was a poet of extraordinary ingenuity. Less than five foot in height, she was an award-winning poet, a scriptwriter, a librettist and a proud Welsh woman. I wrote this biography after asking myself – if I don't, then who will? If not now, then when? This is Eluned: the poet from Cenarth, and later from California. Let all disparagement turn to praise.

I feel blessed, Eluned, in that I grew to know you through the journey I took writing this book: A woman who 'saw the bright star through the black cloud.' And through it all, she beamed. If she did indeed live on the periphery of Wales, she lived as a kindhearted woman, satisfied with her life. She did not let any system grind her down and crush her self-belief. The daughter of the wonderful poet from Llan-y-bri, Lynette Roberts, said about her mother, 'She always knew her own worth.' The same could be said of Eluned. She defended her self-image with dignity. Her life story deserves to be appreciated by all.

•

Maybe I will visit again the Garden of Remembrance on her birthday, to sit on the bench by the river Teifi. She will not be there, of course, but the weather will be warm and sunny all the same. I will be comforted by the fact that I and many others will no longer think of her life or fame as 'the sun that never was'. Emily Dickinson said once that 'phosphorescence' was a word one should raise one's hat to. It is a word that describes the light of Eluned's abilities perfectly. Let the light of getting to know her through her words take me home energised. Two of her words, though a paradox, linger in my mind: in this day and age, it does not pay to be anything other than, in Eluned's words, an 'absolute optimist'.

The Two Poems that Won the Crown

Folds (*Corlannau*)
Here, in the fold of the East
The devotional imam is on his travels under idle palm trees,
his respectable gown licking the threshold
of poor people's tents.
'Where will you go, Mohammed grandson of Abdul?'
'To the childless widow who lives beyond the Orangery.'
When the religious knives were like hailstones
In the Year of Plunder
His father died, his tongue loose like a tired camel,
Before pulling a son from the womb and placing him on the fleece
of the sacrificial sheep from the holy-day of El Kabir,
Before the witchlike midwife throws the traditional salt
To chase away the spirits from the birthing room.

In the Beginning
Allah created man from a blood clot.

One Almighty Friday
I saw the Yellow Heifer whipping the flies
At the mosque gable-end in Al-Madinah.
On the sixteenth of July
The Voice between the bones and the green marrow
Through to the soulful poetry under the flow of the river of the mind.

And to the ears of the Shepherd came the words –
'Write on the sheep's shoulder blade,
on the palm leaf,
And on the skin of the perished animal.'

In the Forbidden Month
When the camels laugh derisively
The sunset is fiery on the buttocks of the flock;
Their grey backs quivering like a herd in the heat
Their noses burrowing into the dust of the hour of blessing.
'Allah's words to us dripped from the holy tongue –
From the Cave that laments in the storm,
From the Cattle that stagger their bones down the street,
And from the Wind-that-sifts on the restless hills.'
I saw the yellow hands blessing the donkeys and goats before
Weaning the baby, and before wiping the breasts.
'Like a hurricane blowing dust from the rock,
Will his breath denude the soul in Judgment?'
The dance of playful eyes
Under the headscarf of lineage,
Looking for a fertile woman on her way to the pit.
A pile of gold,
A horse with his master's mark on his forehead,
Cattle and lands – all carnal bliss.

In the Battle of the Trenches
And the bloody thrusting between the folds the Shepherd kneels
In the consecrated dust.
'The virgins' love warms the loins
And the clouds of soil sweeten the body.'

When the moon is torn
The stars fall between the pomegranate leaves;
The goat laughed when he discovered his beard
In the depths of Tasmin.

From the planets' wrathful sockets
Comes the Day of Promise to stoke the fire,
And the morning's whip to call the camel from his dreams.

Did you see Allah flooring the Elephant's master, did you see
Claggy clotted dirt on the donkey's tails?
The quick steps of the man who does the burials
As he runs the race against pollution.
A green net around remains
Before taking the bier-bed from Death's stable,
Before placing the dead on his side facing Mecca.
Leaving him there in the state of his conscience.
Between two quarrelsome angels on the morning of reckoning.

In the dawn of the Last Day
The bird comes to sip from the pitcher
When the soul-child wears wings
And his resurrected flesh nests high in the palm-tree.

From the territory of the fold –
'I swear by the Fig and the Olive tree,'
By the Undefiled Soil,
Near Haram – the sacred forest.

The soul's asylum in the earth's cellar,
I run into the lap of Lord of all Creation
Away from the Vandals' evil
And the wolf's eyes,
From the maliciousness of the night
That congeals the blood in the valley,
From the arms of whores in their tents.
There are mystical whispers between the breastbones;
My feet bled where there is Abu Lahab's deceit
Hiding the thorns under the sand's pathways.'
The cucumbers are young and tender tonight
When the donkey brays at the coldness of summer.
The birds of the heavens swear at the miser
And the files sing in the sheep's carcass.

The cockerel on his heap rebukes his lineage with the fox
The hen harem search his wonders.
Poverty like a red saddle on a white steed;
The dogs chew the walking meat,
And the cat and mouse in the brotherhood of the skeleton.

When the knees of men are denuded,
When the fruit reproaches his debt to the leaf
In the Valley of the Ants,
The clot kneels before the Shepherd.

And on the fourth day
When the salt sweats out of the host
There will be blood on the flanks of the gates,
And Allah will close his eyes
Before falling from the shower of vultures in the faraway valley.

A white robe sweeping under the lazy palm trees
The hem licking the threshold of tents belonging to the poor.

•

Into the Christian fold
Lazarus walked home from his grave to eat
And washed the greyness of Death from his resurrected body;
He changed from his calico shroud into his everyday clothes.
He reached for the bread and the figs for his Guest.
The funeral wine was drunk in the wedding of life.

Bethania is as bright as whitewash in the sun.
The Pharisee kicks his wife out of the prayer room.
Right back in the Beginning
Pharaoh's daughter's breasts were dried up for the Hebrew baby.

In the fullness of the time of our Fate
The toads climbed to the sovereign's bed;
The dust became fleas
The river of blood flows,
Women and camels, donkeys and cows like open mouthed corpses;
Fire walked the earth.
The locusts destroyed the trees' greenery.
And there was night
Before the lamb bleated its innocence at Easter.
The bread appeared like hoar-frost in the fold of the chosen.
There was the sound of live things' wings touching each other
When the son of man opened his jaws to eat the book;
At the top of the cypress tree sits the sneering eagle
And the willow grows like the spreading vine.

Who separates the fatted beast from the lean?
Taking the young bullock at the new moon,
Turning out the animal king to graze the grass?

The lion with the eagle's wings devours the seas
And the Almighty sits on the ruins of thrones;
The flies came to die in the apothecary's ointment.
The Lord's Sword is full of blood –
Growing large on the fat kidneys of rams;
The Valley fills with the smell of rotting hedgehogs.

In the small hours of the world
A mother walked amongst the lions to eat men.
Her daughters losing blood
Like the haemorrhage of horses.
The beast walked
Through the shame of the world,
Its metal teeth grinding the rocks,
And his great paws ripping apart the flesh

Of the descendants of the Swamp.
The Shepherd became flesh
Became feeble in the hay in the year of the Murder of the Innocents;
The sparrow's chest puffed up,
And Judas' body swings like a pendulum on a tree on the common.

The hen gathers her chicks under her wing.
So that the hawk cannot pluck the eyes of the helpless.
His breath is here
Like the wind that blows where it will;
In the awakening of buds, and in the fall of leaves,
In the anaesthetic that is sleep before slashing the flesh.
When the century was barely walking
Between Loughor and the sea,
He jumped into the fold to protect the prostitutes
His Church – for Salem and Seilo, for Our Chapel and for Their Chapel.
The sluggish beer turned sour in the White Horse cellar,
Domino eyes turn yellow in the bar,
And nobody knew that the draft was lost;
The director of the paraffin company smiled.

Today
Meaning is empty like Moreia's collection box,
And the faithful chestnut tree
Waits by the chapel-house door.

But nothing is said anywhere –
'This is where he lies.'
Two angels were called home from their three-day vigil ...
When the forest withers on the streets' chimneys
Choking from the whorled gutters of the flesh
He will be a kiss on the lips
And his scarred hands shall mend the fold.

He will be here and there,
His tired eyes watching the fold
Until He washes his feet on the banks of Jordan
Pulling Charon to the land of the living after the final journey,
Leaving the boat to dance into destruction.

•

Between the sea of doom and the Great Wide Wall
are the folds of the yellow flock; Here at the beginning
When Mother Earth aborted
The Monkey and the Pig and the Monk take a journey.

The rice fields are ancient,
Old like mice, and lice, and sparrows.

This year, the privet flowers
On the Fifth Day of the Ninth Moon;
White rain falls on the banana leaves,
And the gentle willow is green in the mist.
Beyond the Wei river
Spring gallops through the forest
Beyond the straw hat that follows the goat,
Beyond the chestnut tree by Lin Wang's wine-cellar.

Animal paths, cows and sheep, between the primitive tombs
And the living dead chatter in the graveyard's plants.

Once,
The phoenix nested near Red Bird Bridge
When the lily scent clung to the Mandarin's sandals.
Seeing
A willow next door, hunched and weak,
The movement of the washerwomen
As they beat the cotton.

A yellow stork singing in lightning.
A cormorant, his collar too tight to swallow fish
And the great Unthinking crouching to speak of literature
To the undergrowth.

With a brush of camel hair
The art of a language without an alphabet is painted
Back to the beginnings of the beauty of books
Before the arrow pierced the rock
In the Yu-Chang hills.

In the fold of animisim
The bamboo table talks, and the son bows to his father.
In Sikang
The dragon bares her teeth on the temple's eaves
As she watches Kuan Yin's boat
Hurrying to take the souls of the faithful to paradise
Leaving behind
The riot of noisy funerals and bodies between the colourful vials.

Who is this walking laboriously
Through the mulberry garden,
His silken cap dancing in the sun?

Chu Chin Chou,
As old as sin,
His two-pointed beard brushing his knees,
His hair plait on his hump
Lying like a dead snake,
The candles of his eyes snuffed out in the crevices of his skull.
'Where will you go tonight, old man?'
'To deliberate with the camphor tree near the well
Away from the wearisome cough of Death,
There my father's soul still gives warnings
Between the leaves of the third branch.'

Love in chains in the kitchen and the laundry,
Virginity is more valuable than the teachings of the world,
Young fingers embroider dreamily,
Doves and lovers are captive on the indigo plates.
The silken thread escapes from the needle's eye,
She bit her lip sick with love
Before closing them on two rows of pomegranate seeds.
Her eyebrows like new moons,
Bridges over her apricot eyes
The light like the autumn in a pond.

The vegetarian monk
Washes the she-dog in the waters of the Yellow river
So that the lice do not vex his grand-mother's soul.
A beggar takes his sores
Door to door, over the pink piglets along the street,
He was once a monk
Cold moons ago, eating pork on the sly.

The nun is young, oh so young,
She kneels on her hay cushion;
Her head is shaved
And her skin like bamboo buds;
She spends her virginity with the cheek in her hand
And the prior, his mind lustful
for the smoothness of her flesh between the altar's candles.

When Ch'ingming comes
The barren widow shall lie on her husband's grave
Before taking his soul home like a cosseted pup.
But the Great Bird will come
To earth to roost away from the moon and the stars.
Tomorrow,
He will hatch the steel eggs.

Bonds. Knots. Ties.
1865
Through the mist, sounds of moving at Pant Glas
and a woman's wailing;
the muteness of remembering;
a locked gate a final sting.

A voiceless yard groans noisily; in the barn
mice squeaking merrily;
an anchorless family
pushed rudderless out to sea.

An oppressive squirearchy
breaks up a home without mercy;
the orphaned furniture
dragged on a dray along a lane of mud.

A pot-bellied dictator geared into power
by plebeian robots;
a pompous traitor
preening himself in the cuckoo's nest.

The dispossessed, a man of God, honouring
his acres of heritage;
willing for his generation, freedom of thought
without the shadow of fear.

The Court Bailiff took up duties; stock and implements
shied under the hammer.
The day, a day of burial.
Work ceased. The joy of living ended.

•

Venturing into Liverpool, as yet
a mystic name in the mother tongue;
whirlwinds of emotion churning into currents,
flooding their souls with nightmares of horror.
Ties of family tighten, the love of Pant Glas
binding them in its tendrils of grief.

Slowly, slowly moved the Mimosa
towards the heaven of Patagonia.
A voyage of vomit and plague.

Shaking off the dust of oppression,
an awakened conscience eyeing on a fair horizon
a land of plenty, and the pride of freedom
to restart a new life of hope.

Ailing centuries of sailing,
the anguish of hiraeth like the tear of a claw;
gallantly singing in the presence of the English
who had no cause to suffer their indignity of heart.

Children, trampling the boards of adventure,
wildly uncaring in an uneasy storm,
not yet having recognised pain.

Losing a daughter in their adversity,
abandoning the golden tresses to the wastes of ocean,
and the sea closing around her.

He, who defied the law,
humbly on his knees, eyes full of dried tears,
his remaining family his only hope.

A broken-hearted mother bending beneath her burden,
craving with emotion,
an answer to the age-old question.

They blamed the oppressive law; they bow to Fate.
They lose a daughter in spite of prayer;
one who was flesh of their flesh.

Through trials of despair and covering of weals,
there comes a peace
an ecstasy of hope in the sighting of land,
and a journey's end.

Taking leave of the mountains of ocean;
of a cabin that was an altar;
of a daughter cradled at the bottom of the sea.

The heart is knotted in grief
for the fairness amid the sea-weed.
Losing her was losing the sight of one's eye.

•

A never-ending July throws a snowy welcome;
Mimosa dances on the ocean edge.
Parcels of dishearted flesh unloaded their dreams
once more ground into dust.

Headland thrusting their jowls into a bleak sea
at the end of the bay;
dried out skeletons
like the remains of wizened old dragons.

A tight knot of hiraeth
strangles their heroism.
And the waves laugh on the sea shore.

•

An exile, folding his family like a blanket around him,
hurls his mattocks at the root of a sturdy thorn;
raping unceasingly the virginity of desert, his eyes
reflecting the garden of Eve.

Churning in a wilderness, his pickaxe
bouncing uncaringly off the face of parched earth;
aching for a patch of the green grass of tomorrows,
and the day an eternity of nothingness.

Exploring daily through diligent hours,
like the legend Arthur seeking the Holy Grail.
And a day of wonder. A crystal stream gushing
out of the vessel of desolation.

Building a house; planning a home. A second Pant Glas
out of the mountainous ashes of nightmares;
a shelter from the storm of uprooting;
a crude structure. A seventh heaven.

Weary of work, their spirits uplifted by the rousing hymns
of a Bethel reborn.
And the God of Wales, God of the prairie.

•

1982

Briars have spun a death-wish over the Mansion;
rats are at-home in its cowsheds and stables;
co-bedding hippies carpeting floors, and the Squire's cellar,
without lock, a lair for the homeless.

Privileged rich swarm the Fair Valley sucking
the nectar of summer homes;
Rudely ravishing local ties of togetherness, a pleasure boat
grinning in the old cart-house.

The Mill has become a retreat
for the super-annuated childless;
sold for a fat £40,000.
There is no one left at the Chapel House, no one
but a red-lipped foreigner
and a nanny goat worshipping at the door.

Tombstones groan between earth-nut flowers;
the churchyard gate wide open
like the mouth of the mindless forever gaping.

A yew tree weeps
over the remains of old characters.
The ties of the grave cannot be undone.

•

The son of Pant Glas is on the Brecon Beacons, a young lad
clad in Khaki, his toy gun grown real;
lured by promises of joy times roving the world,
his wallet bulging.
Abandoning the plough and harrow to a rusty death,
to take up shooting and stabbing with bayonet.

Turning his back on a pregnant dole-queue, his horizon
undimmed by the shadow of war.
Could one ever wish for a better choice?

Grovelling through coarse growth,
screaming madly across green grass
to stab men of straw.

A General, golden leeks, cap and tunic, poring
over detail sketch-maps, sending troops
to pin-pricked swamps.

Lips of red roses
and dirt black faces
attack, wave after wave.

Feeling, without seeing, in the light of day, eyes
staring from enemy terrain;
when the sun falls asleep, night glasses gaze back
like the two querying eyes of an ox.

A soldier clad in a fair weather suit, as yet
not accepting the technique of killing.

Through tedious hours of hell, he sees
with closed eyes, his paradise Pant Glas;
the face of his sweetheart in a crystal clear pool,
and he locks the image of love in his heart.

A kiss of sunshine peeping through leaves, encircling a finger
of a gorse bush with a golden band;
sipping the virtue of ripe blackberry wine;
the moon's ballet a smile on the smoothness of lake.

The harsh bark of the sergeant-major
shatters the ties of romantic dreams
to lie buried in the churchyard of memory.

There comes a payday at the end of the week,
and the riotous joy of a night to remember.
War will not enter his domain.
Pant Glas shall forever be free of pain.

A short respite of hope; a retreat from duty,
with his passionate girl from Cae Meillion farm;
and the blackthorn needles busily sewing
a fence of love enclosing two hearts.

Drowning the sorrows of a grizzly life;
wrapping peace in a cloak of fur;
peering at Spring calling a tree to life;
carving a memory in the bark of an oak.

Like a clap of thunder, the call to rejoin.
Bidding farewell to hopes and desires, he spies
at the corner of the field of gorse; a ewe
in the seething pangs of birth.

Sir Galahad, beast of prey, is waiting, mouth ajar
like the jaws of a whale;
tanks sinking dutifully into her belly;
hoary guns
bristling on the nape of her neck.
The warring pride of her ilk on the ocean
as she thrusts anchor before the storm.

The son of Pant Glas at the centre of conflict, henceforth
an atom in the ship's manifest.

A machine to kill, a robot on a voyage of doom
across acres of water.
A lad at the Spring of life, his gun night and day
his close, lonely companion.

•

When the waves snarl into a temper, he recalls
the saga of the adventure to Patagonia, and the sighting
of land after aeons of time
in the entrails of the Mimosa.

He, voyaging in the same direction, his passage paid
from the nation's purse.
In his heart there glows the same desire of reaching land,
his training geared to another conquest.
He sees endless seas stretching to far horizons, and a whale,
a lookalike of the beast in the Book of Revelation.

A chill falls, like icicles on a day of battle,
in spite of bonds that tie Patagonia and the homeland of Wales;
two small countries under a cloud, their anguish
an unbearable burden to hold.

Fear of seeing a battleship on the horizon;
fear of a fatal weapon darting its snare;
fear of a submarine creeping lowly;
fear of a bomb born to explode.
Fear of the silent calm in its aching monotony; and fear
of a grave forever between the coral.

There will be no tears or gilded memorials
above the bones on 'No Man's Seas'.

•

Buenos Aires in cloud and sunshine resounds
to the tramp of celtic feet;
proud descendants of the old heroic who fled
the oppression of a land of love.
We have met in reunion on the Thursdays of Hiraeth –
kindred rejoicing in our Festival of Hope.

The City of adoption a bubble of passion;
the Casa Rosada a hive full of dance;
years on through dispute and blinkered obstructions
the Malvinas are surely theirs to hold.

Dawns a day of Armageddon;
darkness over the whiteness of waves.
A day of black sun; of clawing of breasts.

A Mirage swoops,
dropping death from its clutches,
before fleeing home over rocky banks.

Sir Galahad is a ball of fire;
bundles of khaki writhe in water
to escape the lips of a hellish flame.

Wasps of helicopters
sucking the breathing into their bellies
before the closing of the eyes of hope.

A cruel death to their tomorrows
in the Valhalla of scorching pain.
From their heroism they will not return.

271

The truth is born on a day of insanity; false values
are decrutched and fall by the way.

Britain and Argentina, homes of compatriots, are carrying
the indelible mark of Cain.

Burying the dead who will see no summer on a June day
in a winter of discontent;
carting the wounded willy-nilly
to a freezer shed, once for animal flesh.
Urging the near-dying to an impromptu ward and the lads
sons, husbands, sweethearts, and dutiful enemies,
co-suffering under a roof with a Cross.

From the mouth of a bottle, a Britisher's blood
flows slowly into an Argentinian arm;
warm blood of men, lovers of homeland,
mingling in harmony in each other's veins.

•

Who is he who sees but blackness
in a hospital ward in the shed in San Carlos?
A lad whose every day is now a one night.

He listens to the sounds of the busyness of living,
staring emptily without seeing, fingering
the vastness of his calamity.

Eyeless sockets gaping,
gaping unceasingly
into the long night of groan.

When morphia eases the weals of wounds,
he again walks tall on endearing paths,
across the pastures from Pant Glas to Cae Meillion,
and a winsome maiden leaps into his arms.
He sees the carving of love in the bark of an oak;
a cluster of blood-buds on a mountain ash;
Jesus of Bethel hanging on a nearby bush, and Death
lurking in the shadow of an old yew tree.

With sightless eyes he sees a meadow thrilling with lambs,
and the face of a mother whom he will see no more.

But who is this approaching his tortuous bed?
A youth from Buenos Aires in battle.

A kindred of the peasant poor
who fled the City one harsh winter
from the reality of Cwm Hyfryd.

Years on, a legacy remains on lip;
little words of mystic virtue
urging themselves into unmanageable slots.

The one-armed greeting the blind.
And a bond is forged
despite two nations in conflict.

Celts, with warm blood of belonging coursing through veins;
sharing the legacy of an ancient tongue;
two souls apart, yet of common heritage.

The bonds are stronger than the wounds.
Is there a hope of bridging the gap?

Raggedly fitful the communication.
Then, sadly, separation.

Is a black future the only forever?

Nothing remains but the scars of remembrance,
and the Biblical mite of a country to its glorious brave.
Endless days of fingering the letterings
of the carving of memory
in the bark of the oak tree of hope.
A lock seals the door of Cae Meillion.

What is a maid but the figment of passion
and the arrow that stabs through the heart?

    The definitive fragile bond
    for a son deprived of a summer.

Glossary

Awdl: A long poem consisting of several of the 24 strict-metre forms containing *cynghanedd*. The Chair is awarded for this form of poetry in the National Eisteddfod.

Cyfansoddiadau a Beirniadaethau (Compositions and Adjudications): The title of a book that is published and sold at the end of the Eisteddfod week. It contains all the adjudications, the names of the winners in the literary competitions and winning entries including the Crown and Chair poems. All competitors are anonymous when they enter under a nom de plume (pseudonym) and these are given to the adjudicators to judge. This book allows the readers to look at the winning entries as well as the adjudications published.

Cynghanedd: Lines of poetry with strict rules of alliteration, rhymes, accents and syllables. As poetry was an oral tradition for centuries, listening to the lines should be as pleasant as music to the ear of the listener. *Cynghanedd* as a Welsh word means harmony and is popular today with contests between poets who write in this way.

Englyn : One of the 24 strict-metre forms. This consists of a four-line stanza comprised of thirty syllables which are usually subdivided into ten, six, seven and seven syllables. There is one end-rhyme throughout and internal rhyming may occur. Each line must consist of *cynghanedd*. It is very much a form used in social poetry, often used to congratulate or lament, as the brevity of its form is an ideal medium for sharp observation.

Eluned wrote *'Clymau'*, in *Awdl* form, containing several of the 24 strict-metre forms including *englynion* but omitting the *cynghanedd*, retaining only the end rhymes. This demonstrated her unique talent at creating anew from an old form.

Gorsedd y Beirdd: A society of poets, musicians and other representatives of Welsh culture. During *Eisteddfod* week, five *Gorsedd* ceremonies are held, two in the open air around the specially erected *Gorsedd* stones, and three ceremonies in the Pavilion where competitions are held. The Archdruid, elected for a term of three years by fellow Druids, presides over these ceremonies.

Pryddest: A long poem of several hundred lines without *cynghanedd*. Both *'Corlannau'* and *'Clymau'* were written in this form.

The National Eisteddfod of Wales : An annual event focussing on the Arts and Sciences held for a week in August, with competitions held solely in the medium of Welsh. To many, the Crown , Chair and Prose Medal ceremonies are the main attractions of the week, presided over by the Archdruid and other members of *Gorsedd y Beirdd*. It's a week-long celebration of all aspects of Welsh cultural life.

Y Babell Lên (The Literature Pavilion) : The Literature Tent or Pavilion is where poetry contests are conducted as well as literary discussions and lectures. In the past, even though the Crown and Chair ceremonies took place in the big pavilion, the winners of these competitions were expected to be greeted (often a rapturous reception) by their fellow poets and writers. They would often be expected to discuss and share their winning poems with the audience.

Eluned Phillips' Bibliography

Published work:
Caneuon i Blant (*Songs for Children*), music by Pencerddes Emlyn
and words by Luned Teifi, Gwasg Gomer, 1936
Cofiant Dewi Emrys (*Remembering Dewi Emrys*), Gwasg Gomer,
1971
Cerddi Glyn-y-mêl (*Glyn-y-mêl Poems*), Gwasg Gomer, 1985
The Reluctant Redhead, Gwasg Gomer, 2007

Series scripts –as a part of a script-writing team (1955–64):
Teulu Tŷ Coch (*The Tŷ Coch Family*)
Teulu'r Mans (*The Family in the Manse*)
Y Sgwlyn (*The Schoolmaster*)
Y Gwyliwr (*The Guard*)

Feature programme scripts and plays:
Ar Bwrs y Wlad (*Living on the State*) (15 March – no date but
sometime during the 1960s)
Chwilio am Dŷ (*Looking for a House*) (October 1964)
Brethyn Cartref – Bois yr Hewl (*Homespun* – The Boys on the
Road) (no date)
Brethyn Cartref – Pysgotwyr Glannau Teifi (*Homespun*– The Teifi
Riverbank Fishermen) (no date)
Diwrnod Ffair (*Fair Day*) (November 1951)
Dyn y Banc (*The Man from the Bank*) (no date)
Galwch y Plymer (*Call the Plumber*) (January 1958)
Ffoniwch y Fet (*Phone the Vet*) (October 1956)
Yr Hen Felinydd neu *Hen Ŷd y Wlad* (*The Old Miller* or *The Old
Country Corn*) (no date)

Miss Jones y Post (*Miss Jones from the Post Office*) (June 1961)
Nyrs y Wlad (*The Country Nurse*) (no date)
Yr Ocsiyner (*The Auctioneer*) (March 1955)
Oes Lle ar yr Aelwyd? (*Is there Room at Home?*) (no date)
O Flaen eich Gwell (*Up Before the Beak*) (no date)
Bywyd y Sipsiwn (*Gypsy Life*) (no date)
Cartref – Cynhaeaf (*Home – Harvest*) (no date)
Dal Pen Rheswm (*Good Reasons/Justifications* discussion programme), producers Ruth Price, Rhydderch Jones, October 1967. Taking part: Eluned Phillips, Dyfnallt Morgan, Eiri a Caryl. Eluned's history is discussed and her reaction to the criticism about the poem *'Corlannau'*.

Stage play (unpublished):
Robot
(National Library of Wales Archive)

Libretti (published):
'Cenarth'
'Llwyd Bach y Baw' ('Little Sparrow')
'True Love – Cariad Pur'

Television programmes:
Eluned Bengoch (*Redheaded Eluned*) – producer/director Gareth Rowlands (1994)
Llwyd Bach y Baw (*Little Sparrow*) – producer/director Gareth Rowlands (1994)
Clymau (*Ties*) – a television film, director Gareth Rowlands (1984)
Rhith y Lloer (*Ruffled Water*) by Ewart Alexander: a film based on the life of Eluned Phillips (1989)
Feu Follet – the same film in Breton, shown during the Minority Nations Film Festival, Douarnenez, Brittany (1988)
Paned 'da Picasso (*Tea with Picasso*): a celebration of her life when she was 90 – with Gwenno Dafydd; producer Euros Wyn, director Rhodri Davies (2004)

Radio programmes:
Y Llwybrau Gynt (*The Old Pathways*) – an autobiography for the radio
Gwaith Merched yn ystod y Rhyfel (*Women's Work in Wartime*)
Pe Meddwn i'r Ddawn (*If I had the Talent*)

Unpublished works:
'Yr Ifaciwî' ('The Evacuee') – a short story
Giovanni – part of a novel
Shadows – an autobiographical novel
Cyfrinachau (*Secrets*) – an autobiographical novel
Nest – a musical play in English
Moliant i Ddewi Sant (*In Praise of St David*) (Welsh and English versions) – oratorio
The Lost Miners – Requiem (a part of a planned work)

Index

Abercych 26, 27

Aberdwylan 11, 17

Academi Gymreig, Yr (the Welsh Academy) 193

Acumen 218

Adams, John 207

'Afon Cenarth' 4

Alexander, Ewart 67, 92, 278

Anti Hannah 10, 16, 17, 19, 20, 21

Antoinette, Marie 126, 127, 128

ap Gwilym, Gwynn 39, 41, 146, 195, 201

Apollinaire 47

Asimov, Isaac 118

Auden, W. H. 162

Augustus John 33, 34, 41, 56

Banc y Brain (nom de plume) 26, 151, 152

Banc y Shifftwn 3, 12

Baner ac Amserau Cymru (see also *Y Faner*) 42, 66, 168

Bardd Mawr 79

Barddas 150, 195, 200, 202

Barddas Society 193

Barddoniaeth y Chwedegau, Alan Llwyd 171

Barn 197, 203, 250, 263

Beard, Rosemary x, 238, 239

Bestreben (school) 28, 29, 30, 32, 49

Beulah Community Council 2

Bezen Perrot 64

Blaenachddu 30

Blodeugerdd o Farddoniaeth yr Ugeinfed Ganrif, eds Alan Llwyd and Gwynn ap Gwilym 195

Bois de Boulogne 52, 53

Boswell (the family) 12, 15

Bowen, David 203

Bowen, Euros 42, 76

Bowen, Geraint 76

Brenhinbren, Y, Derec Llwyd Morgan 188, 190

Brethyn Cartref (radio programme) 17, 277

Breton, André 47

Breton National Party 64, 65

Breton nationalists 55, 62-66

Broadway 220, 221

Brown, Curtis (literary agents) 99, 247

Bruchet, Jacques 72, 74, 75, 78

Bruchet, Monique 78

Bryn Seion 2, 22, 229, 230, 234

Burrows, Stuart 203

Cadwaladr, Dilys 43, 45, 148, 149, 191

Calvin, Wyn x, 231

Cameron, Euan 48

Campbell, Roy 34

Caneuon i Blant , Pencerddes Emlyn and Luned Teifi 217, 277

Čapek, Karel 118

ABOUT HONNO

Honno Welsh Women's Press was set up in 1986 by a group of women who felt strongly that women in Wales needed wider opportunities to see their writing in print and to become involved in the publishing process. Our aim is to develop the writing talents of women in Wales, give them new and exciting opportunities to see their work published and often to give them their first 'break' as a writer. Honno is registered as a community co-operative. Any profit that Honno makes is invested in the publishing programme. Women from Wales and around the world have expressed their support for Honno. Each supporter has a vote at the Annual General Meeting. For more information and to buy our publications, please write to Honno at the address below, or visit our website: www.honno.co.uk

Honno, 14 Creative Units, Aberystwyth Arts Centre
Aberystwyth, Ceredigion SY23 3GL

Honno Friends

We are very grateful for the support of the Honno Friends: Jane Aaron, Annette Ecuyere, Audrey Jones, Gwyneth Tyson Roberts, Beryl Roberts, Jenny Sabine.

For more information on how you can become a Honno Friend, see: http://www.honno.co.uk/friends.php